CONTENTS

THANKS AND ACKNOWLEDGEMENTS

In the preparation of this new edition I would like to thank:

Sally Mellersh (formerly of Hammersmith and West London College) for updating and expanding the *List of likely errors* to accompany the new editions of *Ship or Sheep?* and *Tree or Three?* by its inclusion on the website (http://www.cambridge.org/elt/elt_projectpage.asp?id=2500905).

David McCreath for IT assistance and contribution to my computer literacy. Sandra Turner for help with typing.

My editors Nóirín Burke, Frances Amrani and Yvonne Harmer, as well as the following teachers from all over the world who commented during development and gave me such practical advice:

Michele Chartrand-Hirsch, France; Ian Chitty, UK; David Deterding, Singapore; Sylvie Donna, UK; Elizabeth Downey, New Zealand; Lynda Edwards, UK; Laura Hancock, UK; David Hill, Australia; Kip Kelland, Italy; Kathy Keohane, UK; Andrea Paul, Australia; Gordon Francis Robinson, Singapore; Julietta Ann Schoenmann, UK; Roger Scott, UK

Peter Hobbs and other teachers of International House Sydney, who allowed me to observe and co-teach their classes; Shân Jones, for class observation at Blacktown TAFE College.

I would like to continue to thank Amir Pirouzan, Jean Crocker and John Lipscomb for their advice and encouragement during the preparation of the original edition of *Ship or Sheep?* Also Philippa Lipscomb and other teachers of the British Council, Teheran, who helped with the first class try-outs.

The publisher has used its best endeavours to ensure that the URLs for external websites referred to in this book are correct and active at the time of going to press. However, the publisher has no responsibility for the websites and can make no guarantee that a site will remain live or that the content is or will remain appropriate.

Illustrations by: Johanna Boccardo, Pat Murray, Felicity House and Tony Wilkins

Cover design by Pentacor Book Design

Designed and typeset by Hart McLeod

INTRODUCTION FOR STUDENTS

- Seven of the 50 units in this book are review units. Each of the other units introduces a different English sound, as well as other aspects of pronunciation (e.g. stress, intonation) which are also important for successful communication in English.
- You can use this book either working alone or with a class + teacher.
- You will need:
  - equipment to listen to the CD, and equipment to record your voice
  - a small mirror to compare your lip positions with the pictures
  - Your mask (cut it out from page 185). You will use it at the beginning of most units (but not Unit 1). You can also use it for extra practice of sounds that are difficult for you.
- First, find out which units are most important for you. To do this:
  - If possible, check your mother tongue in the *List of likely errors* (see website: http://www.cambridge.org/elt/elt_projectpage.asp?id=2500905) and make a printout of that part of the list.
  - Do at least one of the Diagnostic Tests (see pages ix–xi). If you are working alone, do Test A. Test B needs the help of a teacher, native speaker or near-native speaker. If you are working with a teacher, he/she will decide whether you do the tests.
- Decide whether you want to:
  - work first on the most important units for you, or
  - begin at the beginning and work through the book, spending more time on the most important units for you. You can choose to work simultaneously on Section A (vowels) and Section B (consonants). You can also do the seven review units.
- Read *Making English sounds* before beginning each section (see pages 1–2, 79–80). This introduces some essential vocabulary.
- Symbols used in the book:

means this material is recorded.

means the answers are in the Key (see pages 186–224).

means this exercise is suitable for a group or pair of students. If you are a student working alone, you could try it by using your imagination, e.g. by imagining another student.

means 'use the mask' (see page vi).

means 'visit the website to practise'.

- Other symbols used:

Intonation is shown with arrows:

The main word stress is shown in bold, e.g. pronun**cia**tion, **stu**dent.

Sentence stress is shown with underlining, e.g. <u>Sen</u>tence <u>stress</u> is <u>shown</u> with under<u>lin</u>ing, or sometimes with big and small circles:

OoOoOoooOo (<u>Sen</u>tence <u>stress</u> is <u>shown</u> with under<u>lin</u>ing).

- Phonetic symbols used in this book are the International Phonetic Alphabet (IPA) (the Contents page shows all the symbols used). You can use this book without knowing these symbols, but it is useful to learn them so that you can check the pronunciation of new words in a dictionary. The *Cambridge Advanced Learner's Dictionary* uses these symbols.
- In most units (but not in Unit 1), Exercise 2 *Minimal pairs* gives you practice in contrasting two sounds in words and sentences. If you don't have one of the two sounds in your language, practising the pairs of sounds can sometimes help you to hear – and then produce – the English sound.
- Dialogues are recorded. You can backtrack on the CD to repeat them as many times as you want. If you don't like backtracking, listen to the dialogue after you have done the dialogue tasks.

The Mask

There are two ways in which you can use the mask (which you cut out from page 185):

1 *At the beginning of the minimal pair exercises* Here, you are instructed to use the mask in most units after Unit 1. The mask symbol 👽 at the beginning of the exercise indicates 'use the mask'. You can start the minimal pair practice with the mask covering the written words, just looking at the pictures and listening to the pair sounds (first in words and then in sentences). This will help you to focus on really listening to the sounds first. After you have listened for the first time, you can backtrack on the CD to listen again and repeat.

2 *Extra practice of difficult sounds* You can also use the mask, for example at the end of a unit, to enjoy extra practice of sounds that are difficult for you. Here, your task with the mask is to try to produce the contrasting sounds correctly while trying to remember the words and sentences. (e.g. 1 Mask on – listen and repeat. 2 Mask off – read aloud. 3 Mask on – remember and say aloud. 4 Mask off – read aloud to check.)

Other ways of having extra practice of difficult sounds

1 Make playing cards by photocopying the minimal pair charts (e.g. four copies) and cutting out the pairs. You can then play some of the card games described in the review units. If working alone, play *Pick up pairs*, Unit 7, page 27 or *Pick up same sounds*, Unit 14, page 52.

2 Check on the website (http://www.cambridge.org/elt/elt_projectpage.asp?id=2500905) to see if there is any extra practice material for this sound.

INTRODUCTION FOR TEACHERS

- Please read the Introduction for Students on pages v–vi.
- **Level** This book is written for intermediate students, but previous editions have also been used by students at other levels. *Tree or Three?* is written for beginner–elementary level.
- **Class/Student working alone** The instructions are written for a student working alone, but can be used for classroom teaching as well. See the symbols in the students' introduction, especially 👥 .
- **Diagnostic Tests** You can use these if you need to assess students' difficulties. But if you already know this for your class, you can choose to skip the tests and decide whether you want the students to work through the book or focus only on some units.

  Students working alone can self-administer Test A with or without your input. To administer Test B, students can be asked to record their individual performances for your assessment. Or you may prefer to do this with them so that you can immediately check possible 'reading' rather than pronouncing mistakes, by asking them to listen and repeat the item.
- **List of likely errors** This is on the website so that it can be added to. It can be found at

  http://www.cambridge.org/elt/elt_projectpage.asp?id=2500905.

  It would be useful for each student to have a printout of the relevant part of this list.
- **Minimal pairs** In this book, these are pairs of words/sentences which differ by only one sound, e.g. *Bill bought a sheep./Bill bought a ship.* These sometimes help students to hear – and then pronounce – sounds that are difficult for them. You may want to extend students' class practice of particular minimal pairs by inventing games or playing the following:
  - *Card games* These are described in Exercise 1 of the review units. Make more copies if using pairs from only one unit. This book is copyright, but permission is granted to make a single copy of the cards described in the review units, for the sole purpose of playing the card games outlined.
  - *'Fingers'* For each pair, say words rapidly at random, e.g. *sheep sheep sheep ship ship sheep ship*. Students show with one or two fingers if they hear sound 1 or sound 2. Students practise in pairs and then back to back.

- *'Mingling'* Each student has one of the minimal pair cards. Students mingle (move around randomly), not showing their cards but repeating their word to find the others with the same sound. They form a group, which checks correct membership. The first group to complete their set of words with the same sound wins. Students swap cards within their group and check pronunciation of new words before all mingling again to find the person in the other group with the other half of their minimal pair. Students change cards with that person and check each other's pronunciation. Then start the mingling game from the beginning so both sounds are used.

• **The mask** (See Introduction for Students.) The purpose of the mask is twofold:
  - to allow students to listen to and practise the minimal pair sounds first in words and then in sentences without being distracted by the written word
  - for extra practice of sounds they find difficult.

DIAGNOSTIC TESTS

All students should do Test A.

Test B requires the help of a teacher, native speaker or near-native speaker of English.

The tests are not to give you a mark. They may help you to find out which sounds and other aspects of English pronunciation could be the most difficult for you. You should also check this in the *List of likely errors* on the website: http://www.cambridge.org/elt/elt_projectpage.asp?id=2500905.

TEST A

Section 1 Sound discrimination

A2 Do not stop the recording or repeat. In each item you will hear two words. Sometimes the two words are the same. Sometimes they have one sound that is different. Listen once only to each item and tick the S (same) column or the D (different) column. If you are not sure, tick the question mark (?) column.

	S	D	?
EXAMPLE If you hear, 'sheep sheep' tick the S column.	✓		
If you hear, 'sheep ship' tick the D column.		✓	
If you are not sure, tick the ? column.			✓

	S	D	?		S	D	?		S	D	?		S	D	?
1a				6a				12a				17a			
1b				6b				12b				17b			
2a				7a				13a				18a			
2b				7b				13b				18b			
2c				7c				14a				19a			
3a				8a				14b				19b			
3b				8b				14c				20a			
4a				9a				14d				21a			
4b				9b				15a				22a			
5a				10a				15b				22b			
5b				10b				16a				23a			
5c				11a				16b				23b			
				11b				16c				24a			

Section 2 Intonation

A3 Do not stop the recording or repeat. Listen to Lucy talking to Lesley on the telephone. In some items her voice goes up (⟋) at the end. In some items her voice goes down (⟍). Tick the ⟋ or ⟍ column for each item. If you are not sure, tick the ? column. Listen to the example first.

	⟋	⟍	?
EXAMPLE a) That's Lesley, isn't it?	✓		
b) That's Lesley, isn't it?		✓	

	⟋	⟍	?		⟋	⟍	?
1				6			
2				7			
3				8			
4				9			
5				10			

Section 3 Word stress

A4 Do not stop the recording or repeat. In each item, tick the one word that is different from the others.

EXAMPLE items   column   number   alone ✓   listen

1 nowhere   birthday   mistake   toilet   postcard
2 guitar   eighteen   today   machine   English
3 away   brother   breakfast   frightened   valley
4 comfortable   vegetables   photograph   lemonade   minimal
5 telephoning   supermarket   conversation   exercises   helicopter

TEST B

(Note: This test requires the help of a teacher, native speaker, or near-native speaker of English.)

Ask the student to read each test item, and record the grading on the result sheet (page xii).

A student's performance can be recorded, or the student can be asked to repeat an item as many times as necessary to record a result. The reasons for mispronunciation are many, and some may be caused by reading difficulty. To check this, say the mispronounced word correctly and ask the student to repeat it. If the student can then say it correctly, add the symbol R to your grading on that item, indicating that the student can pronounce this sound but may have difficulty when reading it.

Suggested symbols for grading: ✓ no difficulty with this sound
          X difficulty with this sound
          R may have difficulty reading this sound

Shopping list

1 some cheese (cheap cheese); some tea (Chinese tea)
2 fifty biscuits; four fish
3 ten eggs (big eggs)
4 jam; apples and oranges; a cabbage
5 ten tomatoes (large tomatoes)
6 five kilos of veal (very good veal)
7 some strong string (long string)
8 four forks (small forks); spoons; cups; small paper plates
9 some good sugar; milk; coffee; a cake
10 pick up Jude's blue shoes at the shoe shop; two kilos of brown rice; a grapefruit
11 nuts; honey; half a dozen hot buns
12 one lemon; nine brown onions; flowers for the house
13 some paper for my mother's letters; collect Grandfather's leather jacket from the cleaner's
14 a girl's shirt and skirt (size thirteen); cold drinks (don't get dry ginger); some good bread
15 eight small cakes and paper plates; some sausages for supper
16 some yellow roses for your sister
17 white wine (sweet wine); some ice
18 beer for Bob (buy it from the pub near here)
19 some shampoo for Claire's hair; some pears
20 some tins of New Zealand peas, or frozen beans
21 fresh English fish from the fish shop
22 a toy for the little boy (a blue or yellow ball)
23 something for Mr Smith (it's his birthday on Thursday)
24 a small cheap television for the garage

RESULTS SHEET AND FINDINGS from *List of likely errors*

In any of the three columns, place a cross against the sound where there may be difficulty.

SOUNDS	page	(Diagnostic Test B)	Diagnostic Test A	Findings from *List of likely errors*
1 /iː/ (sheep)	3		1a	
/tʃ/ (chip)	120		1b	
2 /ɪ/ (ship)	7		2a	
/f/ (fan)	131		2b, 2c	
3 /e/ (pen)	11		3a	
/g/ (girl)	101		3b	
4 /æ/ (man)	15		4a	
/dʒ/ (jam)	124		4b	
5 /ɑː/ (heart)	23		5a, 5b	
/t/ (table)	89		5c	
6 /v/ (van)	135		6a, 6b	
7 /ɒ/ (clock)	29		7a	
/ŋ/ (ring)	168		7b, 7c	
8 /ɔː/ (ball)	174		8a	
/p/ (pen)	81		8b	
9 /ʊ/ (book)	36		9a	
/k/ (key)	97		9b	
10 /uː/ (boot)	39		10a	
/r/ (rain)	176		10b	
11 /ʌ/ (cup)	19		11a	
/h/ (hat)	147		11b	
12 /n/ (nose)	165		12a	
/aʊ/ (house)	63		12b	
13 /ə/ (camera)	48		13a	
/ð/ (the feather)	155		13b	
14 /ɜː/ (girl)	43		14a, 14b, 14c	
/d/ (door)	93		14d	
15 /eɪ/ (male)	54		15a	
/s/ (sun)	107		15b	
16 /əʊ/ (phone)	66		16a, 16b	
/j/ (yellow)	143		16c	
17 /aɪ/ (fine)	57		17a	
/w/ (window)	139		17b	
18 /ɪə/ (year)	70		18a	
/b/ (baby)	85		18b	
19 /eə/ (chair)	73		19a	
/m/ (mouth)	162		19b	
20 /z/ (zoo)	110		20a	
21 /ʃ/ (shoe)	114		21a	
22 /ɔɪ/ (boy)	60		22a	
/l/ (letter)	172		22b	
23 /θ/ (thin)	151		23a, 23b	
24 /ʒ/ (television)	117		24a	

Section A
Vowels

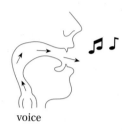

voice

Use your voice to make all vowels.

Making English sounds

short vowels
(make a short sound)
/ɪ/ (ship)
/e/ (pen)
/ʊ/ (book)
/æ/ (man)
/ʌ/ (cup)
/ɒ/ (clock)
/ə/ (camera)

long vowels
(make a long sound)
/ɔː/ (ball)
/uː/ (boot)
/iː/ (sheep)
/ɑː/ (heart)
/ɜː/ (girl)

diphthongs
(two vowel sounds)
/əʊ/ (phone)
/ɪə/ (year)
/ɔɪ/ (boy)
/aʊ/ (house)
/eɪ/ (male)
/aɪ/ (fine)
/eə/ (chair)

1 Spot the different sound.

EXAMPLE /ə/ /e/ /ʊ/ /eə/ /ɪ/

> *Answer:* The fourth sound is a diphthong. All the others are short vowels.

1 /əʊ/ /ʊ/ /ʌ/ /ə/ /ɔ/   2 /ɔɪ/ /e/ /ɪə/ /aɪ/ /aʊ/   3 /ɒ/ /iː/ /ɔː/ /ɑː/ /ɜː/

2 Match these words with the pictures below.

a the back of the tongue
b the lips
c the tip of the tongue
d the front of the tongue

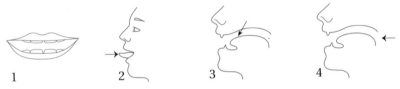

3 Match the pictures (1–9) in A with the instructions (a–i) in B.

A

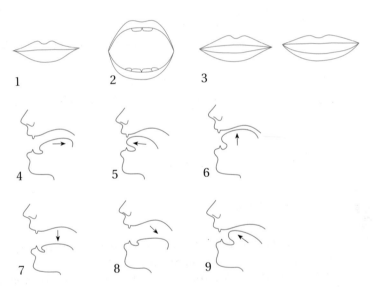

B

a) Open your mouth.
b) Close your mouth.
c) Put your tongue forward.
d) Open your mouth a little. Then open mouth a little more.
e) Put your tongue back.
f) Put your tongue down.
g) Put your tongue up.
h) Put your tongue forward and up. Practise /iː/: eat, easy, he, she, we.
i) Put your tongue down and back. Practise /ɑː/: ask, are, arm, car.

UNIT 1 /iː/ sheep

– Do you like your tea sweet?
– Yes. Three sugars, please.

1 Target sound /iː/

 Open your mouth very little to make the target sound iː. /iː/ is a long sound. Listen and repeat: /iː/.

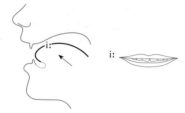

2 Sound /iː/

	sheep Look out for that sheep.	**leak** Stop it leaking!	
	cheeks What lovely cheeks!	**peel** This peel's got vitamin C in it.	
	bean Throw out that bean.	**leave** He's going to leave.	

Sound /iː/ words

 a Listen and repeat the words.

Sound /iː/ sentences

b Listen to the sentences.

c Sentence stress

Notice that the most important words for the meaning of a sentence are pronounced more **LOUD**ly and s l o w ly .
The less important words are said more quietly and quickly.
Listen to the sentences again and this time look at the <u>underlined</u> syllables below. Notice that they are louder and slower.

Look <u>out</u> for that <u>sheep</u>.   <u>Stop</u> it <u>lea</u>king!
What <u>lovely</u> <u>cheeks</u>!   This <u>peel's</u> got vitamin <u>C</u> in it.
Throw <u>out</u> that <u>bean</u>.   He's <u>go</u>ing to <u>leave</u>.

d Listen again and repeat the sentences.

3 Dialogue

a First practise the sound /iː/ in some of the words from this unit. Read the words aloud or visit the website to practise.

One-syllable words: cheese beef tea eat meal
three cheap please me

Two-syllable words: **Pe**ter **peo**ple **E**dam **eve**ning
Eastfield **bis**cuit **cheese**cake

(The stress is always on the first syllable.)

Two-syllable words: Ja**nine** re**peat**

(The stress is always on the second syllable.)

Note on word stress: **bold** is used here to show you which part of the word is strongly stressed, i.e. which syllable is pronounced more **LOUD**ly and s l o w ly than the other(s). Word stress doesn't usually change, except in some longer words with stress near the end. (See 4c and 4d.)

A8 b Listen to the dialogue, paying attention to the target sound. Then read the dialogue and fill the gaps (1–10) with the correct words from the box.

> cheese Peter eat please tea beef
> three me teas beef

In a café: 'It's cheaper to eat at Marguerite's'

CHRISTINA: What would you like to eat, 1_____ ? The cheese sandwiches are the cheapest.

PETER: Er … mmm … oh, a 2_____ sandwich, please, Christina.

CHRISTINA: Cheese … mmm … Janine? Would you like a 3_____ sandwich or a cheese sandwich?

JANINE: A cheese sandwich, 4_____.

PETER: What about you, Christina? Would you like cheese or 5_____ ?

WAITRESS: Are you all ready to order? What would you like to 6_____ ?

CHRISTINA: Er, we'll have one beef sandwich, two cheese sandwiches and, mmm, 7_____ for me.

JANINE: Tea for 8_____ too, please.

PETER: Yes, make that three 9_____ , please.

WAITRESS: (writing down the order) One beef sandwich, two cheese sandwiches and 10_____ teas.

A8 c Listen to the dialogue again to check your answers. Practise reading the dialogue aloud, and record your voice to compare your production of the target sound with the recording.

4 Intonation of questions with 'or'

Intonation is the voice going up or down.

This movement up or down begins on the most important word in a phrase or sentence.

In questions with 'or' the intonation usually goes down at the end.

 a Listen and repeat.

Would you like <u>veal</u> or <u>beef</u>?

Would you like <u>coffee</u> or <u>tea</u>?

Would you like <u>coffee</u>, <u>tea</u> or <u>milk</u>?

b Role play

Use the menu to practise a conversation in a group of four or five. You are in a restaurant. Take turns to be the waiter. Ask each other questions, e.g. *Would you like … or …?* Then one person gives the order to the waiter, who repeats the order to check it. If possible, also practise using other menus. If it is an expensive restaurant, the waiter or waitress can be more formal, saying *Good evening* before asking for the order.

EASTFIELD RESTAURANT

MENU

Soup
leek soup OR pea soup

Meat
veal OR beef

Vegetables
beans OR peas

Sweets
cheesecake OR ice cream OR peaches

Drinks
coffee OR tea

Biscuits and Cheese
Edam cheese OR Brie

A10 c Word stress – nationalities ending in 'ese'

As you listen to the sentences about these nationalities, draw a line connecting the country and nationality in the two lists below.

Countries	Nationalities (Note the stress on the last syllable.)
China	Vietnamese
Bali	Maltese
Malta	Balinese
Portugal	Japanese
Lebanon	Chinese
Japan	Nepalese
Nepal	Lebanese
Vietnam	Portuguese

A11 d Moving stress

The stress of these 'ese' nationalities changes if the next word is strongly stressed. So we say, *This __beef__ is Japan__ese__* but, *It's __Jap__anese __beef__*.

Listen and respond, like the example.

EXAMPLE Is this bread from Beirut?

Response: Yes, it's Leba**nese**. It's **Leb**anese bread.

5 Spelling

Look back over this unit at words with the target sound, and write what you noticed about how to spell the sound /iː/.

UNIT 2 /ɪ/ ship

– What about this fish? Can I eat it?
– Yes. Eat it.
– What about this cheese? Can I eat it?
– No, don't eat it. It's six weeks out of date.

1 Target sound /ɪ/

A12a **a** First practise the sound /iː/
(see page 3). Listen and repeat.

A12b **b** Open your mouth a *little* more to
make the target sound /ɪ/.
Listen and repeat.

A12c **c** Listen and repeat both sounds together.
/iː/ is long. /ɪ/ is short.

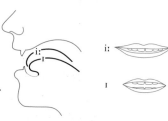

2 Minimal pairs

Sound 1 /iː/	Sound 2 /ɪ/

sheep | **ship**
Look out for that sheep. | Look out for that ship.

leak | **lick**
Stop it leaking! | Stop it licking!

cheeks | **chicks**
What lovely cheeks. | What lovely chicks.

peel | **pill**
This peel's got vitamin C in it. | This pill's got vitamin C in it.

bean | **bin**
Throw out that bean. | Throw out that bin.

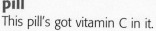

leave | **live**
He's going to leave. | He's going to live.

Minimal pair words

A13a a Listen and repeat the words.

A13b b You will hear five words from each minimal pair. For each word, write *1* for /iː/ (sound 1) or *2* for /ɪ/ (sound 2).

EXAMPLE Pair 1: 1, 2, 2, 2, 2

Minimal pair sentences

A14a c Listen to the minimal pair sentences.

A14b d Listen to six of the sentences and write *1* for /iː/ (sound 1) or *2* for /ɪ/ (sound 2).

e Sentence stress

The most important words in a sentence are strongly stressed. They are pronounced **LOUD**er and s l o w e r. Look at these examples from the minimal pair sentences. (In the brackets on the right, the big circles are the strongly stressed syllables and the small circles are the weakly stressed syllables.)

Pair 1: <u>OUT</u> ... <u>SHIP</u>   Look <u>OUT</u> for that <u>SHIP</u>! (**oOooO**)
Pair 2: <u>STOP</u> ... LEAK   <u>STOP</u> it <u>LEAK</u>ing. (**OoOo**)
Pair 3: <u>LOVE</u> ... <u>CHICKS</u>   What <u>LOVE</u>ly <u>CHICKS</u>! (**oOoO**)
Pair 4: <u>PILL'S</u> ... <u>C</u>   This <u>PILL'S</u> got vitamin <u>C</u> in it. (**oOooooOoo**)

A14a Listen to the minimal pair sentences again and <u>underline</u> the strongly stressed words in each sentence (on page 7).

A15 f Tick the words a) or b) that you hear in the sentences.

1 a) sheep ☐   b) ship ☐
2 a) bean ☐   b) bin ☐
3 a) cheeks ☐   b) chicks ☐
4 a) cheap ☐   b) chip ☐
5 a) heel ☐   b) hill ☐
6 a) peel ☐   b) pill ☐

3 Dialogue

a First practise the sound /ɪ/ in some of the words from the dialogue. Read the words aloud or visit the website to practise.

One-syllable words: film ill miss kids quick Kim Bill
Two-syllable words: (1st syllable) **cricket** **tickets** **children**
                 minutes **quickly** **listen** **pity**
             (2nd syllable) be**gins**
Three-syllable words: (1st syllable) **history** **festival** **cinema**
                 interesting **prize**-winning **Africa**
             (2nd syllable) gym**nastics** o**lympic** ex**cited**
                 be**ginning** te**rrific** go**rilla**
             (3rd syllable) chimpan**zee**

A16 **b** Listen to the dialogue, paying attention to the target sound. Then read the dialogue and fill the gaps (1–8) with the correct three-syllable words from the list in 3a.

Three interesting films

BILL: Good evening, Mrs Lee.

GINA: Is Kim in?

BILL: Is he coming to the cinema, Mrs Lee? It's the Children's Film 1_____ .

MRS LEE: Kim's ill.

BILL: Here he is!

GINA: Hi, Kim!

KIM: Hi, Gina! Hi, Bill!

BILL: Kim, we've got these three free tickets to see three 2_____ films for children!

MRS LEE: Listen, Kim …

KIM: Is it 3_____ ?

GINA: *We* think it is. First there's a short film about gorillas and 4_____ in Africa, and …

BILL: … then the next film is about the six best Olympic 5_____ competitions, and then …

GINA: … then it's the big film – *The* 6_____ *of English Cricket.*

KIM: Cricket!

BILL: It's a 7_____ film.

MRS LEE: If you're ill, Kim …

GINA: It would be a pity to miss it.

MRS LEE: Now listen, you kids …

BILL: And it begins in fifty minutes.

MRS LEE: KIM!

KIM: Quick! Or we'll miss the 8_____ of the gorilla film!

A16 **c** Listen to the dialogue again to check your answers. Practise reading the dialogue aloud, and record your voice to compare your production of the target sound with the recording.

d Perform the dialogue in a group of four and, if possible, record your voices. In your group, first practise speaking with feeling. Mrs Lee is getting more and more angry. The others are getting more and more excited.

In English, if you get more angry, you usually speak more loudly. if you get more excited, you usually speak more quickly.

4 Numbers

A17 a Word stress
Stressed syllables are in **bold**. Listen and repeat.

three	thir**teen**	**thir**ty	3	13	30
four	four**teen**	**for**ty	4	14	40
five	fif**teen**	**fif**ty	5	15	50
six	six**teen**	**six**ty	6	16	60
seven	seven**teen**	**seven**ty	7	17	70
eight	eigh**teen**	**eigh**ty	8	18	80
nine	nine**teen**	**nine**ty	9	19	90

b Moving stress
The stress in these 'teen' numbers is different when we are counting.

thirteen, **four**teen, **fif**teen, **six**teen, **seven**teen, etc.

c Other moving stress
The stress in these 'teen' numbers is also different when there is a strong stress in the next word.

<u>Tim</u> lives at number fif**teen**.

<u>Tim</u> lives at number **fif**teen <u>Green</u> Street.

A18 Practise giving A's reply in the conversations you hear, like the example.

Example
A: The <u>den</u>tist is at <u>sev</u>enteen <u>Mill</u> Street.
B: <u>Sev</u>enty?
A: <u>No</u>, not **sev**enty – seven**teen**.

d Mini Bingo game
Play in a group of 3–5. One person calls out the numbers from 4a but in a random order. (Take turns to call the numbers.) The others each choose one of the boxes A, B, C or D below. Listen to the numbers and if a number is in your box, cover it with a small piece of paper. When all the numbers in your box are covered, you are the winner and you shout, BINGO!

A			B			C			D		
13	3	80	60	4	16	5	15	16	60	6	15
7	19	50	40	30	13	70	90	3	8	14	17
17	90	8	70	5	90	40	7	18	9	90	80

Self study student: first make a recording, saying clearly all the numbers from 4a but in a random order. Then listen and play as many boxes as you can simultaneously.

5 Spelling

Look back over this unit at words with the target sound, and write what you noticed about how to spell the sound /ɪ/.

UNIT 3 /e/ pen

- Is this milk fresh?
- Yes. Everything in this fridge is fresh.

1 Target sound /e/

A19a **a** First practise the sound /ɪ/ (see page 7).

A19b **b** Open your mouth a *little* more to make the short target sound /e/. Listen and repeat.

A19c **c** Listen and repeat both sounds together: /ɪ/ and /e/.

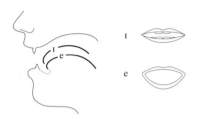

2 Minimal pairs

	Sound 1 /ɪ/	**Sound 2** /e/	
	pin I need a pin.	**pen** I need a pen.	
	bin That's my bin.	**Ben** That's my Ben.	
	tin It's a big tin.	**ten** It's a big ten.	
	pig Where's the pig?	**peg** Where's the peg?	
	bill There's the bill.	**bell** There's the bell.	
	chick She wants a chick.	**cheque** She wants a cheque.	

Minimal pair words

A20a **a** Listen and repeat the words.

A20b **b** You will hear five words from each minimal pair. For each word, write *1* for /ɪ/ (sound 1) or *2* for /e/ (sound 2).

EXAMPLE Pair 1:   2, 2, 1, 1, 2

Minimal pair sentences

A21a c Listen to the minimal pair sentences.

A21b d Listen to six of the sentences and write *1* for /ɪ/ (sound 1) or *2* for /e/ (sound 2).

A21a e Sentence stress

The most important words in a sentence are strongly stressed. If the minimal pair sentences were spoken with only one strong stress, which word would it be? Read the sentences and guess which word it might be. Then listen to the minimal pair sentences again and <u>underline</u> the strongly stressed word in each sentence (on page 11).

A22 f Tick the words a) or b) that you hear in the sentences.

1 a) pin ☐   b) pen ☐

2 a) pig ☐   b) peg ☐

3 a) tins ☐   b) tens ☐

4 a) sit ☐   b) set ☐

5 a) disk ☐   b) desk ☐

6 a) pick at ☐   b) peck at ☐

3 Dialogue

a First practise the sound /e/ in some of the words from the dialogue. Read the words aloud or visit the website to practise. In words with two or more syllables, **bold** is used to show which syllable is strongly stressed. In the brackets, write the number of syllables in each word before you practise.

EXAMPLES friend (1) **terri**bly (3) **Emm**a (2) ex**pen**sive (3)

jealous ( ) help ( ) **every**body ( ) **any** ( ) bench ( ) **Kev**in ( )

A**mer**ica ( ) **Mex**ican ( ) **Emil**y ( ) Ben ( ) **ver**y ( ) bread ( ) **Edd**ie ( )

Notice that many words in English have the strong stress on the first syllable, but some words have the strong stress on the last syllable.

hel**lo** A**dele** a**gain** ex**cept** your**self** lemon**ade**

A23 b Listen to the dialogue, paying attention to the target sound. Then read the dialogue and fill the gaps (1–7) with the correct questions (a–g) below.

a) Can I get you a drink, Adele?

b) Is that better?

c) Was it expensive?

d) Are you listening to the Red Hot Chili Peppers?

e) How did you spend your holiday, Adele?

f) Are you a friend of Emma's?

g) Have you met my friend Adele yet, Kevin?

Friends

ADELE: Hi, Emma! Hi, Ben! Hello, Emily! Hello, Eddie! Hi, everybody!

EVERYBODY EXCEPT KEVIN: Hi, Adele!

EMILY: Nice to see you again, Adele. Kevin, this is Adele. Adele, this is Kevin.

ADELE: Hi, Kevin. 1_____ ? It's terribly loud.

KEVIN: Yes … *(turns the music down)* 2_____ ? *(Adele nods her head)* 3_____ ?

ADELE: Yes.

KEVIN: Emma said she had a friend called Adele.

EDDIE: Help yourself to Mexican food, Adele. It's on the kitchen bench.

EMILY: And there's French bread on the shelf.

BEN: 4_____ ?

ADELE: Yes, thanks, Ben. Some lemonade with a bit of ice in it.

EMMA: 5_____ ?

KEVIN: Yes. I've just met her. She's very friendly.

BEN: 6_____ ?

ADELE: I went to South America with my best friend Kerrie.

EVERYBODY: Well!

EMMA: We're all jealous.

EDDIE: 7_____ ?

ADELE: Not very. But I spent everything. I haven't any money left.

A23 **c** Listen to the dialogue again to check your answers. Then practise reading the dialogue aloud. Record your voice to compare your production of the target sound with the recording.

4 Intonation

Intonation is the voice going up or down on the strongest syllable of the most important word in a phrase or sentence.

Intonation statements usually goes down at the end.

Intonation in *WH* questions (*Who? What? Why? When? Where? How?*) usually goes down at the end.

Intonation in *Yes/No* questions usually goes up at the end.

A24 **a** Listen and repeat.

WH question: <u>How</u> did you spend your **holi**day?

Statement: I <u>went</u> to A**mer**ica.

Yes/No question: Was it ex**pen**sive?

Statement: <u>**Yes**</u>**. Very.**

<u>**No**</u>. Not <u>**very**</u>.

A25 **b** Word stress

Practise the word stress in these place names. In many place names the strong stress is on the first syllable.

Denmark **Ven**ice **Ed**inburgh **Mex**ico
Mecca **Mel**bourne **Leb**anon

A smaller number of place names have the strong stress on the last syllable.

Ja**pan** Mum**bai** Ma**drid** Bei**rut** New **York**

In longer place names the strong stress is sometimes in the middle of the word.

the Rivi**e**ra   the Medi**ter**ranean   Aus**tral**ia   A**mer**ica   Hel**sin**ki
Phila**del**phia

c Now practise the conversation below, using the place names in 4b.

A: How did you spend your holiday?
B: I went to …
A: Was it expensive?
B: Yes. Very. / Not very.

d Dictionary work: word stress

When you meet a new word, you can check which syllable is strongly stressed in a good dictionary (e.g. *Cambridge Advanced Learner's Dictionary*). The pronunciation of the word is shown in the International Phonetic Alphabet (IPA), with the symbol ˈ in front of the main strong stress of the word, e.g. electric /ɪˈlektrɪk/. Your dictionary will also show the secondary stress (usually in longer words) with the symbol ˌ , e.g. electricity /ɪˌlekˈtrɪsəti/.

In *Ship or Sheep?* only the main strong stress in a word is in **bold** to show you where the stressed syllable ends, e.g. e**lec**tric, electr**ic**ity.

Look up some of these words in a dictionary and mark which syllable has the main strong stress.

EXAMPLE ex<u>cept</u> or exˈcept

except	exercise	expect	expedition
expel	experiment	expenditure	expert
expression	extend	extra	extrovert

5 Spelling

Look back over this unit at words with the target sound, and write what you noticed about how to spell the sound /e/.

UNIT 4 /æ/ man

- Let's have a chat about that cat.
- My cat?
- Yes … em … it's too fat.
- Well, it is a bit fat. But it's … mm … a very happy cat.

1 Target sound /æ/

A26a **a** First practise the sound /e/
(see page 11). Listen and repeat.

A26b **b** Open your mouth a little more to
make the target sound /æ/.
Listen and repeat.

A26c **c** Listen and repeat both sounds together:
/e/ and /æ/.

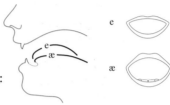

2 Minimal pairs

	Sound 1 /e/	Sound 2 /æ/	
	x Put the 'x' here.	**axe** Put the axe here.	
	pen Can I borrow a pen?	**pan** Can I borrow a pan?	
	men Look at the men.	**man** Look at the man.	
	send I'm sending the table.	**sand** I'm sanding the table.	
	gem It's a lovely gem.	**jam** It's a lovely jam.	
	bread We had bread for lunch.	**Brad** We had Brad for lunch.	

Minimal pair words

A27a **a** Listen and repeat the words.

A27b **b** You will hear five words from each minimal pair. For each word write *1* for /e/ (sound 1) or *2* for /æ/ (sound 2).

EXAMPLE Pair 1: 2, 2, 1, 1, 2

Minimal pair sentences

A28a **c** Listen to the minimal pair sentences.

A28b **d** Listen to six of the sentences and write *1* for /e/ (sound 1) or *2* for /æ/ (sound 2).

A28a **e** Sentence stress

Listen to the first two minimal pair sentences again and look at the circles on the left. The big circles are the strongly stressed syllables, and the small circles are the weakly stressed syllables.

OoOO   Put the '<u>x</u>' here./<u>Put</u> the <u>axe</u> here.
ooOooO   Can I <u>borrow</u> a <u>pen</u>?/Can I <u>borrow</u> a <u>pan</u>?

A28a Listen to the rest of the sentences and <u>underline</u> the sentence stress (the **strong**ly stressed syllables in the most important words in the sentence).

OooO   Look at the men./Look at the man.
oOooOo   I'm sending the table./I'm sanding the table.
ooOoO   It's a lovely gem./It's a lovely jam.
ooOoO   We had bread for lunch./We had Brad for lunch.

A29 **f** Tick the words a) or b) that you hear in the sentences.

1 a) pen	☐	b) pan	☐
2 a) men	☐	b) man	☐
3 a) end	☐	b) and	☐
4 a) feta	☐	b) fatter	☐
5 a) pet	☐	b) pat	☐
6 a) bed	☐	b) bad	☐

3 Dialogue

a First practise the sound /æ/ in some of the words from the dialogue. Read the words aloud or visit the website to practise.

1 **All**en **sal**ad **hab**it **trav**el **Jan**et **ab**sent **sand**wich **contr**acts **canc**elled

2 **an**imals **Af**rica **an**telope **Ann**abelle **Anth**ony **pass**engers **an**chovy

3 **all**igator **ad**vertising

Which of the list of words (1, 2, 3) above have the word stress patterns below? The big circles are the strongly stressed syllables and the small circles are the weakly stressed syllables.

a) **O**oo   b) **O**ooo   c) **O**o

Match the sentences (1–3) below with the sentence stress patterns (a–c). The big circles are the strongly stressed words and the small circles are the weakly stressed words.

1 He hasn't done the backup. a) ooOooO
2 Aaron doesn't have to come back. b) oOoooOo
3 The computer has crashed. c) OoooOooO

b Aaron's recorded messages

A30 Listen to the recorded messages, paying attention to the target sound.

Now listen again and complete the sentences below. Each missing word has the sound /æ/. Number 1 has been done as an example.

1 Aaron works at the _Ajax Travel_ Agency.
2 He's on holiday in _____ .
3 His boss is Mrs _____ .
4 Aaron left an _____ and _____ on his desk.
5 He _____ to contact Anthony about the _____ of _____
   he _____ on _____ .
6 Aaron has a _____ habit of being _____ from work.
7 Aaron booked a _____ to San _____ with three _____ : an
   anteater, an _____ , and an _____ .
8 The computer has _____ and Aaron hadn't done the _____ up
   for the _____ programmes. Mrs Allen is very _____ .
9 The best advertising _____ have been _____ because of Aaron's
   bad _____ .
10 Aaron doesn't _____ to come _____ to the _____ agency
   because he's been _____ .

A31 Listen to the complete sentences and check your answers then practise reading the sentences aloud. Record your voice to compare your production of the target sound with the recording.

4 Sentence stress: the rhythm of English

A32 a Practise first with the names Annabelle and Janet. Notice how the important words are strongly stressed – we say them **LOUD**er and s l o w er. Listen and repeat.

Question: How do you shorten Annabelle and Janet?
Answer: Ann and Jan.

Listen to seven possible answers to the next question (see page 18).

A33 Notice that when we add more weakly stressed words or syllables to these sentences, we still say them in about the same length of time. We do this by saying all the weakly stressed words more quickly and quietly.

Question: Who works with Aaron?
Answers:
1 OO   Ann, Jan.
2 OoO   Ann and Jan.
3 OoooOo   Annabelle and Janet.

4 oOooooOo	There's <u>Ann</u>abelle and there's <u>J</u>anet.
5 ooOooooooOo	Well there's <u>Ann</u>abelle and then there's <u>J</u>anet.
6 oooOoooooooooOo	Well first there's <u>Ann</u>abelle and then there's also <u>J</u>anet.
7 oooooOoooooooooooOo	Well first of all there's <u>Ann</u>abelle and then you know there's also <u>J</u>anet.

(Note that although sometimes native speakers of English do speak like this with a lot of weakly stressed words, at other times they may use more strongly stressed words, e.g. 'Well, <u>first</u> of <u>all</u> there's <u>Ann</u>abelle and <u>then</u> you <u>know</u> there's <u>al</u>so <u>J</u>anet.' Both are correct. Both have the same rhythm of strong and weak stress.)

A34 b Listen to the seven answers in 4a again and try to say them all in the same length of time. Try a few times. First practise putting your energy into the strongly stressed words. Next practise saying the weakly stressed words with less energy, so that you say them more quietly. Then practise saying the weakly stressed words more and more quickly. Record your voice and compare this with the recording.

c Match the questions (1–3) with the pairs of answers (a–c) below. (In the brackets, the big circles are the strongly stressed syllables and the small circles are the weakly stressed syllables.)

Questions:
1 <u>What</u> kind of <u>an</u>imals did Aaron <u>book</u> on the San <u>Sal</u>vador flight?
2 What were <u>two</u> of the mis<u>takes</u> Aaron <u>made</u> before he went on <u>hol</u>iday?
3 Who <u>else</u> works at the <u>tra</u>vel agency?

Answers:
a) <u>An</u>thony, Mrs <u>All</u>en. (Ooo, ooOo)
   Well, there's <u>An</u>thony, and then there's Mrs <u>All</u>en. (ooOoo, ooooooOo)
b) An <u>ant</u>eater, an <u>an</u>telope, and an <u>all</u>igator. (oOoo, oOoo, ooOooo)
   He booked an <u>ant</u>eater, as well as an <u>an</u>telope, and also an <u>all</u>igator.
   (oooOoo, ooooOoo, ooooOooo)
c) The <u>map</u>, the <u>back</u>up, (oO, oOo)
   He lost the <u>map</u>, and he didn't do the <u>back</u>up. (oooO, ooooooOo)

Practise reading the questions and answers aloud. Try to say the pairs of answers in the same length of time.

5 Spelling

Look back over this unit at words with the target sound, and write what you noticed about how to spell the sound /æ/.

UNIT 5 /ʌ/ cup

> – I'm hungry. How much money's in the hat?
> – Nothing.
> – Nothing? I'm hungry too.
> – Oh shut up! Everybody's hungry.

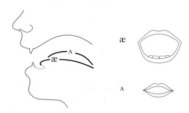

1 Target sound /ʌ/

A35a **a** First practise the sound /æ/
(see page 15). Listen and repeat.

A35b **b** Put your tongue back a little to make
the short target sound /ʌ/.
Listen and repeat.

A35c **c** Listen and repeat both sounds:
/æ/ and /ʌ/.

2 Minimal pairs

	Sound 1	Sound 2	
	/æ/	/ʌ/	
	cap Where's my cap?	**cup** Where's my cup?	
	hat There's a hat in the garden.	**hut** There's a hut in the garden.	
	track See the tracks on the road.	**truck** See the trucks on the road.	
	ban There's a ban on it.	**bun** There's a bun on it.	
	bag She's got a bag.	**bug** She's got a bug.	
	ankle My ankle was injured.	**uncle** My uncle was injured.	

Minimal pair words

A36a **a** Listen and repeat the words.

A36b **b** You will hear five words from each minimal pair. For each word write *1* for /æ/ (sound 1) or *2* for /ʌ/ (sound 2).

EXAMPLE Pair 1:   2, 1, 2, 1, 1

Minimal pair sentences

A37a **c** Listen to the minimal pair sentences.

A37b **d** Listen to six of the sentences and write *1* for /æ/ (sound 1) or *2* for /ʌ/ (sound 2).

A37a **e** Sentence stress

Listen to the pairs of sentences again and match them with the sentence stress patterns below. The big circles are the strong syllables and the small circles are the weak syllables.

EXAMPLE ooO (Pair 1) Where's my <u>cap</u>? / Where's my <u>cup</u>?

a) oooO   **b)** ooOoo   **c)** ooOooO   **d)** ooOooOo   **e)** oOooOo

Notice that if we put too many strong stresses in a sentence, we may sound angry, especially if the intonation keeps going down. Practise the sentences below.

OOO   Where's my cup?

OOooOo   My uncle was injured.

A38 **f** Tick the words a) or b) that you hear in the sentences.

1 a) cap ☐   b) cup ☐

2 a) hat ☐   b) hut ☐

3 a) bag ☐   b) bug ☐

4 a) mad ☐   b) mud ☐

5 a) hang ☐   b) hung ☐

6 a) ran ☐   b) run ☐

3 Dialogue

a First practise the sound /ʌ/ in some of the words from the dialogue. Listen and repeat.

lunch   just   much   one   love   **cous**in   **doesn't**   **funny**   **rubb**ish
enough   un**true**   shut up   un**happy**   under**stand**   unat**tractive**
worry   **lovely**   **honey**   **brother**   **other**   **nothing**   **company**
wonderful   month   does

A39 **b** Listen to the dialogue, paying attention to the target sound. Then read the dialogue and fill the gaps (1–10) with the correct words from the box. They are all words like *love* spelled with *o* but pronounced /ʌ/.

worry lovely honey brother other nothing company wonderful month does

She doesn't love him

JASMINE: Honey, why are you so sad?

(Duncan says 1_____ .)

JASMINE: 2_____ , why are you so unhappy? I don't understand.

DUNCAN: You don't love me, Jasmine.

JASMINE: But Duncan, I love you very much!

DUNCAN: That's untrue, Jasmine. You love my cousin.

JASMINE: Justin?

DUNCAN: No, his 3_____ .

JASMINE: Dudley?

DUNCAN: No. Stop being funny, Jasmine. Not that one. The 4_____ brother. Hunter. You think he's 5_____ and I'm unattractive.

JASMINE: Duncan! That's utter rubbish!

DUNCAN: And Hunter loves you too.

JASMINE: No he doesn't.

DUNCAN: Yes he 6_____ .

JASMINE: Duncan, just once last 7_____ I had lunch with Hunter. You mustn't 8_____ . I like your 9_____ much better than Hunter's. Hunter's …

DUNCAN: Oh, just shut up, Jasmine!

JASMINE: But honey, I think you're 10_____ .

DUNCAN: Oh, shut *up*, Jasmine.

JASMINE: Now that's enough! You're just jealous, Duncan. *You* shut up!

 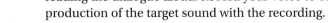 **c** Listen to the dialogue again to check your answers. Then practise reading the dialogue aloud. Record your voice to compare your production of the target sound with the recording.

4 Stress and intonation

Stress and intonation are used to show feelings in English. In the dialogue in 3b, you may have noticed that Jasmine's stress and intonation changed at the end when she got angry with Duncan.

A40 **a** Study the sentences below, and then listen to the recording.

Emotions	N (neutral)	A (angry)
1 No, he doesn't.	ooOo	OOOo
2 Yes, he does.	ooO	OOO
3 Now that's enough.	oooO	OOoO
4 I don't understand.	ooooO	OOOoO
5 Oh just shut up.	oooO	OOOO

A41 Listen to the sentences and write *A* for angry or *N* for neutral.

1 ___ 2 ___ 3 ___ 4 ___ 5 ___

Complete this statement.

If someone speaks with a lot of _____ly stressed words, with the intonation going _____ all the time, they can sound very angry.

A42 **b** Intonation in a list

The intonation goes up on the last strongly stressed word in each phrase, and then down at the end. Listen and repeat.

He bought a cup and some nuts.
He bought a cup, some nuts and some honey.
He bought a cup, some nuts, some honey and a brush.

c Game

'My uncle (mother/brother/cousin) went to London'

Practise this game with a group of five people. Choose any words from the list below.

EXAMPLE

A: My uncle went to London and he spent a lot of money. He bought a bus company.

B: My uncle went to London and he spent a lot of money. He bought a bus company and a toy duck.

Each player remembers what the others have said and then adds something to the list.

Practise saying these phrases before you start.

a **cup**	an **on**ion field	some sacks of **nuts**
a cuddly **monk**ey	a **bus** company	a toy **duck**
some **hon**ey	a **brush**	a lovely **butt**erfly
some comfortable **gloves**	a **bun** shop	a hundred **butt**ons
some **sun**glasses		

5 Spelling

Look back over this unit at words with the target sound, and write what you noticed about how to spell the sound /ʌ/. Make a list of all the words in this unit that are pronounced /ʌ/ but spelt with the letter *o*, like *love*. Add other words to this list when you see them.

UNIT 6 /ɑː/ heart

– Marvellous cars, aren't they?

– Wonderful ... fantastic ... so fast ...

– They are ... they are ...

1 Target sound /ɑː/

A43a **a** First practise the sound /æ/
(see page 15). Listen and repeat.

A43b **b** Put your tongue further back and
down to make the longer target
sound /ɑː/. Listen and repeat.

A43c **c** Listen and repeat both sounds together.
/æ/ is short. /ɑː/ is long.

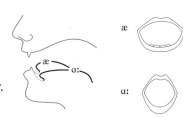

2 Minimal pairs A

	Sound 1 /æ/	Sound 2 /ɑː/	
	cap What a lovely cap!	**carp** What a lovely carp!	
	hat He touched his hat.	**heart** He touched his heart.	
	cat It's a farm cat.	**cart** It's a farm cart.	
	ban There's a ban on it.	**barn** There's a barn on it.	
	pack I'll pack the car.	**park** I'll park the car.	

Minimal pair words

A44a **a** Listen and repeat the words.

A44b **b** You will hear five words from each minimal pair. For each word write *1*
for /æ/ (sound 1) or *2* for /ɑː/ (sound 2).

EXAMPLE Pair 1:   2, 1, 1, 2, 2

Minimal pair sentences

A45a c Listen to the minimal pair sentences.

A45b d Listen to five of the sentences and write *1* for /æ/ (sound 1) or *2* for /ɑː/ (sound 2).

A45a e **Sentence stress**

In English sentences, the important words have a strongly stressed syllable that is **LOUD**er and s l o w er. The unstressed syllables are quieter and quicker. This gives English its rhythm.

Listen to the minimal pair sentences again and <u>underline</u> the sentence stress (on page 23).

EXAMPLE What a <u>love</u>ly <u>carp</u>!

Minimal pairs B

	Sound 1 /ʌ/	**Sound 2** /ɑː/	
	cup What a beautiful cup!	**carp** What a beautiful carp!	
	hut There's a problem with my hut.	**heart** There's a problem with my heart.	
	cut He covered his cut.	**cart** He covered his cart.	
	bun What's in that bun?	**barn** What's in that barn?	
	come 'Come down,' she said.	**calm** 'Calm down,' she said.	

Minimal pair words

A46a a Listen and repeat the words.

A46b b You will hear five words from each minimal pair. For each word write *1* for /e/ (sound 1) or *2* for /æ/ (sound 2).

EXAMPLE Pair 1: 1, 2, 1, 2, 2

Minimal pair sentences

A47a c Listen to the minimal pair sentences.

A47b d Listen to five of the sentences and write *1* for /ʌ/ (sound 1) or *2* for /ɑː/ (sound 2).

A47a e **Sentence stress**

Listen to the minimal pair sentences again and <u>underline</u> the sentence stress (above).

EXAMPLE <u>What's</u> in that <u>bun</u>?

A48 f Tick the words a), b) or c) that you hear in the sentences.

1 a) hat ☐ b) hut ☐ c) heart ☐

2 a) cat ☐ b) cut ☐ c) cart ☐

3 a) cap ☐ b) cup ☐ c) carp ☐

4 a) bun ☐ b) barn ☐

5 a) come ☐ b) calm ☐

6 a) Patty's ☐ b) parties ☐

3 Dialogue

a First practise the sound /ɑː/ in some of the names in the dialogue. Read the names aloud or visit the website to practise. Remember that when we say both the first and last names, the last name has the strongest stress.

It's **Tar**a.   It's Tara **Dar**ling.

Bart Jackson   **Mar**garet   Markus **Marsh**   A**la**na

The sound /ɑː/ is also in some of the words in your instructions.

example   **an**swer   the **tar**get <u>sound</u>   the **mask**   the <u>last</u> name

A49 b Listen to the dialogue, paying attention to the target sound. Then read the dialogue and fill the gaps (1–5) with the correct adjectives from the box.

| **mar**vellous   at**trac**tive   fan**tas**tic   **fab**ulous   smart |

At a party

(Margaret and Alana are at the bar. People are laughing in the garden.)

ALANA: What a 1_____ party this is! I'm having so much fun, Margaret.

MARGARET: Where's your glass, Alana?

ALANA: Here you are. Thanks. That's enough.

MARTIN: Alana! Margaret! Come into the garden. Tara Darling and Markus Marsh are dancing on the grass.

MARGARET: In the dark?

MARTIN: They're dancing under the stars.

ALANA: 2_____ ! And Bart Jackson is playing his guitar.

MARGARET: Just look at Tara! She can't dance but she looks very 3_____ .

MARTIN: Look at Markus. What a 4_____ dancer!

ALANA: What an 5_____ couple they are! Let's take a photograph of them.

A49 c Listen to the dialogue to check your answers. Then practise reading the dialogue aloud. Record your voice to compare your production of the target sound with the recording.

4 Intonation in exclamations

We often show the feeling of surprise in an exclamation where the intonation goes a long way up and then down.

A50 a Listen and repeat.

What a fast car!

What a funny dancer!

What a marvellous photograph!

What a fantastic guitar!

b Use these words to make exclamations about the pictures.

dark   **dir**ty   **fast**   **mar**vellous   **smart**   **un**usual   **funny**   **fantastic**

carpet

guitar

dancer

car

scarf

glass

photograph

star

5 Spelling

Look back over this unit at words with the target sound, and write what you noticed about how to spell the sound /ɑː/.

UNIT 7 REVIEW

Card game: Pick up pairs

Photocopy and cut out cards from all minimal pairs in units 1–6.

Shuffle the cards and deal them face down all over the table.

Turn over any two cards and read their sentences aloud. If they are minimal pairs, you keep them and you continue playing.

If these two cards aren't minimal pairs, turn them face down again and the next person plays.

Collect as many pairs as you can in a time limit, e.g. ten minutes.

TEST

You can use a dictionary if you wish, but you don't need to understand every word to do this test.

A51 1 For each line (1, 2, 3, 4, 5), first listen to the whole line. Then circle the one word that is said twice. Note that meaning is not important in this exercise. The purpose is to review the sounds by hearing them in contrast. Some of the words are rarely used in everyday English, and this is shown by an asterisk *.

	/iː/	/ɪ/	/e/	/æ/	/ʌ/	/ɑː/
1	bean	bin	Ben	ban	bun	barn
2	beat	bit	bet	bat	but	Bart
3	bead	bid	bed	bad	bud	bard*
4	peak	pick	peck	pack	Puck*	park
5	peaty*	pity	petty	Patty	putty	party

Score ☐ /5

2 Circle the words with the same vowel sound as 1–3.

1 cup
/ʌ/

done sad
doesn't does
match comb
copy come hot
us yes

2 heart
/ɑː/

jump half
am arm cut
home are
aren't can
carry
can't

3 sheep
/iː/

slip people
bread piece any
these stick shop
she this need

Score ☐ / 15

3 **Intonation jumble**

Match the correct intonation pattern items a–f with the conversation items 1–6. Number 1 has been done.

1 'I'm going to make some jelly.' ——
2 'Would you like lemon or cherry?'
3 'Cherry.'
4 'Can I help?'
5 'I need a spoon, a bowl, some jelly crystals and some hot water.'
6 'What a lovely colour!'

a) ⌐⌐⌐ (a list)
b) ⌐ (yes/no question)
c) ⌐ (statement)
d) ⌐ (short statement)
e) ⌐ (exclamation)
f) ⌐ (question with 'or')

Score ☐ / 5

4 **Word stress**

<u>Underline</u> the main stressed syllable in these words. (Score half a mark per item.)

advertising   understand   Lebanon   lemonade   sandwich
expensive   sunglasses   fantastic   photograph   guitar

Score ☐ / 5

Total score ☐ / 30

Additional review task using dialogues from Units 1–6

Unit	1	2	3	4	5	6
Target sound	/iː/	/ɪ/	/e/	/æ/	/ʌ/	/ɑː/
	sheep	ship	pen	man	cup	heart

From the above table, choose any target sounds that you had difficulty with.

1 Listen again to the dialogue in that unit, listening for the target sound.
2 Circle the target sound in any words in the dialogue.
3 Listen to the dialogue again and check your answers.
4 Check your answers in the key.
5 Listen to the dialogue again, listening for the target sound.
6 Practise reading the dialogue aloud, and record your voice to compare your production of the target sound with the recording.

You can also use this review task as a quick self-test, by doing steps 2 and 4 only.

UNIT 8 /ɒ/ clock

> – What's wrong?
> – I've got a really bad backache.
> – I'm sorry to hear that.

1 Target sound /ɒ/

A52a **a** First practise the sound /æ/
(see page 15). Listen and repeat.

A52b **b** Put your tongue slightly back and
bring your lips slightly forward to make
the target sound /ɒ/. Listen and repeat.

A52c **c** Listen and repeat both sounds together:
/æ/ and /ɒ/.

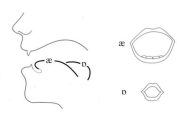

2 Minimal pairs

Sound 1 /æ/	Sound 2 /ɒ/
hat It's hat weather.	**hot** It's hot weather.
cat He's got a white cat.	**cot** He's got a white cot.
fax Look for the fax.	**fox** Look for the fox.
sack Put it in a sack.	**sock** Put it in a sock.
tap Turn that tap slowly.	**top** Turn that top slowly.
backs I can see their backs.	**box** I can see their box.

Minimal pair words

A53a a Listen and repeat the words.

A53b b You will hear five words from each minimal pair. For each word, write *1* for /æ/ (sound 1) or *2* for /ɒ/ (sound 2).

EXAMPLE: Pair 1:   2, 2, 1, 2, 1

Minimal pair sentences

A54a c Listen to the minimal pair sentences.

A54b d Listen to six of the sentences and write *1* for /æ/ (sound 1) or *2* for /ɒ/ (sound 2).

A54a e Sentence stress

The most important words for the meaning of a sentence are spoken with a strong stress. Listen to the minimal pair sentences again and match them with the sentence stress patterns below. The big circles are the strong syllables and the small circles are the weak syllables.

EXAMPLE oOOo (Pair 1) It's <u>hat</u> <u>weath</u>er./It's <u>hot</u> <u>weath</u>er.

a) **OooO**   b) **oooOO**   c) **ooOoO**   d) **OoOOo**   e) **OoooO**

A55 f Tick the words a) or b) that you hear in the sentences

1 a) cat ☐   b) cot ☐

2 a) sack ☐   b) sock ☐

3 a) tap ☐   b) top ☐

4 a) Pat ☐   b) pot ☐

5 a) baddie ☐   b) body ☐

6 a) black ☐   b) block ☐

3 Dialogue

a First practise the sound /ɒ/ in some of the words from the dialogue. Read the words aloud or visit the website to practise.

soft   hot   long   strong   **pop**ular   **horr**ible   wants   what   wrong socks   job   got   **of**ten   **sorr**y   **wash**ing   Mrs **Bloggs**

A56 b Listen to the dialogue, paying attention to the target sound. Then read the dialogue and fill the gaps (1–6) with the correct adjectives from the box.

soft   hot   long   strong   **pop**ular   **horr**ible

TV advertisement for 'Onwash'

VOICE A: What's wrong with you, Mrs Bloggs?

MRS BLOGGS: What's wrong with me? I want a holiday from this 1_____ job of washing socks!

VOICE B: Buy a bottle of 'Onwash', Mrs Bloggs!

VOICE C: 'Onwash' is so 2_____ and 3_____ .

VOICE D: You don't want lots of 4_____ water with 'Onwash'.

VOICE A: It's not a 5_____ job with 'Onwash'.

VOICE B: Use 'Onwash' often.

VOICE C: You won't be sorry when you've got 'Onwash'.

VOICE D: Everybody wants 'Onwash'.

EVERYBODY: 'Onwash' is so 6_____ !

 A56 c Listen to the dialogue again to check your answers. Then practise reading the dialogue aloud. Record your voice to compare your production of the target sound with the recording.

4 Intonation in suggestions and commands

Intonation is the voice going up or down. Sometimes this shows whether the speaker is more polite and friendly or less friendly.

 A57 a Listen.

Intonation goes up in a suggestion, and this sounds polite and friendly:

Have a holiday, Mrs Bloggs.

Stop washing, Mr Wong.

Don't drop that pot, Ms Morris.

Put it on the box, Miss Johnson.

Intonation goes down in a command, and this sounds less friendly:

Have a holiday, Mrs Bloggs.

Stop washing, Mr Wong.

Don't drop that pot, Ms Morris.

Put it on the box, Miss Johnson.

A58 **b** Intonation dictation

Listen to the intonation in the sentences below. Decide if they are suggestions (which are polite and friendly as the intonation is going up) or commands (which are less friendly as the intonation is going down). Draw an arrow up or down in the space before the <u>strong</u>ly stressed word. Number 1 has been done.

1 Put these socks in the top ↘ <u>draw</u>er, John. *command*
2 Put it on top of the <u>box</u>. _____
3 Make the coffee <u>hot</u>, Mrs Wong. _____
4 Don't wash these socks in the <u>wash</u>ing machine, Robin. _____
5 Don't go to the wrong <u>off</u>ice. _____
6 Go to the <u>shops</u>, Oscar. _____
7 Don't go to the wrong <u>doc</u>tor, Bronwen. _____

A58 **c** Listen again and then practise the sentences. Record your voice to compare your production of the intonation with the recording.

5 Spelling

Look back over this unit at words with the target sound, and write what you noticed about how to spell the sound /ɒ/.

UNIT 9 /ɔː/ ball

– Dawn always goes for a jog in the morning.
– Don? Jogging? In the morning?
– No, not Don! His daughter-in-law, Dawn. She's very sporty.

1 Target sound /ɔː/

A59a **a** First practise the sound /ɒ/
(see page 29). Listen and repeat.

A59b **b** The back of your tongue goes up a
little more to make the long target
sound /ɔː/. Listen and repeat.

A59c **c** Listen and repeat both sounds together.
/ɒ/ is short. /ɔː/ is long.

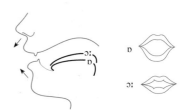

2 Minimal pairs

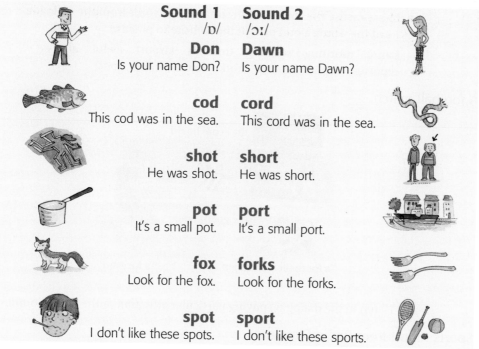

Sound 1 /ɒ/	Sound 2 /ɔː/
Don Is your name Don?	**Dawn** Is your name Dawn?
cod This cod was in the sea.	**cord** This cord was in the sea.
shot He was shot.	**short** He was short.
pot It's a small pot.	**port** It's a small port.
fox Look for the fox.	**forks** Look for the forks.
spot I don't like these spots.	**sport** I don't like these sports.

Minimal pair words

A60a **a** Listen and repeat the words.

A60b **b** You will hear five words from each minimal pair. For each word write *1*
for /ɒ/ (sound 1) or *2* for /ɔː/ (sound 2).

EXAMPLE Pair 1: 1, 1, 2, 2, 1

Minimal pair sentences

A61a **c** Listen to the minimal pair sentences.

A61b **d** Listen to six of the sentences and write *1* for /ɒ/ (sound 1) or *2* for /ɔ:/ (sound 2).

A61a **e** Sentence stress

Listen to the minimal pair sentences again and <u>underline</u> the sentence stress (on page 33). Notice that the strongly stressed words are **LOUD**er and s l o w er. The weakly stressed words are quieter and quicker.

A62 **f** Tick the words a) or b) that you hear in the sentences.

1 a) spots ☐   b) sports ☐
2 a) pots ☐   b) ports ☐
3 a) cod ☐   b) cord ☐
4 a) shot ☐   b) short ☐
5 a) Rod ☐   b) roared ☐
6 a) what a ☐   b) water ☐

3 Dialogue

a First practise the sound /ɔ:/ in some of the words from the dialogue. Read the words aloud or visit the website to practise.

Laura   morning   walking   towards   airport   awful   always reporter   report   sports   York   fault (/fɔːlt/ or /fɒlt/)

A football match

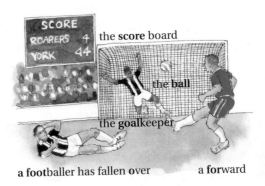

the score board

the ball

the goalkeeper

a footballer has fallen over   a forward

A63 **b** Listen to the dialogue, paying particular attention to the target sound.

Sports report from Radio Station 4

ANNOUNCER: This morning the Roarers football team arrived back from York. Laura Short is our sports reporter, and she was at the airport.

LAURA SHORT: Good morning, listeners. This is Laura Short. All the footballers are walking towards me. Here's George Ball, the goalkeeper. Good morning, George.

GEORGE BALL: Good morning. Are you a reporter?

LAURA SHORT: Yes. George. I'm Laura Short from Radio Station 4. Tell us about the football match with York.

GEORGE BALL: Well, it was awful. We lost. And the score was forty-four, four. But it wasn't my fault, Laura

LAURA SHORT: Whose fault was it, George?

GEORGE BALL: The forwards.

LAURA SHORT: The forwards?

GEORGE BALL: Yes. The forwards. They were always falling over or losing the ball!

c Practise reading the dialogue aloud. Record your voice to compare your production of the target sound with the recording.

4 Intonation

Intonation is the voice going up or down. We can show a feeling of surprise with an intonation that goes a long way up.

A64 a Listen to the speakers expressing surprise.

A: Mr Short always plays football in the morning.

B: In the morning?

C: Mr Short?

D: Football?

E: Always?

In this conversation B, C, D and E are all surprised by what A says. B is surprised that he plays *in the morning*. C is surprised that *Mr Short* plays. D is surprised that he plays *football*. E is surprised that he *always* plays.

A65 b Listen and then express surprise about the part of the sentence in *italics*, like the example.

EXAMPLE I saw Victoria *at the airport*.

Response: At the airport?

1 I've put the ball *in the drawer*.
2 *It's too warm* to go walking.
3 *Georgia* was looking gorgeous this morning.
4 Morgan has bought *forty-five forks*.
5 I'm going to buy *a horse*.
6 You ought to get up *at four in the morning*.
7 I saw *Orlando* when I was *in New York*.
8 It's *your fault*.

5 Spelling

Look back over this unit at words with the target sound, and write what you noticed about how to spell the sound /ɔː/.

UNIT 10 /ʊ/ book

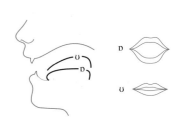

> – We should put all these books in that box *now*, shouldn't we?
> – Yes, we should.

1 Target sound /ʊ/

A66a **a** First practise the sound /ɒ/
(see page 29). Listen and repeat.

A66b **b** The back of your tongue goes forward
and up a little more to make the target
sound /ʊ/.

A66c **c** Listen and repeat both of these short
sounds: /ɒ/ and /ʊ/.

2 Minimal pairs

	Sound 1 /ɒ/	Sound 2 /ʊ/	
	pot Pot the plant in the garden.	**put** Put the plant in the garden.	
Cod	**cod** How do you spell 'cod'?	**could** How do you spell 'could'?	*Could*
	lock I'll lock you up.	**look** I'll look you up.	
	rock The wind blew around the rock.	**rook** The wind blew around the rook.	
	box Give me the box.	**books** Give me the books.	

Minimal pair words

A67a **a** Listen and repeat the words.

A67b **b** You will hear five words from each minimal pair. For each word write *1*
for /ɒ/ (sound 1) or *2* for /ʊ/ (sound 2).

EXAMPLE Pair 1:   2, 2, 1, 2, 1

Minimal pair sentences

A68a **c** Listen to the minimal pair sentences.

A68b **d** Listen to five of the sentences and write *1* for /ɒ/ (sound 1) or *2* for /ʊ/
(sound 2).

A69 **e** Sentence stress

Any word in a sentence can become *the* most important word, and have the strongest stress to give the sentence a special meaning. Listen to the minimal pair sentences again and write the word which has the strongest stress in each pair in the table. Then read the special meanings.

	Strongest stress	Special meaning
Pair 1	in	Not just anywhere, e.g. near or beside it.
Pair 2		Everybody else has a different answer.
Pair 3		Nobody else would do that.
Pair 4		But not under it or above it.
Pair 5		Don't trust anybody else.

A70 **f** Tick the words a) or b) that you hear in the sentences:

1 a) cock ☐ b) cook ☐

2 a) lock ☐ b) look ☐

3 a) god ☐ b) good ☐

4 a) cod ☐ b) could ☐

3 Dialogue

a First practise the sound /ʊ/ in some of the words from this unit. Read the words aloud or visit the website to practise.

good   book   foot   cook   look   took   should   could   would   full
sugar   **foot**ball   **book**shelf   **cook**ery   **should**n't   **could**n't   **would**n't

A71 **b** Listen to the dialogue, paying attention to the target sound.

A lost book

MR COOK: Could you tell me where you've put my book, Bronwen?

MRS COOK: Isn't it on the bookshelf?

MR COOK: No. The bookshelf is full of your cookery books.

MRS COOK: Then you should look in the bedroom, shouldn't you?

MR COOK: I've looked. You took that book and put it somewhere, didn't you?

MRS COOK: The living room?

MR COOK: No. I've looked. I'm going to put all my books in a box and lock it!

MRS COOK: Look, John! It's on the floor next to your foot.

MR COOK: Ah! Good!

c Practise reading the dialogue aloud. Record your voice to compare your production of the target sound with the recording.

4 Intonation: down tags

EXAMPLE We should put all these books in that box *now*, **should**n't we?

The intonation in most question tags is going down. This means that the speaker expects agreement. So down tags are used a lot in conversations to create agreement and rapport between the speakers.

A72 **a** Listen and repeat.

should you?   shouldn't you?   could you?   couldn't you?   would he?

wouldn't he?

He couldn't cook, could he?   She could play football, couldn't she?

You wouldn't look, would you?   They would like sugar, wouldn't they?

A73 **b** Practise in pairs. Listen and respond, like the example.

EXAMPLE She couldn't cook.

   A: She couldn't cook, could she?

   B: No, she couldn't.

1 We couldn't cook a cake without sugar.
2 Good footballers shouldn't eat too much pudding.
3 You should look at some good cookery books.
4 You wouldn't 'put your foot in it'*.
 (*idiom meaning say or do the wrong thing)
5 They wouldn't 'cook the books'*.
 (*idiom meaning change the accounts to steal money)

5 Spelling

Look back over this unit at words with the target sound, and write what you noticed about how to spell the sound /ʊ/.

UNIT 11 /uː/ boot

– I'm full of good food.
– Such beautiful puddings!
– But too much sugar …
– *I* had a huge serving of chocolate mousse with stewed fruit.
– *I* had the blueberry soufflé *and* the rhubarb strudel.
– *I* was very foolish. I had two servings of gooseberry fool.
– What a fool you are!

(Note: *fool* has two meanings: 1 a stupid person; 2 mousse, soufflé, strudel and fool are desserts)

1 Target sound /uː/

B2a a First practise the sound /ʊ/ (see page 36). Listen and repeat.
B2b b Put your tongue up and back a little more to make the long target sound /uː/. Listen and repeat.
B2c c Listen and repeat both sounds together. /ʊ/ is short. /uː/ is long.

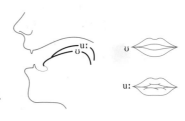

2 Minimal pairs

	Sound 1 /ʊ/	Sound 2 /uː/	
	look Look, a new moon!	**Luke** Luke, a new moon!	
	pull The sign said 'Pull'.	**pool** The sign said 'Pool'.	
	full This isn't really full proof.	**fool** This isn't really foolproof.	
	could The bird could.	**cooed** The bird cooed.	
	would 'He would, Julie, at the full moon.'	**wooed** He wooed Julie at the full moon.	

(Note: *proof* has two meanings: 1 evidence that something is true; 2 *foolproof* – made so that it can't be damaged, even by a fool)

Minimal pair words

B3a a Listen and repeat the words.

B3b b You will hear five words from each minimal pair. For each word write *1* for /ʊ/ (sound 1) or *2* for /uː/ (sound 2).

EXAMPLE Pair 1:   2, 2, 1, 2, 1

Minimal pair sentences

B4a c Listen to the minimal pair sentences.

B4b d Listen to five of the sentences and write *1* for /ʊ/ (sound 1) or *2* for /uː/ (sound 2).

B5 e Listen to the strong and weak stresses in: oOooOo a **fool**proof com**pu**ter. Then listen and <u>underline</u> the strong stresses in:

OooO waterproof boots   oOoOo a wind-proof jacket
OooOo childproof containers   oOooO an ovenproof dish
oOooO a waterproof coat   oOooO a bullet-proof vest.

B6 f Tick the words a) or b) that you hear in the sentences.

1 a) look ☐   b) Luke ☐
2 a) full ☐   b) fool ☐
3 a) pull ☐   b) pool ☐
4 a) fullish ☐   b) foolish ☐
5 a) would ☐   b) wooed ☐

3 Dialogue

a First practise the sound /uː/ in some of the words and phrases from the dialogue. Read the words aloud or visit the website to practise.

who   school   soup   threw   unit   **rude**ness   **rud**est   **stu**dent continue   computer   **chew**ing gum   ex**cuse** me   good after**noon** it was **you**!

B7 b Listen to the dialogue, paying attention to the target sound. Then read the dialogue and guess which words are strongly stressed. The number in brackets tells you how many strong stresses there are in that line. The first line has been done.

B7 c Listen to the dialogue again and <u>underline</u> the strong stresses. Check your answers.

The two rudest students in the school

MISS LUKE: (1) Good after<u>noon</u> girls.

GIRLS: (2) Good afternoon, Miss Luke.

MISS LUKE: (4) This afternoon we're going to learn how to cook soup.

(5) Turn on your computers and look at unit twenty-two.

LUCY: (2) Excuse me, Miss Luke.

MISS LUKE: (1) Yes, Lucy?

LUCY: (2) There's some chewing gum on your shoe.

MISS LUKE: (5) Who threw their chewing gum on the floor? Was it you, Lucy?

LUCY: (2) No, Miss Luke. It was Susan.

MISS LUKE: (1) Who?

LUCY: (2) Susan Duke.

SUSAN: (3) It wasn't me, stupid. It was Julie.

JULIE: (1) It was you!

SUSAN: (8) It wasn't me! My mouth's full of chewing gum. Look, Miss Luke!

JULIE: (4) Stop pulling my hair, Susan. It was you!

SUSAN: (1) YOU!

JULIE: (1) YOU!

MISS LUKE: (11) Excuse me! If you two continue with this rudeness, you can stay after school instead of going to the pool.

4 Sentence stress

B8 a Listen to this conversation. Notice how the strongly stressed words are **LOUD**er, and the weakly stressed words are said very quickly.

A: Ex<u>cuse</u> <u>me</u>.

B: <u>Yes</u>?

A: Could you <u>tell</u> me where I can get some (1) <u>shoe</u>laces?

B: <u>Yes</u>. There's a <u>shop</u> next to the (2) <u>su</u>permarket that sells <u>very</u> good (1) <u>shoe</u>laces. <u>I'm</u> going there <u>too</u>.

b Use the words below to make more conversations like the one in 4a. Try to say the unstressed syllables quickly.

1	**2**
shoelaces	supermarket
herbal sham**poo**	**swimm**ing pool
toothpaste	compu**ter** shop
tools	**news**paper stand
football boots	**school**
tuna	
chewing gum	
fresh **fruit** juice	

5 Spelling

Look back over this unit at words with the target sound, and write what you noticed about how to spell the sound /uː/.

UNIT 12 /ɜː/ girl

> – All my co-workers have started ... er ... walking
>   to work ... er ... very early in the morning.
> – Oh. And do *you* walk to work?
> – Not me ... er ... I'm the world's worst walker.

1 Target sound /ɜː/

B9a **a** First practise the sound /ɔː/
(see page 33). Listen and repeat.

B9b **b** Put your tongue forward and up a
little more to make the target sound
/ɜː/. Listen and repeat.

B9c **c** Listen and repeat both of these
long sounds together: /ɔː/ and /ɜː/.

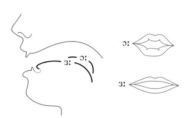

2 Minimal pairs A

	Sound 1 /ɔː/	Sound 2 /ɜː/
	four She's got four.	**fur** She's got fur.	
	torn It's a torn sign.	**turn** It's a turn sign.	
	**warm** I wouldn't like warm soup.	**worm** I wouldn't like worm soup.	
	walker He's a fast walker.	**worker** He's a fast worker.	

Minimal pair words

B10a **a** Listen and repeat the words.

 B10b **b** You will hear five words from each minimal pair. For each word write *1*
for /ɔː/ (sound 1) or *2* for /ɜː/ (sound 2).

EXAMPLE Pair 1: 1, 2, 1, 1, 2

Minimal pair sentences

B11a c Listen to the minimal pair sentences.

B11b d Listen to four of the sentences and write *1* for /ɔː/ (sound 1) or *2* for /ɜː/ (sound 2).

B11a e Sentence stress
Listen to the minimal pair sentences again and <u>underline</u> the sentence stress (on page 43).

EXAMPLE I <u>would</u>n't like <u>warm</u> soup.

Minimal pairs B

	Sound 1 /e/	Sound 2 /ɜː/
	ten The sign says ten.	**turn** The sign says turn.
	Ben Look at it, Ben.	**burn** Look at it burn.
	bed It's a colourful bed.	**bird** It's a colourful bird.
	west It's the west wind.	**worst** It's the worst wind.

Minimal pair words

B12a a Listen and repeat the words.

B12b b You will hear five words from each minimal pair. For each word write *1* for /e/ (sound 1) or *2* for /ɜː/ (sound 2).

EXAMPLE Pair 1: 2, 2, 2, 1, 1

Minimal pair sentences

B13a c Listen to the minimal pair sentences.

B13b d Listen to four of the sentences and write *1* for /e/ (sound 1) or *2* for /ɜː/ (sound 2).

B13a e Sentence stress
Listen to the minimal pair sentences again and <u>underline</u> the sentence stress (above).

EXAMPLE It's the <u>west</u> wind.

Minimal pairs C

	Sound 1	**Sound 2**	
	/ʌ/	/ɜː/	
	fun	**fern**	
	Fabulous fun!	Fabulous fern!	
	bun	**burn**	
	Look at that bun.	Look at that burn.	
	bud	**bird**	
	That's a tiny little bud.	That's a tiny little bird.	
	gull	**girl**	
	There's a gull on the beach.	There's a girl on the beach.	

Minimal pair words

B14a **a** Listen and repeat the words.

B14b **b** You will hear five words from each minimal pair. For each word write *1* for /ʌ/ (sound 1) or *2* for /ɜː/ (sound 2).

EXAMPLE Pair 1: 1, 2, 1, 2, 1

Minimal pair sentences

B15a **c** Listen to the minimal pair sentences.

B15b **d** Listen to four of the sentences and write *1* for /ʌ/ (sound 1) or *2* for /ɜː/ (sound 2).

B15a **e** Sentence stress

Listen to the minimal pair sentences again and <u>underline</u> the sentence stress (above).

EXAMPLE Fabulous <u>fun</u>!

B16 **f** Tick the words a) or b) that you hear in the sentences:

1 a) bed ☐   b) bud ☐   c) bird ☐
2 a) Ben's ☐   b) buns ☐   c) burns ☐
3 a) ward ☐   b) word ☐
4 a) walk ☐   b) work ☐
5 a) short ☐   b) shirt ☐
6 a) or ☐   b) er ☐

3 Dialogue

a First practise the sound /ɜː/ in words from the dialogue below. Read the words aloud or visit the website to practise.

were   weren't   nurse   worst   world   shirts   hurts   **thirsty**
Thursday   **dirty**   Sir **Herbert**   Colonel **Burton**

B17 **b** Listen to the dialogue, paying attention to the target sound.

The worst nurse

SIR HERBERT: Nurse!

COLONEL BURTON: Nurse! I'm thirsty!

SIR HERBERT: Nurse! My head hurts!

COLONEL BURTON: Nurse Sherman always wears such dirty shirts.

SIR HERBERT: He never arrives at work early.

COLONEL BURTON: He and … er … Nurse Turner weren't at work on Thursday, were they?

SIR HERBERT: No, they weren't.

COLONEL BURTON: Nurse Sherman is the worst nurse in the ward, isn't he, Sir Herbert?

SIR HERBERT: No, he isn't, Colonel Burton. He's the worst nurse in the world!

c Practise reading the dialogue aloud. Record your voice to compare your production of the target sound with the recording.

4 Intonation: up or down tags

B18 a The intonation of question tags is usually going down. This means the speaker expects agreement. Down tags are used a lot to create agreement and rapport between the speakers.

EXAMPLE A: We were at work early, weren't we?
 B: Yes, we were.

Sometimes the intonation goes up. This means the speaker is not sure if the information is correct and is asking the listener to check it. Before an up tag there is often a slight pause..

EXAMPLE A: The nurses were at work on Thursday, weren't they?
 B: Yes, they were.

B19 b **Up or down?**

Listen and mark intonation arrows on the tags: ↘ (expects agreement) or ↗ (not sure). Number 1 has been done.

1 They weren't <u>walk</u>ing to work, <u>were</u> they? ↗ _not sure_

2 Those dirty shirts were Nurse <u>Tur</u>ner's, <u>weren't</u> they? _____

3 The wards weren't <u>dir</u>ty, <u>were</u> they? _____

4 They weren't speaking <u>Ger</u>man, <u>were</u> they? _____

5 Those nurses were <u>thir</u>sty, <u>weren't</u> they? _____

6 The Colonel and Sir Herbert were the worst patients in the <u>ward</u>,
<u>weren't</u> they? _____

c Practise reading the questions above with the same intonation. Record your voice to compare your production of the intonation with the recording.

5 Spelling

Look back over this unit at words with the target sound and write what you noticed about how to spell the sound /ɜː/.

UNIT 13 /ə/ a camera

> – Remember to telephone your sister the day after tomorrow, for her birthday.
> – And don't forget to send a letter to your brother.
> – Shall I send *you* a letter?
> – Of course. But don't forget to telephone as soon as you arrive.

1 Target sound /ə/

B20a a First practise the sound /ɜː/
(see page 43). Listen and repeat.

B20b b Make the same sound but very very short to make the target sound /ə/. Listen and repeat.

B20c c Listen and repeat both sounds together: /ɜː/ is long. /ə/ is very short.

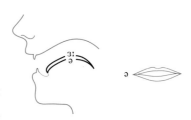

2 /ə/ in unstressed words and syllables

B21a a Listen and repeat. The spelling has been changed in the words on the right to show you when to use the sound /ə/.

a photograph of Barbara	1 ə photəgraph əf Barbərə
a glass of water	2 ə glass əf watə
a pair of binoculars	3 ə pair əf binoculəs
a photograph of her mother and father	4 ə photəgraph əf hə mothər ənd fathə
a book about South America	5 ə book əbout South əmericə

b Cover the words on the left and practise questions and answers.

EXAMPLE A: What's in picture two?

B: ə glass əf watə

B21b c Telling the time

Listen and repeat.

Look at the clock.
What's the time?

It's six o'clock.

It's a quarter to seven.

Look ət thə clock.
What's thə time?

It's six ə'clock.

It's ə quartə tə sevən.

Now practise these.

EXAMPLE A: What's thə time?

B: It's ə quartə tə twelve.

3 Reading aloud

a Read this story aloud or visit the website to practise. The spelling has been changed to show you when to make the sound /ə/. Record your voice to listen to your production of the target sound.

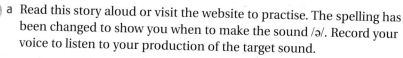

Barbərə spent Satəday aftənoon looking ət ə beautifəl book əbout South əmericə.

'I want tə go tə South əmericə,' she said tə həself.

Thə next morning, when Barbərə woke up it wəs six ə'clock, ənd hə brothəs ənd sistəs wə still əsleep. Barbərə looked ət thəm, ənd then closed hər eyes əgain.

Then she quiətly got out əf bed ənd started tə pack hə suitcase.

She took səme comfətəble clothes out əf thə cupbəd. She packed ə pair əf binoculəs ənd hə sistə's camərə. She packed ə photəgraph əf həself ənd one əf hə mothər ənd fathə.

'I musn't fəget tə have səme breakfəst,' she said tə həself. Bət then she looked ət thə clock. It wəs ə quartə tə seven.

'I'll jəst drink ə glass əf watə,' she said.

'ə glass əf watə,' she said.

'Watə,' she said, ənd opened hər eyes.

She wəs still in hə bed, and hə brothəs ənd sistəs wə laughing ət hə.

'Tell əs what you wə dreaming əbout,' they said tə hə.

Bət Barbərə didn't answə. She wəs thinking əbout hə wondəful journey tə South əmericə.

B22 b **Weak forms**

Listen to the example of the weak form and the strong form of *was*.

EXAMPLE

Wəs she dreaming?
This is the sound /ə/. This is the weak form of *was*.

Yes, she **was.**
This is a different sound. This is the strong form of *was*

Then listen and repeat.

Wəs she thinking about South America?	Yes, she **was.**
Wə her brothers and sisters asleep?	Yes, they **were.**
Də they like reading?	Yes, they **do.**
Həve you read about South America?	Yes, I **have.**
Dəs your friend like reading?	Yes, he **does.**
ə we working hard?	Yes, we **are.**
Həs your friend been to South America?	Yes, he **has.**
Cən you swim?	Yes, I **can.**

B23 c Tick the words a) or b) that you hear in the sentences.

1 a) **has** ☐ b) həs ☐

2 a) **can** ☐ b) cən ☐

3 a) **was** ☐ b) wəs ☐

4 a) **does** ☐ b) dəs ☐

5 a) **am** ☐ b) əm ☐

6 a) **them** ☐ b) thəm ☐

4 Dialogue

a Read this dialogue and circle the sound /ə/. The first line has been done for you.

Shopping

A: I'm going to the library.

B: Can you buy something for me at the newsagent's?

A: But the newsagent's is a mile from the library.

B: No. Not that newsagent's. Not the one that's next to the fish and chip shop.

I mean the one that's near the butcher's.

A: Oh, yes. Well, what do you want?

B: Some chocolates and a tin of sweets and an address book.

B24 b Listen and check your answers, then practise reading the dialogue aloud. Record your voice to compare your production of the target sound with the recording.

5 Spelling

Look back over this unit at words with the target sound, and write what you noticed about how to spell the sound /ə/.

UNIT 14 | REVIEW

Card game: Pick up same sounds

Photocopy and cut out cards from all minimal pairs in Units 8–13.

Shuffle the cards and deal them face down all over the table.

Turn over any two cards and read their sentences aloud. If they are the same vowel sound you keep them and you continue playing.

If those two cards aren't the same vowel sound, turn them face down again and the next person plays.

Collect as many same sound pairs as you can in a time limit, e.g. ten minutes.

TEST

You can use a dictionary if you wish, but you don't have to understand every word to do this test.

B25 **1** For each line (1, 2, 3, 4), first listen to the whole line. Then circle the one word – or part of a word – that is said twice. Note that meaning is not important in this exercise. The purpose is to review the sounds by hearing them in contrast. Some of the words are rarely used in everyday English, and this is shown by an asterisk*. Incomplete words have the rest of the word written in brackets, e.g. *foll(ow)*.

	/ɒ/	/ɔː/	/ʊ/	/uː/	/ɜː/
1	Poll(y)	Paul	pull	pool	Pearl
2	foll(ow)	fall	full	fool	furl*
3	cod	cord	could	cooed	curd*
4	wad	ward	would	wooed*	word

Score ☐ / 4

2 Circle the words with the same vowel sound as 1–4.

1 bird
/ɜː/

bed   were
rude   burn
early   board   shirt
worst   shot

2 ball
/ɔː/

torn   water
girl   all   glass
four   log
talk   nurse

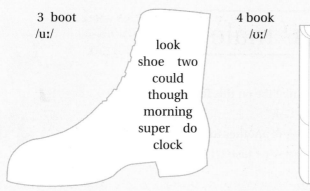

3 boot
/uː/

look
shoe   two
could
though
morning
super   do
clock

4 book
/ʊː/

full   box
cook   who
lock   threw
would   look
tool   good

Score [/20]

B26 **3** Listen to the sentences and mark which kind of question tag is being used:

↘ agreement (expected)   ↗ unsure (so checking the information)

1 You can buy bootlaces at the shoeshop, can't you? _____
2 That carpet shop sells cushions too, doesn't it? _____
3 Sue bought her flute at the music shop, didn't she? _____
4 You'd like a new cookery book, wouldn't you? _____
5 The bookshop's next to the newsagent's, isn't it? _____
6 You do want your birthday presents to be a surprise,
   don't you? _____

Score [/6]

Total score [/30]

Additional review task using dialogues from Units 8–12

Unit	8	9	10	11	12	13
Target sound	/ɒ/	/ɔː/	/ʊ/	/uː/	/ɜː/	/ə/
	clock	ball	book	boot	girl	a camera

From the above table, choose any target sounds that you had difficulty with.

1 Listen again to the dialogue in that unit, listening for the target sound. If you have chosen the target sound /ə/, listen for that sound in any of the dialogues from Units 8–12.
2 Circle the target sound in any words in the dialogue.
3 Listen to the dialogue again and check your answers.
4 Check your answers in the key.
5 Listen to the dialogue again, listening for the target sound.
6 Read the dialogue aloud, and record your voice to compare your production of the target sound with the CD.

You can also use this review task as a quick self-test, by doing steps 2 and 4 only.

UNIT 15 /eɪ/ male

– I'm afraid I've made a mistake on this form.
Is your name spelt J–A–C–K?
– No. It's J–A–H–K. And here's another mistake.
My occupation. I'm not a wine taster. I'm a food tester.

---

1 Target sound /eɪ/

B27a **a** First practise the sound /e/ (see page 11). Then practise the short sound /ɪ/ (see page 7). Listen and repeat.

B27b **b** Join the two sounds: /eeeɪ/.

B27c **c** Listen and repeat the target sound /eɪ/. The second part of the sound is shorter.

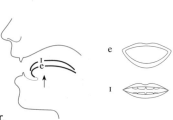

2 Minimal pairs

	Sound 1 /e/	Sound 2 /eɪ/	
	pen What an awful pen!	**pain** What an awful pain!	
	shed The dog's in the shed.	**shade** The dog's in the shade.	
	edge It's a difficult edge.	**age** It's a difficult age.	
	wet Just wet.	**wait** Just wait.	
	test Test this food.	**taste** Taste this food.	
	pepper That's too much pepper.	**paper** That's too much paper.	

Minimal pair words

B28a **a** Listen and repeat the words.

B28b **b** You will hear five words from each minimal pair. For each word, write *1* for /e/ (sound 1) or *2* for /eɪ/ (sound 2).

EXAMPLE Pair 1:   1, 1, 2, 2, 1

Minimal pair sentences

B29a **c** Listen to the minimal pair sentences.

B29b **d** Listen to six of the sentences and write *1* for /e/ (sound 1) or *2* for /eɪ/ (sound 2).

B29a **e** Sentence stress

First read the minimal pair sentences and try to guess which words will be stressed. Notice which words are nouns, adjectives or main verbs. These are often important, and the most important words for the meaning of a sentence are stressed.

Then listen to the sentences again and <u>underline</u> the sentence stress (on page 54).

EXAMPLE What an <u>awful pen</u>! / What an <u>awful pain</u>!

B30 **f** Tick the words a) or b) that you hear in the sentences.

1 a) pen ☐ b) pain ☐
2 a) shed ☐ b) shade ☐
3 a) pepper ☐ b) paper ☐
4 a) let ☐ b) late ☐
5 a) letter ☐ b) later ☐
6 a) get ☐ b) gate ☐

3 Dialogue

a First practise the target sound /eɪ/ in some words from the dialogue. Read the words aloud or visit the website to practise.

made   late   changed   may   say   train   **wai**ting   eight
Grey   **time**table   April   **sta**tion   ages   **Ba**ker   eigh**teen**
afraid   mis**take**   to**day**

B31 **b** Listen to the dialogue, paying attention to the target sound.

At the railway station

(Mr Grey is waiting at the railway station for a train.)

MR GREY: This train's late! I've been waiting here for ages.

PORTER: Which train?

MR GREY: The 8.18 to Baker Street.

PORTER: The 8.18? I'm afraid you've made a mistake, sir.

MR GREY: A mistake? My timetable says: Baker Street train – 8.18.

PORTER: Oh no. The Baker Street train leaves at 8.08.

MR GREY: At 8.08?

PORTER: They changed the timetable at the end of April. It's the first of May today.

MR GREY: Changed it? May I see the new timetable? What does it say?

PORTER: It says: Baker Street train – 8.08.

MR GREY: Oh no, you're right. The train isn't late. I am.

c Practise reading the dialogue aloud. Record your voice to compare your production of the target sound with the recording.

4 Intonation

B32 a In a conversation we can show surprise by repeating the other person's words with the intonation going up. Listen.

EXAMPLES

A: I'm afraid you've made a mistake, sir.   B: A mistake?

A: They changed the timetable.   B: Changed it?

B33 b Write B's part in the conversation below by repeating the part in *italics*. Note that number 7 needs a different word in the answer. Draw intonation arrows following the example in 1. Check your answers by listening to the recording and then practise the intonation. Record your voice to compare your production of the intonation with the recording.

1 A: It's *the eighth* of May. B: *The eighth?*_____

2 A: Yes. It's Mrs Grey's birthday *today*. B: _____

3 A: Yes. She's *eighty-eight*. B: _____

4 A: Yes. And she's *going away* for a holiday B: _____

5 A: That's right. And she's going *by plane*. B: _____

6 A: Yes. She wants to go *to Spain*. B: _____

7 A: That's right. Why don't *you* go with her? B: _____

5 Spelling

Look back over this unit at words with the target sound, and write what you noticed about spelling the sound /eɪ/.

UNIT 16 /aɪ/ fine

> – ... er ... Hi! ... Are you all right? ... er ...
> Would you like a ride in my cart?
> – No thanks. I'm fine. I'm just flying my kite
> and enjoying the sunshine.
> – Oh ... er ... alright! Have a nice time!

1 Target sound /aɪ/

B34a   **a** First practise the long sound /ɑː/ (see
page 23). Then practise the short
sound /ɪ/ (see page 7). Listen and repeat.

B34b   **b** Join the two sounds: /ɑːɑːɑːɪ/.

B34c   **c** Listen and repeat the target sound /aɪ/.
The second part of the sound is shorter.

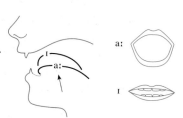

2 Minimal pairs

	Sound 1 /ɑː/	**Sound 2** /aɪ/	
	bar That was a good bar.	**buy** That was a good buy.	
	bark What a noisy bark.	**bike** What a noisy bike.	
	Pa He loves his Pa.	**pie** He loves his pie.	
Carry	**R** It's got two R's.	**eye** It's got two eyes.	
	cart It's a cart.	**kite** It's a kite.	
	heart Check the heart.	**height** Check the height.	

Minimal pair words

B35 a Listen and repeat the words.

B36 b You will hear five words from each minimal pair. For each word write *1* for /aː/ (sound 1) or *2* for /aɪ/ (sound 2).

EXAMPLE Pair 1: 2, 2, 1, 1, 1

Minimal pair sentences

B37a c Listen to the minimal pair sentences.

B37b d Listen to six of the sentences and write *1* for /aː/ (sound 1) or *2* for /aɪ/ (sound 2).

B37a e Sentence stress

Listen to the minimal pair sentences again and <u>underline</u> the sentence stress (on page 57). Strongly stressed words are **LOUD**er and s l o w er. Weakly stressed words are quieter and quicker.

EXAMPLE That was a <u>good</u> <u>buy</u>.

B38 f Tick the words a) or b) that you hear in the sentences.

1 a) cart ☐ b) kite ☐

2 a) darning ☐ b) dining ☐

3 a) star ☐ b) sty ☐

4 a) laugh ☐ b) life ☐

5 a) hard ☐ b) hide ☐

6 a) Pa ☐ b) pie ☐

3 Dialogue

a First practise the target sound /aɪ/ in words from the dialogue. Read the words aloud or visit the website to practise.

hi right **ride** smile five nine drive Miles **Heidi** **Riley**
Nigel **Caroline** bike nice type iced **mo**bile **climb**ing
spider **Friday** **library** to**night**

B39 b Listen to the dialogue, paying attention to the target sound. Then read the dialogue and fill the gaps 1–10 with the correct words from the box.

> bike nice type iced **mo**bile **climb**ing **spi**der **Friday**
> **library** to**night**

Heidi, Caroline and Nigel

(*Heidi and Caroline are both typing.*)

HEIDI: (*Stops typing. She's smiling.*) Hi, Nigel.

NIGEL: Hi, Heidi. Hi, Caroline. You're looking 1_____ , Caroline.

(*Silence from Caroline. She keeps typing.*)

NIGEL: Would you like some 2_____ coffee, Caroline?

CAROLINE: *(Keeps on typing.)* No thanks, Nigel. I'm busy typing. I have 99 pages to 3_____ by Friday.

NIGEL: Never mind. Do you like motor 4_____ riding, Caroline?

CAROLINE: Sometimes. *(Mobile phone rings.)* … My 5_____ ! … Hello … *(Smiles.)* … Hi, Riley! Mmmm! … *(Laughs.)* … I'd like that … Mmmm … at five … at the 6_____ … it's 19 High Street … bye bye! *(Caroline puts away her mobile and starts typing.)*

NIGEL: Would you like to come riding with me 7_____ , Caroline?

CAROLINE: Not tonight, Nigel. I'm going for a drive with Riley. *(Smiles to herself and keeps typing.)*

NIGEL: What about 8_____ ?

CAROLINE: Friday? I'm going 9_____ with Miles.

NIGEL: All right then. Bye.

HEIDI: Caroline, Nigel's put something behind your computer.

CAROLINE: Is it something nice, Heidi?

HEIDI: No. It's a 10_____ .

B39 c Listen to the dialogue to check your answers. Then practise reading the dialogue aloud. Record your voice to compare your production of the target sound with the recording.

4 Word stress

B40 a Listen and repeat.

flying   **ice** skating   **sky** diving   **driv**ing   **horse** riding   **wine** tasting
kite flying   **climb**ing   **cyc**ling

b Use the words above to practise this conversation.

A: I think _____ is quite exciting. Do you like it?

B: Yes. Would you like to come _____ with me on Friday?

A: I'd really like to. But I'm busy on Friday. Would some other time be all right?

5 Spelling

Look back over this unit at words with the target sound, and write what you noticed about how to spell the sound /aɪ/.

UNIT 17 /ɔɪ/ boy

> – I put all this oil in the rice?
> – Yes, all the oil, and then let it boil.

1 Target sound /ɔɪ/

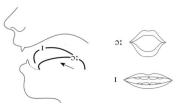

B41a **a** First practise the sound /ɔː/ (see page 33). Then practise the short sound /ɪ/ (see page 7). Listen and repeat.

B41b **b** Join the two sounds: /ɔːɔːɔːɪ/.

B41c **c** Listen and repeat the target sound /ɔɪ/. The second part of the sound is shorter.

2 Minimal pairs

	Sound 1 /ɔː/	Sound 2 /ɔɪ/	
	all It's all there.	**oil** It's oil there.	
	ball It's a ball on his head.	**boil** It's a boil on his head.	
	corn Look at that golden corn.	**coin** Look at that golden coin.	
	tore The paper tore.	**toy** The paper toy.	
	roar Hear the engine roar.	**Roy** Hear the engine, Roy.	

Minimal pair words

B42a **a** Listen and repeat the words. Then listen and repeat.

B42b **b** You will hear five words from each minimal pair. For each word, write *1* for /ɔː/ (sound 1) or *2* for /ɔɪ/ (sound 2).

EXAMPLE Pair 1:   1, 2, 1, 2, 2

Minimal pair sentences

B43a **c** Listen to the minimal pair sentences.

B43b **d** Listen to five of the sentences and write *1* for /ɔː/ (sound 1) or *2* for /ɔɪ/ (sound 2).

B43a **e** Sentence stress

Listen to the minimal pair sentences again and notice that the most important words for the speaker's meaning are **LOUD**er. The less important words for the meaning are quieter. <u>Underline</u> the most important words in the sentences (on page 60).

EXAMPLE Hear the <u>engine</u>, <u>Roy</u>.

B44 **f** Tick the words a) or b) that you hear in the sentences.

1 a) corn ☐   b) coin ☐
2 a) bawling ☐   b) boiling ☐
3 a) all ☐   b) oil ☐
4 a) aw ☐   b) oi ☐
5 a) bore ☐   b) boy ☐
6 a) all ☐   b) oil ☐

3   Dialogue

a First practise the target sound /ɔɪ/ in words from the dialogue. Read the words aloud or visit the website to practise.

boy   toy   noise   voice   spoilt   **poin**ting   de**stroyed**   em**ployed**   a**ppoint**ment   a**nnoy**ing   disa**ppoint**ing

Intonation in names

The main stress is on the last name.

Joyce **Roy**al   Roy **Coyne**   Rolls **Royce**

B45 **b** Listen to the dialogue, paying attention to the target sound.

Joyce Royal's Rolls Royce

(Joyce Royal takes her noisy Rolls Royce to the mechanic employed at the garage, a young boy named Roy Coyne. Roy loves Rolls Royces.)

ROY COYNE: What a terrible noise, Mrs Royal!

JOYCE ROYAL: Isn't it annoying, Roy? It's out of oil.

ROY COYNE: A Rolls Royce! Out of oil? … And look! *(pointing)* … The water's boiling! Perhaps you've spoilt the motor. Or even destroyed it. How disappointing! It's such a beautiful Rolls Royce! … *(raising his voice)* … AND A ROLLS ROYCE ISN'T A TOY!

JOYCE ROYAL: How disappointing! I'll be late for my appointment.

c Practise reading the dialogue aloud. Record your voice to compare your production of the target sound with the recording.

4 Word stress

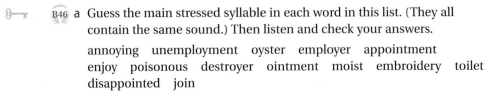

B46 a Guess the main stressed syllable in each word in this list. (They all contain the same sound.) Then listen and check your answers.

annoying   unemployment   oyster   employer   appointment
enjoy   poisonous   destroyer   ointment   moist   embroidery   toilet
disappointed   join

b Dictionary work: secondary stress
In *Ship or Sheep?* the main stress in a word is shown in **bold**,
e.g. *employment.*

When you meet a new word, you can check the word stress in a good dictionary (e.g. *Cambridge Learner's Dictionary*). Most dictionaries use the symbol ˈ in front of the main stressed syllable, and the symbol ˌ to show any secondary stress (usually in longer words),
e.g. /ˌʌnɪmˈplɔɪmənt/.

Choose four of the longest words in the list in 4a and use your dictionary to check if there is any secondary stress.

5 Spelling

Look back over this unit at words with the target sound, and write what you noticed about how to spell the sound /ɔɪ/.

UNIT 18 /aʊ/ house

– How's your cow?
– Better now I'm taking it to Roy Coyne. It's running
around the town using much less oil.
– I didn't ask about your car! I said how's your cow?
You know, your brown cow!

1 Target sound /aʊ/

B47a **a** First practise the sound /æ/ (see
page 23). Then practise the sound /ʊ/
(see page 36). Listen and repeat.

B47b **b** Join the two sounds: /æææʊ/.

B47c **c** Listen and repeat the target sound /aʊ/.
The second part of the sound is shorter.

2 Minimal pairs

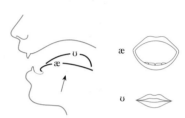

	Sound 1 /aː/	Sound 2 /aʊ/	
	car It's the best car.	**cow** It's the best cow.	
	bar It was a long bar.	**bow** It was a long bow.	
	bra Her bra was wrinkled.	**brow** Her brow was wrinkled.	
	grass There's beautiful grass here.	**grouse** There's beautiful grouse here.	
	arch 'Arch!' he said loudly.	**ouch** 'Ouch!' he said loudly.	

Minimal pair words

B48a **a** Listen and repeat the words.

B48b **b** You will hear five words from each minimal pair. For each word write *1*
for /aː/ (sound 1) or *2* for /aʊ/ (sound 2).

EXAMPLE Pair 1:   2, 1, 1, 2, 2

Minimal pair sentences

B49a **c** Listen to the minimal pair sentences.

B49b **d** Listen to five of the sentences and write *1* for /aː/ (sound 1) or *2* for /aʊ/ (sound 2).

B49a **e** Sentence stress

First read the minimal pair sentences and notice which words are adjectives or adverbs. These are often important for the meaning of a sentence (as well as nouns and main verbs). Then listen to the sentences again and <u>underline</u> the sentence stress (on page 63).

EXAMPLE It's the <u>best car</u>.

B50 **f** Tick the words a) or b) that you hear in the sentences.

1 a) car ☐ b) cow ☐

2 a) grass ☐ b) grouse ☐

3 a) bra ☐ b) brow ☐

4 a) ha ☐ b) how ☐

5 a) ah ☐ b) ow! ☐

6 a) tarn ☐ b) town ☐

3 Dialogue

a First practise the sound /aʊ/ in words from the dialogue. Read the words aloud or visit the website to practise.

ow!   now   how   **shout**ing   house   mouse   couch   **loud**ly   town
down   frown   brown   round   found   lounge   ground   some**how**
mountain   a**round**   pro**nounce**   upside **down**

B51 **b** Correction

There are six items to change in the dialogue. Read the dialogue and listen to the recording at the same time. Make the words the same as the recording.

A mouse in the house

MR BROWN: *(shouting loudly)* I'VE FOUND A MOUSE!

MRS BROWN: Ow! You're shouting too loudly. Sit down and don't frown.

MR BROWN: *(sitting down)* I've found a mouse in the house.

MRS BROWN: A town mouse?

MR BROWN: Yes. A little round mouse. It's running around in the lounge.

MRS BROWN: On the ground?

MR BROWN: Yes. It's under the couch now.

MRS BROWN: Well, get it out.

MR BROWN: How?

MRS BROWN: Turn the couch upside down. Get it out somehow. We don't want a mouse in our house. Ours is the cleanest house in the town!

c Practise reading the corrected dialogue. Record your voice to compare your production of the target sound with the recording.

4 Stress in phrasal verbs

B52 a **EXAMPLE 1** <u>Sit</u> <u>down</u>.

Listen and repeat.
1 He's <u>sitting</u> <u>down</u>.
2 He's <u>lying</u> <u>down</u>.
3 He's <u>standing</u> <u>up</u>.
4 He's <u>turning</u> <u>round</u>.
5 He's <u>shouting</u> <u>out</u>.
6 He's <u>running</u> <u>around</u>.

b Match these pictures with the correct sentences in 4a.

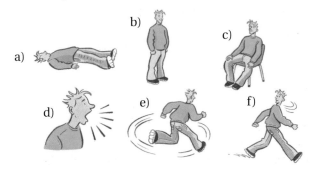

B53 c **EXAMPLE 2** <u>Get</u> it <u>out</u>.

Listen and repeat.
1 <u>Put</u> it <u>down</u>.
2 <u>Take</u> it <u>out</u>.
3 <u>Throw</u> it <u>out</u>.
4 <u>Turn</u> it <u>down</u>.
5 <u>Work</u> it <u>out</u>.

d Match these pictures with the correct sentences in 4c.

$$15 + 73\tfrac{1}{2} \div 3 =$$

5 Spelling

Look back over this unit at words with the target sound, and write what you noticed about how to spell the sound /aʊ/.

UNIT 19 /əʊ/ phone

– Are you going to go to the boat show?
– Mmm … don't know … Maybe I'll go with Bert.
– Does Bert have a boat?
– No.
– Oh.

1 Target sound /əʊ/

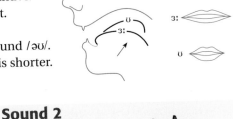

B54a **a** First practise the sound /ɜː/ (see page 43). Then practise the sound /ʊ/ (see page 36). Listen and repeat.

B54b **b** Join the two sounds: /ɜːɜːɜːʊ/.

B54c **c** Listen and repeat the target sound /əʊ/. The second part of the sound is shorter.

2 Minimal pairs A

Sound 1 /ɜː/	Sound 2 /əʊ/
burn	**bone**
It's a large burn.	It's a large bone.
fern	**phone**
It's a green fern.	It's a green phone.
Bert	**boat**
That's my Bert.	That's my boat.
work	**woke**
I work early.	I woke early.
flirt	**float**
He likes flirting.	He likes floating.

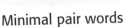
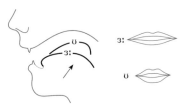

Minimal pair words

B55a **a** Listen and repeat the words.

B55b **b** You will hear five words from each minimal pair. For each word write *1* for /ɔː/ (sound 1) or *2* for /əʊ/ (sound 2).

EXAMPLE Pair 1: 2, 1, 1, 2, 1

Minimal pair sentences

B56a **c** Listen to the minimal pair sentences.

B56b **d** Listen to five of the sentences and write *1* for /ɔː/ (sound 1) or *2* for /əʊ/ (sound 2).

B56a **e** Sentence stress

Listen to the minimal pair sentences again and notice the strong stress on the pair words.

EXAMPLE oooO/oooO It's a green <u>fern</u>./It's a green <u>phone</u>.

Notice how all the other words in the sentence are said more quickly and quietly. <u>Underline</u> the sentence stress in the sentences (on page 66).

Minimal pairs B

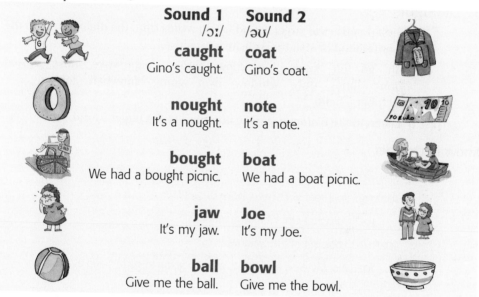

	Sound 1 /ɔː/	Sound 2 /əʊ/	
	caught Gino's caught.	**coat** Gino's coat.	
	nought It's a nought.	**note** It's a note.	
	bought We had a bought picnic.	**boat** We had a boat picnic.	
	jaw It's my jaw.	**Joe** It's my Joe.	
	ball Give me the ball.	**bowl** Give me the bowl.	

Minimal pair words

B57 **a** Listen and repeat the words.

B58 **b** You will hear five words from each minimal pair. For each word write *1* for /ɔː/ (sound 1) or *2* for /əʊ/ (sound 2).

EXAMPLE Pair 1:   2, 2, 1, 1, 2

Minimal pair sentences

B59a **c** Listen to the minimal pair sentences.

B59b **d** Listen to five of the sentences and write *1* for /ɔː/ (sound 1) or *2* for /əʊ/ (sound 2).

B59a **e** Sentence stress

Listen to the minimal pair sentences again and <u>underline</u> the sentence stress (on page 67).

EXAMPLE Gino's <u>caught</u>.

B60 **f** Tick the words a), b) or c) that you hear in the sentences.

1 a) fern ☐ b) phone ☐
2 a) or ☐ b) Oh ☐
3 a) ball ☐ b) bowl ☐
4 a) burn ☐ b) bone ☐
5 a) walk ☐ b) work ☐ c) woke ☐

3 Dialogue

a First practise the target sound /əʊ/ in words from the dialogue. Read the words aloud or visit the website to practise.

oh go no know Joe snow throw coat woke nose closed
don't Jones **only** **win**dow **o**ver **go**ing **snow**ball **jok**ing
October **hel**lo

B61 **b** Listen to the dialogue, paying attention to the target sound.

Snow in October

(Joe Jones is sleeping, but Joanna woke up a few minutes ago.)

JOANNA: Joe! Joe! JOE! Hello, wake up, Joe!

JOE: *(groans)* Oh! What is it, Joanna?

JOANNA: Look out of the window.

JOE: No. My eyes are closed, and I'm going to go to sleep again.

JOANNA: Oh! Don't go to sleep, Joe. Look at the snow!

JOE: Snow? But it's only October. I know there's no snow.

JOANNA: Come over to the window, Joe.

JOE: You're joking, Joanna. There's no snow.

JOANNA: OK. I'll put my coat on and go out and make a snowball and throw it at your nose, Joe Jones!

c Practise reading the dialogue aloud. Record your voice to compare your production of the target sound with the recording.

4 Rhyming

Notice that /əʊ/ may sound different when followed by the letter 'l'.

B62 a Listen and repeat.

old   hole   bowl   cold   hold   stole   sold   told   gold

In the list above five words rhyme with *old*, and two words rhyme with *hole*. Which words are they?

EXAMPLE 'gold' rhymes with 'old'.

b Rhyming crossword

The clues are words which rhyme with the answer but do not have the same meaning.

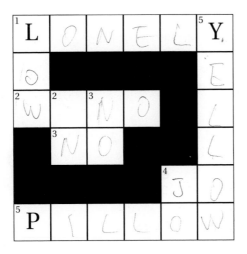

Clues

Across:	*Down:*
1 only	1 slow
2 don't	2 John
3 know	3 snow
4 Joe	4 no
5 billow	5 hello

5 Spelling

Look back over this unit at words with the target sound, and write what you noticed about how to spell the sound /əʊ/.

UNIT 20 /ɪə/ year

– There's a bee in your beer.

– I can't hear.

– I said here's to you, my dear.

– Cheers, dear! I've been hearing that joke about a bee in my beer for nearly sixty-three years.

1 Target sound /ɪə/

B63a a First practise the sound /ɪ/ (see page 7). Then practise the sound /ə/ (see page 48). Listen and repeat.

B63b b Join the two sounds: /ɪɪɪə/.

B63c c Listen and repeat the target sound /ɪə/.

2 Minimal pairs

	Sound 1 /iː/	Sound 2 /ɪə/	
	E	**ear**	
	That E's too big.	That ear's too big.	
	bee	**beer**	
	It's a small bee.	It's a small beer.	
	tea	**tear**	
	This tea tastes salty.	This tear tastes salty.	
	pea	**pier**	
	It's an old pea.	It's an old pier.	
	bead	**beard**	
	He has a black bead.	He has a black beard.	

Minimal pair words

B64a a Listen and repeat the words.

B64b b You will hear five words from each minimal pair. For each word, write *1* for /iː/ (sound 1) or *2* for /ɪə/ (sound 2).

EXAMPLE Pair 1: 2, 1, 1, 2, 2

Minimal pair sentences

B65a **c** Listen to the minimal pair sentences.

B65b **d** Listen to five of the sentences and write *1* for /iː/ (sound 1) or *2* for /ɪə/ (sound 2).

B65a **e** Sentence stress

First imagine how the minimal pair sentences will be spoken if the only stress is on the pair word.

EXAMPLE He has a black <u>beard</u>.

Imagine this word being said more **LOUD**ly and s l o w ly, and all the other words more quickly and quietly. Then listen to the sentences again and <u>underline</u> the sentence stress (on page 70).

B66 **f** Tick the words a) or b) that you hear in the sentences.

1 a) bee ☐	b) beer ☐
2 a) tea ☐	b) tear ☐
3 a) bead ☐	b) beard ☐
4 a) pea ☐	b) pier ☐
5 a) E's ☐	b) ears ☐
6 a) Dee ☐	b) dear ☐

3 Dialogue

a First practise the target sound /ɪə/ in some words from the dialogue. Read the words aloud or visit the website to practise.

dear   Lear   here   **nearly**   **beard**ed   **idea**   Austria   **wind**ier
dis**appear**   **at**mosphere   beer   clear   year   hear   cheers   beard
mountain**eer**   beer

B67 **b** Listen to the dialogue, paying attention to the target sound. Then read the dialogue and fill the gaps 1–8 with the correct words from the box below.

> beer   clear   year   hear   cheers   beard   mountain**eer**   beer

A bearded mountaineer

(Mr and Mrs Lear are on holiday in Austria.)

MR LEAR: Let's have a 1_____ here, dear.

MRS LEAR: What a good idea! They have very good beer here. We came here last 2_____ .

MR LEAR: The atmosphere here is very 3_____ .

MRS LEAR: But it's windier than last year.

MR LEAR: *(speaking to the waiter)* Two beers, please.

MRS LEAR: Look, dear! Look at that 4_____ drinking beer.

MR LEAR: His 5_____ is in his beer.

MRS LEAR: His beard has nearly disappeared into his 6_____ !

MR LEAR: Sh! He might 7_____ .

WAITER: *(bringing the beer)* Here you are, sir. Two beers.

MR LEAR: Thank you. *(drinking his beer)* Cheers!

MRS LEAR: 8_____ ! Here's to the bearded mountaineer!

B67 **c** Listen to the dialogue and check your answers. Then practise reading the dialogue aloud. Record your voice to compare your production of the target sound with the recording.

4 The letter 'r' – pronounced or silent?

When there is no vowel following it, /r/ is silent. This 'rule' only applies to some speakers of English, e.g. in south-east England, South Africa, Australia. But many native speakers always pronounce /r/, e.g. in south-west England, Scotland, America. So you may choose to omit this exercise if you are learning a variety of English where /r/ is always pronounced.

B68 **a** Listen and repeat.

'r' not pronounced	'r' pronounced (before a vowel)
Here they are.	Here_are_all the books.
Here's the beer.	The beer_is here_on the table.

B69 **b** Read these sentences and decide which words have 'r' pronounced. Then listen and check.

I can hear Mr Lear.	He can hear us too.
Mr Lear calls her 'dear'.	Dear old Mrs Lear is here in the kitchen.
He's a mountaineer.	A mountaineer always spends some time each year in the mountains.

5 Spelling

Look back over this unit at words with the target sound, and write what you noticed about how to spell the sound /ɪə/.

UNIT 21 /eə/ chair

– Hello … Oh, Claire! … Oh! … Oh! … Wh …
 Where's the wedding? Here? …
– Oh, there! … What … What are you going to wear? …
– In your hair? … And … Oh, my dear, I wouldn't dare!

1 Target sound /eə/

B70a **a** First practise /e/ (see page 11).
Then practise /ə/ (see page 48).
Listen and repeat.

B70b **b** Join the two sounds: /eeeə/.

B70c **c** Listen and repeat the target sound /eə/.

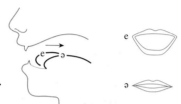

2 Minimal pairs

Sound 1 /ɪə/	Sound 2 /eə/
ear The ear isn't good.	**air** The air isn't good.
beer It's a sweet beer.	**bear** It's a sweet bear.
pier That's an old pier.	**pear** That's an old pear.
hear How do you spell 'hear'?	**hair** How do you spell 'hair'?
tear That's a tear.	**tear** That's a tear.
Cheers! 'Three cheers!' he said.	**chairs** 'Three chairs!' he said.

Minimal pair words

B71a **a** Listen and repeat the words.

B71b **b** You will hear five words from each minimal pair. For each word, write *1* for /ɪə/ (sound 1) or *2* for /eə/ (sound 2).

EXAMPLE Pair 1: 2, 2, 1, 1, 2

Minimal pair sentences

B72a c Listen to the minimal pair sentences.

B72b d Listen to six of the sentences and write *1* for /ɪə/ (sound 1) or *2* for /eə/ (sound 2).

B72a e **Sentence stress**

Listen to the minimal pair sentences again and <u>underline</u> the sentence stress (on page 73).

EXAMPLE <u>How</u> do you spell '<u>hear</u>'?

B73 f Tick the words a) or b) that you hear in the sentences.

1 a) cheers ☐   b) chairs ☐

2 a) beer ☐   b) bear ☐

3 a) pier ☐   b) pear ☐

4 a) here ☐   b) hair ☐

5 a) dear ☐   b) Dare ☐

6 a) clear ☐   b) Claire ☐

3 Dialogue

a First practise the target sound /eə/ in words from the dialogue. Read the words aloud or visit the website to practise.

where   there   they're   pair   hair   chair   Claire   square   **Mary**
up**stairs**   down**stairs**   every**where**

B74 b Listen to the dialogue, paying particular attention to the target sound.

A pair of hairclips

MARY: I've lost two small hairclips, Claire. They're a pair.

CLAIRE: Have you looked carefully everywhere?

MARY: Yes. They're nowhere here. They just aren't anywhere!

CLAIRE: Have you looked upstairs?

MARY: *(getting impatient)* Upstairs! Downstairs! Everywhere! They just aren't there!

CLAIRE: Hm! Are they square, Mary?

MARY: Yes. Why ?

CLAIRE: Well, you're wearing one of them in your hair!

MARY: Oh! Then where's the other one?

CLAIRE: It's over there under that chair.

MARY: Hm!

c Practise reading the dialogue aloud. Record your voice to compare your production of the target sound with the recording.

4 The letter 'r' – pronounced or silent?

When there is no vowel following it, /r/ is silent. This 'rule' only applies to some speakers of English, e.g. in south-east England, South Africa, Australia. But many native speakers always pronounce /r/, e.g. in south-west England, Scotland, America. So you may choose to omit this exercise if you are learning a variety of English where /r/ is always pronounced.

B75 a Listen and repeat.

'r' not pronounced	'r' pronounced (before a vowel)
Claire	Claire_and Mary
a pair	a pair_of shoes
a square chair	a square_envelope

B76 b Read these sentences and decide which words have 'r' pronounced. Then listen and check.

It's there.   There it is.
They're here.   They're under a table.
I've looked everywhere for them.   I've looked everywhere in the house.

5 Spelling

Look back over this unit at words with the target sound, and write what you noticed about how to spell the sound /eə/.

UNIT 22 | REVIEW

Card game: Pairs snap

Photocopy and cut out cards from all minimal pairs in Units 15–21.

Shuffle the cards and deal them face down to make a pile of cards in front of each player.

Take turns to quickly turn your top card face up and put it on top of a new pile in the middle of the table. When you see two cards together that are a minimal pair, quickly say 'Snap!' and put your hand on the pile. Then you can add all those cards to your pile.

Collect as many cards as you can in a time limit, e.g. ten minutes.

TEST

You can use a dictionary if you wish, but you don't have to understand every word to do this test.

B77 1 For each line (1, 2, 3, 4, 5), first listen to the whole line, then circle the one word, or part of a word, that is said twice. Note that meaning is not important in this exercise. The purpose is to review the sounds by hearing them in contrast. Some of the words are rarely used in everyday English, and this is shown with an asterisk *. Incomplete words have the rest of the word written in brackets, e.g. *Woy(Woy)*.

	/eɪ/	/aɪ/	/ɔɪ/	/aʊ/	/əʊ/	/ɪə/	/eə/
1	bay	buy	boy	bow (v)	bow (n)	beer	bear
2	hay	high	Hoy!*	how	Ho!	here	hair
3	A	I	Oy!*	Ow!	Oh!	ear	air
4	weigh	why	Woy(Woy*)	Wow!	woe	weir	wear
5	Tay*	tie	toy	Tao*	toe	tier	tear

Score ☐ / 5

2 Circle the words with the same vowel sound as 1–5.

1 paper
/eɪ/

edge   barge
page   voyage
percentage
weight   fright
pain   poppies
pepper

2 shine
/aɪ/

machine
sing   noise
shy   spoilt
frightened
stars   darn
sigh   shorn

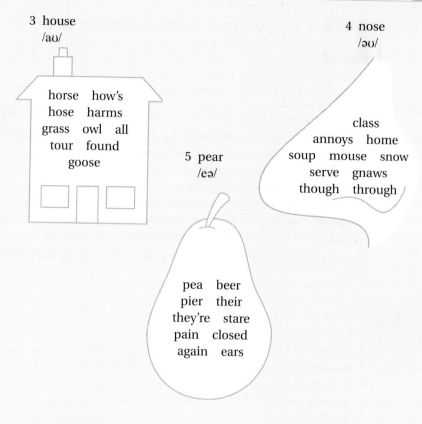

3 house
/aʊ/

horse   how's
hose   harms
grass   owl   all
tour   found
goose

4 nose
/əʊ/

class
annoys   home
soup   mouse   snow
serve   gnaws
though   through

5 pear
/eə/

pea   beer
pier   their
they're   stare
pain   closed
again   ears

Score [/15]

3 Pronounced/silent 'r'
Show where the letter 'r' is pronounced. (Score 1 for each correct line.)
EXAMPLE Ar<u>e Amber and Roger a</u>rchitects?
1 We're looking for a builder or an architect, Adler and Anderson.
2 Where are their offices?
3 They're over there, aren't they?
4 Are you an engineer or an architect, Mr Adler?
5 I'm a structural engineer and this is Blair Anderson, our architect.
Score [/5]

4 Word stress
Underline the stressed syllable in these words or phrases. (Score half a mark per item.)

timetable   today   cycling   horse riding   appointment   snowball
atmosphere   nowhere   work it out   turn it down
Score [/5]

Total score [/30]

Additional review task using dialogues from Units 15–21

Unit	15	16	17	18	19	20	21
Target sound	/eɪ/	/aɪ/	/ɔɪ/	/aʊ/	/əʊ/	/ɪə/	/eə/
	male	fine	boy	house	phone	year	chair

From the above table, choose any target sounds you had difficulty with.

1 Listen again to the dialogue in that unit, listening for the target sound.
2 Circle the target sound in any words in the dialogue.
3 Listen to the dialogue again and check your answers.
4 Check your answers in the key.
5 Listen to the dialogue again, listening for the target sound.
6 Practise reading the dialogue aloud, and record your voice to compare your production of the target sound with the recording.

You can also use this review task as a quick self-test, by doing steps 2 and 4 only.

Section B
Consonants

Making English sounds

Use your voice for some
consonant sounds:
/b/ /d/ /g/ /v/ /z/ /w/ /r/ /l/ /m/
/n/ /ŋ/ (ring) /dʒ/ (jam) /j/ (yes)
/ʒ/ (vision) /ð/ (the feather)

Don't use your voice for some
consonant sounds:
/p/ /t/ /k/ /f/ /s/ /ʃ/ (shoe)
/tʃ/ (cherry) /θ/ (thin)

VOICE
These are 'voiced'.

NO VOICE
These are 'unvoiced'.

1 Are these consonants voiced or unvoiced? Write (v.) or (unv.).

1 /p/ _____   6 /f/ _____

2 /t/ _____   7 /v/ _____

3 /z/ _____   8 /ð/ _____

4 /k/ _____   9 /θ/ _____

5 /g/ _____   10 /ŋ/ _____

                        11 /ʃ/ _____

2 Match these words with the numbers in the pictures.

a) the nose   b) the back of the tongue   c) the top teeth
d) the top lip   e) the roof of the mouth   f) the sides of the tongue
g) the throat   h) the front of the tongue   i) the tip of the tongue
j) the side teeth   k) the bottom teeth   l) the bottom lip

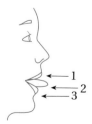

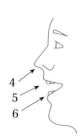

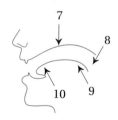

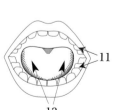

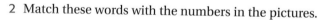

3 Match the pictures (1–7) in A with the words (a–g) in B.

A

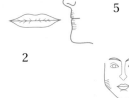

1

5

2

6

3

7

4

B

a) Close your lips.

b) Open your lips

c) Close your lips hard.

d) Touch your side teeth with the sides of your tongue.

e) Touch the front of the roof of your mouth with the front of your tongue.

f) Touch the back of the roof of your mouth with the back of your tongue.

g) Push air forward in your mouth.

How are English consonant sounds made?

air being stopped, then ... released suddenly: /p/ /b/ /t/ /d/ /k/ /g/	air moving between two parts of the mouth (or throat) which are close to each other: /f/ /v/ /s/ /z/ /h/ /θ/ /ð/ /ʒ/	air coming through the nose: /m/ /n/ /ŋ/
stops or **plosives**	**fricatives**	**nasals**

air being released more slowly: /tʃ/ /dʒ/	air moving between two not so close parts: /w/ /r/ /j/	air coming round the sides of the tongue: /l/
affricates	**approximants**	**lateral**

UNIT 23 /p/ pen

– Excuse me. Please could you help me?
– How can I help you? ... Oh, ... you want your parcel up there?
– Yes. Put it on top of that pile of newspapers, please ... Thank you.

1 Target sound /p/

B78a **a** Listen to the sound /p/. This is an unvoiced sound.

B78b **b** To make the louder sound /p/ at the beginning of a word, first close your lips hard. Then push air forward in your mouth. **Then quickly open your lips to release the air suddenly.** Don't use your voice. Listen and repeat: /p/.

B78c **c** Notice that sometimes /p/ is quieter because the air isn't released suddenly. Listen.

up   top   help   helps   help me.

Omit from ** to ** above to make this quieter sound.

2 Sound /p/

/p/

pin
It's a useful pin.

pen
Pen, please!

pear
Look at the yellow pear!

cap
It's an old cap.

pup
What a lively pup!

Poppy
Do you like Poppy?

a In the words on page 81, notice that the target sound is quieter in *cap* and at the end of *pup*. Listen and repeat the words.

b Listen to the sentences.

c Sentence stress
The most important words for the speaker's meaning are strongly stressed. This means that they are pronounced a little more **LOUD**ly and s l o w ly than the other words in the sentence. Practise listening for these important words. They are <u>underlined</u> here.

It's a <u>useful</u> <u>pin</u>.   <u>Pen</u>, please.
<u>Look</u> at the <u>yellow</u> <u>pear</u>.   It's an <u>old</u> <u>cap</u>.
What a <u>lively</u> <u>pup</u>!   Do you <u>like</u> <u>Poppy</u>?

d Listen again and repeat the sentences.

3 Dialogue

 a First practise the target sound /p/ in words from the dialogue. Read the words aloud or visit the website to practise.

The sound /p/ is louder before a vowel, and fairly loud before 'l' or 'r'.

One-syllable words: pot   pie   piece   spoon   plate   plane   please

Two-syllable words: **pen**cil   **Pe**ter   **pep**per   **pock**et   **Pop**py
postcard   **pull**ing   **Pa**ris   **air**port   **stu**pid   **prac**tise   **plas**tic
people   **app**le
(The strong stress is always on the first syllable in these words.)

Two-syllable words: sur**prised**   per**haps**
(The strong stress is always on the second syllable in these words.)

Three-syllable words: **pass**enger   **news**paper   po**ta**to   im**pa**tient
pepper pot.

Note on word stress: Word stress doesn't usually change. **Bold** is used to show you which part of the word is strongly stressed, i.e. which syllable is always pronounced more **LOUD**ly and s l o w l y than the other(s).

Note on sentence stress: Sentence stress changes with the speaker's meaning. <u>Underlining</u> is used here to show you which words in the sentence are being strongly stressed, i.e. which words are pronounced more **LOUD**ly and s l o w l y than the others:

It's a <u>piece</u> of po<u>ta</u>to <u>pie</u> on a <u>plastic</u> <u>plate</u>. <u>Peter</u> is sur<u>prised</u>.

The sound /p/ is often quieter at the end of a word.

an envelope with a stamp   a cup   Help!   a pipe

What happens to the quiet sound if the next word begins with a vowel?

a cup‿of tea   Help‿us!

The sound /p/ is usually quiet and sometimes almost silent before a consonant. Listen and repeat.

empty	upstairs	dropped	help me
helpful	perhaps	Mr Tupman	stop shouting
stop talking	stop pulling		

B80 b Listen to the dialogue, paying attention to the target sound. Notice that it is sometimes louder or quieter. Then read the dialogue and fill the gaps (1–6) and (a–f) with the correct words from the boxes. Numbers 1 and a) have been done as examples.

Words 1–6 have a louder /p/ sound:

> past   pocket   passports   policeman   pepper   potato

Words a–f have a quieter /p/ sound:

> upstairs   stop   envelope   cup   dropped   help

Passports, please

(Mr and Mrs Tupman are at the airport. They have just got off the plane from Paris.)

OFFICIAL: Passports, please!

MR TUPMAN: Poppy! Poppy! I think I've lost the 1 *passports* !

MRS TUPMAN: How stupid of you, Peter! Didn't you put them in your 2_____ ?

MR TUPMAN: *(emptying his pockets)* Here's a pen … a pencil … my pipe … a postcard … an a) *envelope* with a stamp … a pin …

MRS TUPMAN: Oh, b)_____ taking things out of your pockets. Perhaps you put them in the plastic bag.

MR TUPMAN: *(emptying the plastic bag)* Here's a newspaper … an apple … a pear … a plastic c)_____ … a spoon … some paper plates … a piece of 3_____ pie … a 4_____ pot …

MRS TUPMAN: Oh, stop pulling things out of the plastic bag, Peter. These people are getting impatient.

MR TUPMAN: Well, d)_____ me, Poppy.

MRS TUPMAN: *(to official)* We've lost our passports. Perhaps we e)_____ them on the plane.

OFFICIAL: Then let the other passengers 5_____ , please.

MR TUPMAN: Poppy, why don't you help? You aren't being very helpful. Put the things in the plastic bag.

OFFICIAL: Your name, please?

MR TUPMAN: Tupman.

OFFICIAL: Please go f)_____ with this 6_____ , Mr Tupman.

B80 c Listen to the dialogue again to check your answers. Then practise reading the dialogue aloud. Record your voice to compare your production of the target sound with the recording.

4 Stress and intonation

  B81 a Stress

Listen and <u>underline</u> the stressed syllables. The first one in each column has been done as an example. Check your answers, then listen and repeat.

a <u>pin</u>	a <u>pen</u>cil	a paper <u>plate</u>
a pen	a postcard	a pepper pot
a pear	a picture	a plastic spider
some soap	a carpet	a piano
a pipe	a puppy	an expensive present for Poppy
a spoon	an apple	

B82 b Intonation

Intonation usually goes down on the last strongly stressed word in a sentence. In a list, the intonation goes up with each item but down on the last item. Listen and repeat.

He bought a <u>pen</u>.
He bought a <u>pen</u> and a <u>pencil</u>.
He bought a <u>pen</u> and a <u>pencil</u> and a <u>pin</u>.

  c Practise this game in a group of four or five. You must remember what the others have said and then add something to the list.

EXAMPLE A: Peter went to Paris and he bought a pipe.
B: Peter went to Paris and he bought a pipe and a picture.
C: Peter went to Paris and he bought a pipe, a picture and a piano.

5 Spelling

  Look back over this unit at words with the target sound, and write what you noticed about how to spell the sound /p/.

UNIT 24 /b/ baby

– Are those people backpackers? ... They've got packs on their backs.
– But they aren't ... *travelling.* They've just been shopping and they're waiting for a bus or a cab.
– So does that mean they aren't backpackers? They're just ... er ... people with backpacks.
– Mm.

1 Target sound /b/

B83a **a** First practise the unvoiced sound /p/ (see page 81). Listen and repeat.

B83b **b** Use your voice to make the target sound /b/. Listen and repeat.

B83c **c** Listen and repeat both sounds together. /p/ is unvoiced. /b/ is voiced.

B83d **d** Notice that sometimes /b/ is quieter because the air isn't released suddenly. Listen.

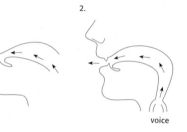

voice

job jobs cab cabs verb verbs

2 Minimal pairs

	Sound 1	Sound 2	
	/p/	/b/	
	**pin**	**bin**	
	It's a useful pin.	It's a useful bin.	
	pen	**Ben**	
	Pen, please!	Ben, please!	
	pear	**bear**	
	Look at the yellow pear.	Look at the yellow bear.	
	cap	**cab**	
	It's an old cap.	It's an old cab.	
	pup	**pub**	
	What a lively pup!	What a lively pub!	
	Poppy	**Bobby**	
	Do you like Poppy?	Do you like Bobby?	

Minimal pair words

B84a **a** Listen and repeat the words. Notice that the target sound is quieter in *cab* and *pub*.

B84b **b** You will hear five words from each minimal pair. For each word, write *1* for /p/ (sound 1) or *2* for /b/ (sound 2).

EXAMPLE Pair 1: 2, 2, 1, 2,

Minimal pair sentences

B85a **c** Listen to the minimal pair sentences.

B85b **d** Listen to six of the sentences and write *1* for /p/ (sound 1) or *2* for /b/ (sound 2).

B85a **e** Sentence stress

Listen and <u>underline</u> the strongly stressed words in the minimal pair sentences (on page 85). Notice that when an important word has more than one syllable, like *yellow*, the sentence stress is only on the strong syllable.

EXAMPLE It's a <u>use</u>ful <u>bin</u>.

B86 **f** Tick the words a) or b) that you hear in the sentences.

1 a) pin ☐   b) bin ☐
2 a) Poppy ☐   b) Bobby ☐
3 a) pup ☐   b) pub ☐
4 a) pig ☐   b) big ☐
5 a) pack ☐   b) back ☐
6 a) peach ☐   b) beach ☐

3 Dialogue

a First practise the target sound /b/ in words from the dialogue. Read the words aloud or visit the website to practise.

/b/ is **LOUD** before a vowel and fairly loud before 'l' and 'r'.

One-syllable words: big   but   been   book   birds   blue   black   blouse

Two-syllable words: **bet**ter   **bus**y   **cabb**ie   **Ru**by   **bro**ther   **butt**ons   **birth**day (first syllable stressed)

Two-syllable words: a**bout** (second syllable stressed)

Three-syllable words: **some**body   **beau**tiful   **Bar**bara   **butter**flies   **terr**ibly   re**mem**ber

/b/ is often quiet before a consonant or at the end of a word.

a cab   Bob   pub   a **prov**erb   Bob's job.

Is it louder when the next word begins with a vowel?

the cab‿over there   the pub‿on the corner   the job‿is interesting

B87 **b** Listen to the dialogue, paying attention to the target sound. Notice that it is sometimes louder or quieter.

Happy Birthday

BOB: Hi, Barbara!

BARBARA: Hi, Bob. It's my birthday today.

BOB: Oh, yes! … Your birthday! … er … Happy birthday, Barbara!

BARBARA: Thanks, Bob. Somebody gave me this blouse for my birthday.

BOB: What a beautiful blouse! It's got … mm … er … blue butterflies on it.

BARBARA: And big black buttons.

BOB: Did … er … mm … Ruby buy it for you?

BARBARA: Yes. And my brother gave me a book about birds.

BOB: I didn't remember your birthday, Barbara. I'm terribly sorry. I've been so busy with my new job. I left my old job. The one in the pub. Guess what? I'm driving a cab.

BARBARA: A cabbie! Congratulations! Don't worry about the birthday present, Bob. But, remember that proverb: 'Better late than never'.

c Find five words in the dialogue where the sound /b/ is quieter.

d Practise reading the dialogue aloud. Record your voice to compare your production of the target sound with the recording.

4 Word stress

B88 a In compound nouns, the stress is on the first word. Listen and repeat.

1 a **shelf**	a **book**shelf	
2 a **brush**	a **hair**brush	a **paint**brush
3 a **card**	a **post**card	a **birth**day card
4 a **ball**	a **foot**ball	a **ping** pong ball
5 a **bag**	a **hand**bag	a **shopp**ing bag
6 a **man**	a po**lice**man	a **post**man

B89 b Talk about these pictures. Follow the example. Listen and respond.

EXAMPLE It's a bookshelf.

shelf

1 bag   2 ball   3 ball   4 bag

5 brush 6 brush 7 card 8 card

9 man 10 man

c **Stop sounds**

The sounds /p/, /b/, /t/, /d/, /k/, /g/ are 'stop sounds'. If they come at the end of a word, stop – don't add another sound.

Match these compound words.

EXAMPLE shopkeeper (Remember to stress the first word.)

shop	ball	book	mint
pet	keeper	bus	robe
hip	board	bath	shop
blood	shop	back	ball
black	pocket	base	stop
beach	bank	pepper	pack

B90   Now listen and check your answers.

5 Spelling

Look back over this unit at words with the target sound, and write what you noticed about how to spell the sound /b/.

UNIT 25 /t/ table

– Excuse me. Could you tell me the time, please?
– Yes. It's exactly twenty minutes to ten.
– Thank you.

1 Target sound /t/

B91a **a** To make the target sound /t/, first put your tongue behind your top teeth. Then push air forward inside your mouth. **Then quickly move the tip of your tongue away from your teeth to release the air suddenly.** Don't use your voice. Listen and repeat: /t/.

1.

2.

B91b **b** Notice that sometimes /t/ is quieter because the air isn't released suddenly. Listen.

what   forget   doesn't   breakfast   minute   minutes   it's exactly

Omit from ** to ** above to make this quieter sound.

2 Sound /t/

/t/

too
You too?

sent
You sent the emails?

cart
Is hers the red cart?

write
Can he write well?

train
Does this train smell?

trunk
Is there a trunk here?

B92a **a** In the words on page 89, notice that the target sound is quieter in the words *sent*, *cart* and *write*. Listen and repeat the words.

B92b **b** Listen to the sentences.

B92b **c** Sentence stress

Listen to the *Yes/No* questions again and repeat. Notice how the voice begins to go up on the most important word for the speaker's meaning. This word is spoken with a very strong stress.

You **too**?   **You** sent the emails?   Is hers the **red** cart?

Can he **write** well?   Does this train **smell**?   Is there a **trunk** here?

3 Dialogue

a First practise the target sound /t/ in words from the dialogue. Read the words aloud or visit the website to practise.

/t/ is **LOUD** before a vowel.

One-syllable words: two   to   top   ten   tell   tins   Thai   time

Two-syllable words: **coun**ter   up**stairs**

Three-syllable words: **cus**tomer   telephone   tomatoes

Four/five-syllable words: pho**tog**rapher   cafeteria

Notice how two /t/ sounds join together.

I want_to take the lift_to the top. The telephone is next_to the cafeteria.

/t/ is often quiet at the end of a word.

hat   coat   skirt   shirt   first   want   what   get   got   right
cricket bat   **opp**osite   **su**permarket

What happens if the next word begins with a vowel?

I want_a hat_and a coat_and a skirt_and a …

Practise a quiet /t/ here before a consonant.

hats   coats   skirts   shirts   eighth   what's   **rest**aurants
cricket bats

Sometimes there will be loud and quiet /t/ in the same word. Decide if these are loud (L) or quiet (Q).

EXAMPLE assistant (L Q)

travel agent ( )   twenty-two ( )   tonight ( )   student ( )
important ( )   department store ( )   tomatoes ( )   toilet

Now look at the words in the box below and decide whether the target sound is loud (L) or quiet (Q).

EXAMPLE to (L), skirts (Q)

to ( )   skirts ( )   basement ( )   telephone ( )   cricket bat ( )
exactly ( )   cafeteria ( )   tomatoes ( )   fruit ( )   tell ( )   top ( )
Thai ( )   time ( )   next ( )

Check your answers in the key before doing the next exercise.

B93 **b** Read the dialogue below and guess the missing words with the sound /t/. Number 1 and a) have been done as examples. 1–7 have a louder /t/; a–g have a quieter /t/. Check your answers by looking in the box of words on page 90, and then by listening to the dialogue.

In a department store

CUSTOMER 1: I want 1 _to_____ buy a skirt.

ASSISTANT: a) _Skirts_____ are upstairs on the next floor.

CUSTOMER 2: Where can I get some 2_____ food?

ASSISTANT: The cafeteria is on the first floor.

CUSTOMER 3: Where's the b)_____ juice, please.

ASSISTANT: The c)_____ counter on your left.

CUSTOMER 4: Tins of 3_____ .

ASSISTANT: Try the supermarket in the d)_____ .

CUSTOMER 5: Could you 4_____ me where the … erm … travel agent's is?

ASSISTANT: Yes. It's right next to the e)_____ on the third floor.

CUSTOMER 6: I want to buy a f)_____ . How do I get to the … the … um … sports equipment?

ASSISTANT: Take the lift to the sports department. It's on the 5_____ floor.

CUSTOMER 7: Where's the 6_____ , please?

ASSISTANT: It's on the next floor opposite the photographer's.

CUSTOMER 8: What's the 7_____ , please?

ASSISTANT: It's g)_____ twenty-two minutes to ten.

c Practise reading the dialogue aloud. Record your voice to compare your production of the target sound with the recording.

4 Intonation in questions: new information/old information

B94 **a** Read the information and listen to the examples on the recording.

In *Yes/No* questions, intonation usually begins to go up on the most important word for the speaker's meaning.

EXAMPLE Could you <u>tell</u> me the <u>time</u>, please?

In *WH* questions, intonation usually begins to go down on the most important word for the speaker's meaning.

EXAMPLES <u>What's</u> the **time**, please?

<u>How</u> do I get to the **sports** equipment?

<u>Where's</u> the **toilet**, please?

Notice that intonation in *WH* questions can change when we are talking about old information. The first time we ask somebody's name, we ask: *What's your **name**?* This is new information. But if we then forget the name and ask again, we ask: ***What's** your name?* because we are asking about old information that has already been given. Intonation goes up to show that this is something we have already shared.

B95 **b** Listen to customers at the information desk in a department store. Some of them are asking for new information. Some of them want to check old information they have already received just now or in the past.

1 Where's the **fruit** juice? (asking for new information)

2 **Where's** the fruit juice? (checking old information)

3 What's on the **next** floor? (asking for new information)

4 How do I get to the **res**taurant? (asking for new information)

5 **How** do I get to the restaurant? (checking old information)

6 **Which** floor are computers on? (checking old information)

B96 **c** Listen to more customers at the information desk and decide if they are asking for new information or checking old information. Numbers 1 and 2 have been done as examples.

1 ＼ *new*   2 ╱ *old*   3 _____   4 _____

5 _____   6 _____   7 _____   8 _____

d Role play

Practise with a group of 4–5 people. Take turns to be the assistant at the information desk in a department store. The others ask questions. You can sometimes choose to check the information (either straightaway or later) by asking the same question again with a different intonation.

First practise the word stress in these words you may use.

restaurant   **tele**phone   **trav**el agent's   **super**market
sports department   **toi**let   cafe**te**ria   pho**tog**rapher's   **fruit** juice
com**pu**ters   **note**books   **prin**ters   **photo**copiers   **crick**et bats
football boots   hot **wa**ter bottles   **blan**kets   **hea**ters

5 Spelling

Look back over this unit at words with the target sound, and write what you noticed about how to spell the sound /t/.

UNIT 26 /d/ door

– Do you want to go out to a restaurant for
  dinner tonight?
– No. It's too cold and dark. And I'm too tired.
  I'd rather stay at home and read a good book.

1 Target sound /d/

a First practise the sound /t/ (see page
   89). Listen and repeat.

b Use your voice to make the target
   sound /d/. Listen and repeat.

c Listen and repeat both sounds together.
   /t/ is unvoiced. /d/ is voiced.

d Notice that sometimes /d/ is quieter
   because the air isn't released suddenly. Listen.

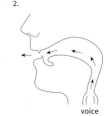

voice

good   food   goodbye   friend   child   bird   birds

2 Minimal pairs

	Sound 1 /t/	Sound 2 /d/	
	too You too?	**do** You do?	
	sent You sent the emails?	**send** You send the emails?	
	cart Is the red cart hers?	**card** Is the red card hers?	
	write Can he write well?	**ride** Can he ride well?	
	train Does this train smell?	**drain** Does this drain smell?	
	trunk Is there a trunk outside?	**drunk** Is there a drunk outside?	

Minimal pair words

C3a   **a** Listen and repeat the words. Notice that the target sound is quieter in the words *send, card, ride*.

C3b   **b** You will hear five words from each minimal pair. For each word, write *1* for /t/ (sound 1) or *2* for /d/ (sound 2).

    EXAMPLE Pair 1:   2, 1, 2, 1, 2

Minimal pair sentences

C4a   **c** Listen to the minimal pair sentences.

C4b   **d** Listen to six of the sentences and write *1* for /t/ (sound 1) or *2* for /d/ (sound 2)

C4a   **e** **Sentence stress**
    Listen to the minimal pair sentences again and <u>underline</u> the sentence stress (on page 93).

    EXAMPLE <u>You</u> send the <u>e</u>mails?

C5   **f** Tick the words a) or b) that you hear in the sentences.

1 a) writing ☐   b) riding ☐
2 a) cart ☐   b) card ☐
3 a) bat ☐   b) bad ☐
4 a) sent ☐   b) send ☐
5 a) sight ☐   b) side ☐
6 a) try ☐   b) dry ☐

3 Dialogue

a First practise the target sound /d/ in some words from the dialogue. Read the words aloud or visit the website to practise.

/d/ is **LOUD** before a vowel.

DIANE   Let's go dancing, darling.

DAISY   Let's listen to the radio, Jordan.

DAVID   You forgot our date yesterday, Daisy.

/d/ is often quiet at the end of a word or before a consonant.

stayed   repaired   It rained.   bad cold   They played cards.

What happens when /d/ at the end of a word is followed by a vowel?

They stayed‿at home.   They repaired‿it today.   It rained‿all day.
I had‿a bad cold.   They played‿a game of cards.

Practise these words with a louder /d/ at the beginning and a quieter /d/ at the end.

did   decide   decided   damaged   David   Donald

Look at the words in the box below and decide whether the sound /d/ is loud (L) or quiet (Q).

EXAMPLE bad (Q) Daisy (L)

nobody ( )   darling ( )   bad ( )   cards ( )   Daisy ( )
date ( )   played ( )   dancing ( )   listened ( )   don't ( )
phoned ( )   tried ( )   today ( )   rained ( )

Check your answers in the key before doing the next exercise.

C6 **b** Read the dialogue below and guess the missing words with the sound /d/. 1–7 have a louder /d/. a–g have a quieter /d/. Number 1 and a) have been done as examples. Check your answers by looking in the box of words above, and then by listening to the dialogue.

A damaged telephone line

DAISY: Hello. This is 22882228.

DAVID: Hello, 1 _Daisy_____ . This is David.

DAISY: Oh, hi, 2_____ .

DAVID: What did you do yesterday, Daisy? You forgot our 3_____ , didn't you?

DAISY: Well, it a)_rained___ all day, David … and … I had a b)_____ cold, so I … er … decided to stay at home.

DAVID: Did you? … I c)_____ twenty times and 4_____ answered.

DAISY: Oh, the telephone line was damaged. They repaired it 5_____ .

DAVID: Well … Daisy!!

DAISY: What, David?

DAVID: Oh! … 6_____ worry about it! … What did … er … Donald do yesterday? Did he and Diane go 7_____ ?

DAISY: No, they didn't yesterday. They just stayed at home and d)_____ e)_____ .

DAVID: And what did you do? Did you play cards too?

DAISY: No … Jordan and I f)_____ to the radio and … er … studied. What did you do yesterday, David?

DAVID: I've just told you, Daisy … I g)_____ to phone you twenty times!

4 Verbs ending in *ed*

Verbs ending in *ed* are pronounced:

/d/ after a vowel or voiced consonant	/t/ after an unvoiced consonant	/ɪd/ after the sounds /t/ or /d/

 C7 a Listen and repeat.

played	brushed	waited
cleaned	laughed	painted
snowed	pushed	shouted
closed	watched	wanted
filled	danced	landed
stayed	walked	departed

C8 b *ed* endings: /d/, /t/, /ɪd/

Talk about these pictures. Work with a partner or listen
to the recording. Follow the example.

EXAMPLE stayed awake/snored

A: He stayed awake, didn't he?
B: No, he didn't. He snored.

combed his hair
brushed it

cried a lot
laughed a lot

painted a room
cleaned it

emptied his glass
filled it

closed a door
opened it

walked away
waited a long time

washed the TV
watched it

pulled his car
pushed it

departed at noon
landed

whispered it
shouted it

danced all night
played cards

rained all day
snowed

5 Spelling

Look back over this unit at words with the target sound, and write what
you noticed about how to spell the sound /d/.

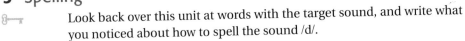

UNIT 27 /k/ key

– Can I have a **c**ouple more of your **c**aramel **c**ookies, please?
– Of **c**ourse you **c**an. ... And some of my chocolate **c**ake?
– No, thanks. I like **c**ake. But I'm allergic to chocolate.

1 Target sound /k/

C9a **a** To make the target sound /k/ first touch the back of the roof of your mouth with the back of your tongue. Then push air forward behind your tongue. **Then quickly move your tongue away to release the air suddenly.** Don't use your voice. Listen and repeat: /k/.

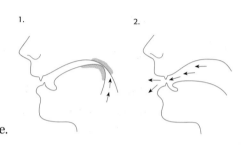

1.

2.

C9b **b** Notice that sometimes /k/ is quieter because the air isn't released suddenly. Listen.

make   music   look   book   like   likes

Omit from ** to ** above to make this quieter sound.

2 Sound /k/

/k/
coat
It's a hairy coat.

curl
He's got a lovely curl.

class
It's a brilliant class.

back
She's got a strong back.

crowing
It's crowing.

C10a **a** In the words on page 97, notice that the target sound is quieter in the word *back*. Listen and repeat the words.

C10b **b** Listen to the sentences.

C10a **c** Sentence stress

First try to guess some of the answers to these questions about the sentences:

Are they all questions or statements?

Does the intonation go up or down?
Which sentences have an adjective + noun?

Which is the most important word for the speaker's meaning?

Then listen to the sentences again and underline the sentence stress (on page 97).

EXAMPLE It's a hairy coat.

C10a **d** Listen and repeat the sentences.

3 Dialogue

a First practise the target sound /k/ in words from the dialogue, plus some others. Read the words aloud or visit the website to practise.

/k/ is **LOUD** before a vowel.

Kate cup sky school course **coff**ee **cuck**oo **Kar**en OK American ex**cuse** me

/k/ is also quite **LOUD** before 'l' and 'r'.

cream cry crowd **Christ**mas **across** class clean clear climb in**clude**

/k/ is often quiet at the end of a word.

look walk ask quick black book work milk Mrs **Clark** **plas**tic electric

What happens when the next word begins with a vowel? Do the two words join together? Is the /k/ louder or quieter?

look	look_up	walk	walk_along
ask	ask_anybody	work	work_out
book	book_out	Mrs Clark	Is Mrs Clark_in?

Notice what happens when a quiet /k/ at the end of a word is followed by a louder /k/ at the beginning of the next word. Make the two sounds different. There can be a slight pause between the two sounds.

black	black cup	quick	quick question
electric	electric clock	plastic	plastic container
like	like cooking	book	book case
speak	speak clearly	walk	walk quickly

/k/ is quieter before most consonants (except 'l' and 'r'). Choose the correct heading from this box for each list of consonant clusters (1–5) below.

/kt/	/kl/	/kw/	/kr/	/ks/

1 _____	2 _____	3 _____	4 _____	5 _____
next	picked	quiet	clock	cricket
exciting	walked	Kwok	class	cream
expensive	worked	question	clever	scream
excuse me	asked	quality	quickly	microwave
forks	electric	quite	chocolate	incredible

In which two lists 1–5 does /k/ sound louder?

Practise saying the clusters.

Look at the words in the box below and decide whether the target sound is loud (L) or quiet (Q).

EXAMPLE like (Q) coffee (L)

| milk ( ) cuckoo (/) like ( ) next ( ) Kate ( )
| fork ( ) make ( ) American ( ) carved ( ) call ( )
| coffee ( ) plastic ( ) course ( ) cream ( ) |

Check your answers in the key before doing the next exercise.

C11 **b** Read the dialogue below and fill the gaps with the correct words from the box above. 1–8 have a louder /k/. a–f have a quieter /k/. Numbers 1 and a) have been done as examples. Check your answers by listening to the dialogue.

The cuckoo clock

KAREN COOK: Would you a)_*like*_____ some cream in your
1_*coffee*___ , Mrs Clark?

KATE CLARK: 2_____ me Kate, Karen.

KAREN COOK: OK … Cream, … 3_____ ?

KATE CLARK: No thanks, Karen. But I'd like a little b)_____ . Thanks.

KAREN COOK: Would you like some little 4_____ cakes … Kate?

KATE CLARK: Thank you. Did you c)_____ them?

KAREN COOK: Yes. Take two. Here's a cake d)_____ , and here's a …

KATE CLARK: Excuse me, Karen. But what's that e)_____ to your bookshelf? Is it a clock?

KAREN COOK: It's an electric cuckoo clock. It's 5_____ .

KATE CLARK: Is it f)_____ ?

KAREN COOK: Oh no, Kate. It's a hand 6_____ wooden clock. It was very expensive.

KATE CLARK: Well, it's exactly six o'clock now, and it's very quiet. Doesn't it say 'cuckoo'?

KAREN COOK: Of 7_____ it does, Kate … Look!

CLOCK: Cuckoo! Cuckoo! Cuckoo! Cuckoo! Cuckoo! 8_____ !

KATE CLARK: Fantastic! How exciting! What a clever clock!

c Practise reading the dialogue aloud. Record your voice to compare your production of the target sound with the recording.

4 Sentence stress patterns

C12 a Listen and repeat.

(adjective + noun)	(adjective + compound noun)
1 a <u>clean</u> <u>shelf</u>	a clean <u>book</u>shelf
2 a <u>clean</u> <u>whisk</u>	a clean <u>egg</u> whisk
3 a <u>black</u> <u>cup</u>	a black <u>coffee</u> cup
4 a <u>plastic</u> <u>ring</u>	a plastic <u>key</u> ring
5 a <u>dirty</u> <u>bottle</u>	a dirty <u>cola</u> bottle
6 an e<u>lectric</u> <u>clock</u>	an electric <u>cuckoo</u> clock
7 an ex<u>pen</u>sive <u>cake</u>	an expensive <u>choc</u>olate cake

b Unjumble these sentences.

1 an it's <u>cuck</u>oo electric clock

2 ring plastic it's <u>key</u> a

3 <u>egg</u> dirty it's whisk a

4 it's bottle dirty a <u>cola</u>

5 expensive cake <u>cream</u> an it's

6 it's <u>car</u> comfortable coat a

7 book black a it's a<u>ddress</u>

5 Spelling

Look back over this unit at words with the target sound, and write what you noticed about how to spell the sound /k/.

UNIT 28 /g/ girl

- – Could you get me some groceries when you go out?
- – What exactly – nutmeg? gherkins? yoghurt?
- – Of course not! Get me some bagels if they've got any …
  mm … sugar, eggs, garlic … and … mm … figs and
  grapes, if they're any good.
- – OK.

1 Target sound /g/

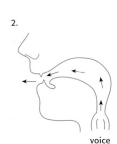

1.   2.

C13a **a** First practise the sound /k/
(see page 97). This is an unvoiced
sound. Listen and repeat.

C13b **b** Use your voice to make the target
sound /g/. Listen and repeat.

C13c **c** Listen and repeat both sounds
together. /k/ is unvoiced. /g/ is voiced.

C13d **d** Notice that sometimes /g/ is quieter
because the air isn't released suddenly. Listen.

voice

big bag fig figs egg eggs example nutmeg

2 Minimal pairs

	Sound 1 /k/	Sound 2 /g/	
	coat It's a hairy coat.	**goat** It's a hairy goat.	
	curl He's got a lovely curl.	**girl** He's got a lovely girl.	
	class It's a brilliant class.	**glass** It's a brilliant glass.	
	back She's got a strong back.	**bag** She's got a strong bag.	
	crow It's crowing.	**grow** It's growing.	

Minimal pair words

C14a **a** Listen and repeat the words. Notice that the target sound is quieter in the word *bag*.

C14b **b** You will hear five words from each minimal pair. For each word, write *1* for /k/ (sound 1) or *2* for /g/ (sound 2).

EXAMPLE Pair 1: 1, 2, 1, 1, 2

Minimal pair sentences

C15a **c** Listen to the minimal pair sentences.

C15b **d** Listen to five of the sentences and write *1* for /k/ (sound 1) or *2* for /g/ (sound 2).

C15a **e** Sentence stress

In spoken English sentences, the most important words for the speaker's meaning are strongly stressed. Strongly stressed words are **LOUD**er and s l o w er. Weakly stressed words are quieter and quicker. This gives English its rhythm.

Listen to the minimal pair sentences again and underline the strongly stressed words (on page 101).

EXAMPLE He's got a lovely girl.

C16 **f** Tick the words a) or b) that you hear in the sentences.

1 a) cold ☐   b) gold ☐
2 a) back ☐   b) bag ☐
3 a) clock ☐   b) clog ☐
4 a) curl ☐   b) girl ☐
5 a) frock ☐   b) frog ☐
6 a) clue ☐   b) glue ☐

3 Phone messages

a First practice the target sound /g/. Some of these words are from the phone messages you will hear. Read the words aloud or visit the website to practise.

/g/ is **LOUD** before a vowel and quite loud before /l/ and /r/.

groups of girls giggling and gossiping together

taking great photographs of a guy in the garden cutting the grass

Maggie isn't in Glasgow. Guess again.

She's gone to Portugal and Greece until August.

/g/ is often quieter at the end of a word or before a consonant.

This is an example.

Another example is fog. Also smog.

rugs   mugs   hugs   rugby

a jog with a big dog   big dogs   a big pig   big pigs

a frog   frog's eggs   frog's legs

Craig   Craig's big bag   Craig has jetlag.

What happens when the next word begins with a vowel? Is /g/ **LOUD**er or quieter?

big dog	There's a big_old dog_in the garden.
fog smog	Fog_and smog_are what we've got.
dialogue	Read the dialogue_aloud.
Greg Craig	Greg_and Craig_and Maggie.

Notice how two /g/ sounds join together.

It's a big garden.   He's a big guy.   Has the fog gone?

/k/ and /g/

Quickly scan all the words in the box below and <u>underline</u> all those with the sound /k/.

---

computer Maggie postcard Glasgow beginning games
weekend Portugal Greece grass catch guess cut camp
August girls gossip couple Carol garden Craig

Check your answers before going on to 3b.

C17 **b** Close your book and listen to Craig and Maggie's phone messages on their answering machine, paying attention to the target sound. Then complete the sentences below. Each missing word has the sound /k/ or /g/, and is in the box above. Number 1 has been done as an example.

Craig and Maggie's answering machine

1 Greg and Carol want to stay for a _couple_ of days at _Craig_ and _Maggie_'s house in _Glasgow_ .

2 They're coming to _____ at the _____ of _____ .

3 _____ is always giggling. She wants to _____ up on all the _____ .

4 The last time they got together, Greg and Craig played _____ _____ while the two _____ went shopping.

5 Carol says, 'I _____ you've gone away for the _____ .'

6 Craig and Maggie sent a _____ from _____ , but they're going to go to Greece.

7 While Craig and Maggie are in _____ , Greg and Carol are going to _____ in their _____ .

8 Greg says they'll be very grateful and they'll _____ the _____ .

C18 **c** Listen to the complete sentences from 3b and check your answers. Then practise reading the sentences aloud. Record your voice to compare your production of the sounds /k/ and /g/ with the recording.

4 Consonant clusters

Choose the correct heading from this box for each list of consonant clusters (1–3) below.

/gl	/gz/	/gr/

1 _____   2 _____   3 _____

exam	English	angry
eggs	glove	hungry
executive	glasses	grammar
earplugs	glamorous	grapefruit
hugs	singly	grateful
exactly	global	congratulations

Use your dictionary to check the word stress and meaning of any words you don't know.

C19 Now listen to the recording of the clusters. Do you think the /g/ is quieter in any of the lists above?

5 Spelling

Look back over this unit at words with the target sound, and write what you noticed about how to spell the sound /g/.

UNIT 29 | REVIEW

Card game: Pick up pairs

Photocopy and cut out cards from all minimal pairs in Units 24, 26 and 28.
Shuffle the cards and deal them face down all over the table.

Turn over any two cards and read their sentences aloud. If they are minimal pairs (consonants), you keep them and you continue playing.

If those two cards aren't minimal pairs, turn them face down again and the next person plays.

Collect as many minimal pairs as you can in a time limit, e.g. ten minutes.

TEST

You can use a dictionary if you wish, but you don't have to understand every word to do this test.

C20 1 For each line (1, 2, 3, 4, 5), first listen to the whole line. Then circle the one word that is said twice. Note that meaning is not so important in this exercise. The purpose is to review the sounds by hearing them in contrast. Some of the words are rarely used in everyday English, and this is shown by an asterisk *.

	/p/	/b/	/t/	/d/	/k/	/g/
1	paw	bore	tore	door	core	gore*
2	pill	Bill	till	dill	kill	gill
3	pay	bay	Tay	day	Kay	gay
4	P	B	tea	Dee	key	ghee*
5	Pooh!	Boo!	two	do	coo	goo

Score ☐ /5

2 Circle the words with the same vowel sound as 1–3.

1 tree
/tr/

dress   strong
understand   retry
distrust   entertain
drunk   entrance
electric   dreaming

2 clock
/kl/

enclosed
glass   class   quite
walked   clothes
microwave   chocolate
glamorous
quickly

3 pram
/pr/

black
appreciate
place   plum
brother   impressive
probably   breakfast
present   prawn

Score [/ 15]

3 **Pick the different one: /t/, /d/ or /ɪd/**
Underline the *ed* ending that has a different pronunciation.
EXAMPLE telephoned   rained   answered   walk<u>ed</u>

1 brushed   washed   emptied   tossed

2 walked   watched   laughed   filled

3 waited   departed   combed   painted

4 pushed   snowed   cleaned   filled

5 whispered   played   rained   shouted

Score [/ 5]

4 **Stress**
<u>Underline</u> the stressed syllable in each item. (Score half a mark per item.)

telephone   remember   cafeteria   photographer's   a policeman
a postcard   a paper plate   American   somebody   a green coffee cup

Score [/ 5]

Total score [/ 30]

Additional review task using dialogues from Units 23–28

Unit	23	24	25	26	27	28
Target sound	/p/	/b/	/t/	/d/	/k/	/g/
	pen	baby	table	door	key	girl

From the above table, choose any target sounds that you had difficulty with.

1 Listen again to the dialogue in that unit, listening for the target sound.
2 Circle the target sound in any words in the dialogue.
3 Listen to the dialogue again and check your answers.
4 Check your answers in the key.
5 Listen to the dialogue again, listening for the target sound.
6 Read the dialogue aloud, and record your voice to compare your production of the target sound with the CD.

You can also use this review task as a quick self-test, by doing steps 2 and 4 only.

UNIT 30 /s/ sun

- Stop screaming! What's upsetting you?
- My sister. She takes my books out of my desk and puts them somewhere else.
- Just tell her to stop it.
- Yes, of course, that's the answer ... but it's not so simple. She makes me so cross! Could *you* speak to her?

1 Target sound /s/

C21 To make the target sound /s/, touch your top teeth with the sides of your tongue. Put the tip of your tongue forward to nearly touch the roof of your mouth. Don't use your voice. Listen and repeat: /s/.

2 Sound /s/

/s/

Sue   **bus**
That Sue was amazing.   I heard a bus.

C   **piece**
It's pronounced /siː/.   I want the big piece.

sip   **price**
Sip it slowly.   What's the price?

C22a **a** Listen and repeat the words.

C22b **b** Listen to the sentences.

C22b **c** Sentence stress
The most important words for the speaker's meaning are strongly stressed. Guess which two words will be strongly stressed in each sentence above. Then listen to the sentences again and <u>underline</u> the sentence stress.

EXAMPLE I want the <u>big piece</u>.

C22b **d** Listen and repeat the sentences.

3 Dialogue

 a First practise the target sound /s/ in some of the words from the dialogue below. Read the words aloud or visit the website to practise.

Sam   Sue   sand   a sum of **mon**ey   **Sat**urday   **sail**ing   **poss**ible **sea**side

/s/ in consonant clusters

let's   that's   it's   six   just   sleep   spend   stay   star   Smith out**side**   in**stead**   **sweet**ie   **swimm**ing   **sen**sible   **small**est   **ski**ing ex**cit**ing   ex**pen**sive   **cheap**skate*

* a person who only spends the smallest amount of money

Notice how /s/ sounds join together.

let's_stay   Six_Star   let's_sleep

c23 b First just listen to the dialogue without looking at your book, paying particular attention to the target sound.

It's expensive

SAM: Let's go to the seaside on Saturday, sweetie.

SUE: Yes! Let's go sailing and water-skiing. That's exciting.

SAM: It's expensive, sweetie. Let's just sit in the sun and go swimming instead.

SUE: Let's stay in the Six Star Hotel and spend Sunday there too.

SAM: Be sensible, Sue. It's too expensive. Let's sleep outside instead.

SUE: Sleep on the sand? You never want to spend more than the smallest possible sum of money, Sam Smith – you're such a cheapskate!

c Practise reading the dialogue aloud. Record your voice to compare your production of the target sound with the recording.

4 /s/ in consonant clusters

c24 a Use the prompts below to make sentences about Sam, Simon, Lucas, Sarah, Chris and Chrissie. Listen and respond, like the example.

EXAMPLE I hate hats. *Response*: Sam hates hats too.

	Sam	Simon	Lucas	Sarah	Chris	Chrissie
1 I hate hats.	✓					
2 I like cats.		✓				
3 I get headaches.						✓
4 I drink milkshakes.			✓			
5 I take good photographs.	✓					
6 I eat chocolate biscuits.					✓	
7 I laugh at jokes.				✓		
8 I want some interesting books.						✓

b Joining /s/ sounds

Find the correct ending to these sentences and practise joining the /s/ sounds as in the example.

EXAMPLE Chrissssspeakssslowly.

1 Chris	sss	silently.
2 In winter let's	sss	such good photographs.
3 Sam takes	sss	such a cheapskate?
4 Sarah laughs	sss	speaks slowly.
5 In summer let's	sss	ski in the snow.
6 Sue likes	sss	sail into the sunset.
7 Lucas	sss	some cats.
8 Is Chris	sss	sends lots of text messages.

C25 Listen to check and repeat.

c Read aloud. Practise the target sound in consonant clusters.

> ## The smile of a snake
>
> She speaks slowly, and eats special, expensive chocolates. As she steps upstairs, her long skirt sweeps over her silver slippers. She is small and smart and sweet-smelling. Her skin is like snow. 'You have stolen my heart!' I once said stupidly, and she smiled. But when she smiled, she smiled the smile of a snake.

5 Spelling

Look back over this unit at words with the target sound, and write what you noticed about how to spell the sound /s/.

UNIT 31 /z/ zoo

- It looks so easy, doesn't it?
- It does. But it isn't.
- Look at those eyes. They're like ice.
- He always draws the bodies so well, doesn't he? Look at the arms ... the legs ... those hands.
- He's such an amazing artist.
- One of these days ... I'm going to buy one of his paintings.

1 Target sound /z/

C26a **a** First practise the sound /s/ (see page 107). Listen and repeat.

C26b **b** Use your voice to make the target sound /z/. Listen and repeat.

C26c **c** Listen and repeat both sounds together. /s/ is unvoiced. /z/ is voiced.

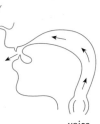

voice

2 Minimal pairs

	Sound 1 /s/	Sound 2 /z/	
	Sue That Sue was amazing.	**zoo** That zoo was amazing.	
	c It's pronounced /si:/.	**z** It's pronounced /zi:/.	
	sip Sip it slowly.	**zip** Zip it slowly.	
	bus I heard a bus.	**buzz** I heard a buzz.	
	piece I want the big piece.	**peas** I want the big peas.	
	price What's the price?	**prize** What's the prize?	

Minimal pair words

C27a a Listen and repeat the words.

C27b b You will hear five words from each minimal pair. For each word, write *1* for /s/ (sound 1) or *2* for /z/ (sound 2).

EXAMPLE Pair 1: 2, 1, 1, 1, 2

Minimal pair sentences

C28a c Listen to the minimal pair sentences.

C28b d Listen to six of the sentences and write *1* for /s/ (sound 1) or *2* for /z/ (sound 2).

C28a e **Sentence stress**

Look at this pattern of strong and weak stresses in the first set of minimal pair sentences.

That <u>Sue</u> was a<u>ma</u>zing. That <u>zoo</u> was a<u>ma</u>zing. oOooOo

Listen to the minimal pair sentences again while looking at the patterns and notice how the weak stresses are quicker and quieter.

Pair 1: **oOooOo**   Pair 2: **ooOO**   Pair 3: **OoOo**
Pair 4: **oOoO**   Pair 5: **oooOO**   Pair 6: **OoO**

C29 f Tick the words a) or b) that you hear in the sentences.

1 a) bus ☐   b) buzz ☐
2 a) sip ☐   b) zip ☐
3 a) price ☐   b) prize ☐
4 a) pence ☐   b) pens ☐
5 a) police ☐   b) please ☐
6 a) Sackville ☐   b) Zackville ☐

3 Dialogue

a First practise the target sound /z/ in words from the dialogue, plus others. Read the words aloud or visit the website to practise.

/s/ and /z/ sounds
The letter 's' is usually pronounced /s/ after an unvoiced sound, and /z/ after a voiced sound.

	/s/ after an unvoiced sound	/z/ after a voiced sound
plurals	snakes sacks units artists zips	animals parcels arms legs
3rd person singular	makes thinks wants repeats	smells contains draws
's	what's it's think's	something's Susan's

Joining /s/ and /z/ sounds

Notice that if the two sounds are different, we say the second one more strongly.

Yes, Zena. (s_z)   This parcel contains six mice. (z_s)   this sack (s_s)
does Susan (z_s)

Say these words that have two /s/ or /z/ sounds. Which sounds are they?

EXAMPLE Mrs (/s/ /z/)

1 smells	6 surprising
2 parcels	7 Lazarus
3 something's	8 sounds
4 boxes	9 sacks
5 Susan	10 zoos

C30 b Listen to the dialogue, paying attention to the /s/ and /z/ sounds. Then practise reading the dialogue aloud. Record your voice to compare your production of those sounds with the recording.

Surprises in the post office

(Zena and Susan work at the post office. They are busy sorting parcels. It's Susan's first day.)

SUSAN: This parcel smells, Mrs Lazarus.

ZENA: Call me Zena, Susan.

SUSAN: Yes … Zena … Something's written on it. What does it say?

ZENA: It says: 'This parcel contains six mice'.

SUSAN: Aw! Isn't that awful, Zena! Poor animals!

ZENA: And listen, Susan! What's in this sack?

SUSAN: It's making a strange hissing noise.

SACK: *(hisses)* Sssssssssssssssss!

SUSAN: Zena! It's a sack of snakes!

ZENA: So it is! … And what do you think's in this box, Susan?

SUSAN: It's making a buzzing sound.

BOX: *(buzzes)* Zzzzzzzzzzzzzzzz!

SUSAN: Those are bees!

ZENA: A parcel of mice … and a sack of snakes … and a box of bees. What do you think about this, Susan, on your first day in the parcels office? Isn't it surprising?

SUSAN: Amazing! This isn't a post office. It's a zoo.

4 Consonant clusters

C31 a **/z/ in consonant clusters**

Use the prompts below to make sentences about Ms Mills, Mr Suzuki, Mrs Moses and Miss Jones. Listen and respond, like the example.

EXAMPLE I love dogs. *Response*: Mr Suzuki loves dogs too.

	Ms Mills	Mr Suzuki	Mrs Moses	Miss Jones
1 I love dogs.		✓		
2 I climb mountains.	✓			
3 I have six cousins.			✓	
4 I listen to jazz records.				✓
5 I read magazines.		✓		
6 I always lose things.	✓			
7 I buy expensive clothes.				✓
8 I have loads of friends.		✓		
9 I prepare horrible meals.	✓			
10 I always remember bad dreams.			✓	

(Note: The following titles are only used with a family name: *Mr* /mistə/ for men and *Ms* /miz/ for women. *Mrs* /misiz/ is also used for married women, and *Miss* /mis/ for unmarried women.)

b **Consonant clusters: occupations, jobs, careers**

Match the sentence halves together.

EXAMPLE A horse trainer trains horses.

1 A horse trainer   a grows only roses.
2 An engineer   b kisses babies.
3 A renovator   c fishes.
4 A housekeeper   d designs garages.
5 A gardener   e sews other clothes besides dresses.
6 A prize giver   f trains horses.
7 A wage clerk   g trims hedges.
8 A rose grower   h sometimes washes clothes.
9 A garage designer   i gives prizes.
10 A fisherman   j builds bridges.
11 A politician   k modernises houses.
12 A dressmaker   l pays wages.

Check your answers in the key. Then read the answers aloud. Finally, cover the second half of the sentences and try to remember them, while still being careful with the clusters.

5 Spelling

Look back over this unit at words with the target sound, and write what you noticed about how to spell the sound /z/.

UNIT 32 /ʃ/ shoe

- She shouldn't be wearing such a shabby skirt at work, should she?
- She certainly shouldn't.
- I do wish she wouldn't.
- Shall I *tell* her?
- ... um ... er ... I'm not sure if you should ...

1 Target sound /ʃ/

C32a **a** First practise the sound /s/ (see page 107). Listen and repeat.

C32b **b** Then put the tip of your tongue back a little to make the unvoiced target sound /ʃ/. Listen and repeat.

C32c **c** Listen and repeat both sounds together. Both are unvoiced: /s/ and /ʃ/.

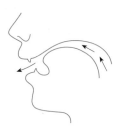

2 Minimal pairs

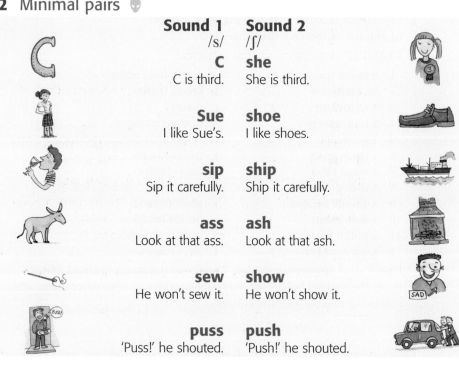

Sound 1 /s/	Sound 2 /ʃ/
C C is third.	**she** She is third.
Sue I like Sue's.	**shoe** I like shoes.
sip Sip it carefully.	**ship** Ship it carefully.
ass Look at that ass.	**ash** Look at that ash.
sew He won't sew it.	**show** He won't show it.
puss 'Puss!' he shouted.	**push** 'Push!' he shouted.

Minimal pair words

C33a **a** Listen and repeat the words.

C33b **b** You will hear five words from each minimal pair. For each word, write *1* for /s/ (sound 1) or *2* for /ʃ/ (sound 2).

EXAMPLE Pair 1: 1, 2, 1, 2, 1

Minimal pair sentences

C34a **c** Listen to the minimal pair sentences.

C34b **d** Listen to six of the sentences and write *1* for /s/ (sound 1) or *2* for /ʃ/ (sound 2).

C34a **e** Sentence stress

First try to guess which two words in each of the minimal pair sentences will be strongly stressed. Then listen, and mark ⌐ where the intonation begins to go down on the most strongly stressed word (on page 114).

EXAMPLE <u>Ship</u> it <u>carefully</u>.

C35 **f** Tick the words a) or b) that you hear in the sentences.

1 a) Sue's ☐   b) shoes ☐

2 a) ass ☐   b) ash ☐

3 a) puss ☐   b) push ☐

4 a) sack ☐   b) shack ☐

5 a) seats ☐   b) sheets ☐

6 a) save ☐   b) shave ☐

3 Dialogue

a First practise the target sound /ʃ/ in words from the dialogue. Read the words aloud or visit the website to practise.

show   Mr Shaw   sure   shop   shut   shall   shake   sheets   shirts shrunk   Mrs Marsh   push   wish   **shouldn't**   English   Swedish **finished**   **washes**   **wash**ing ma**chine**   **spec**ial   demon**stra**tion

C36 **b** First listen to the dialogue and notice that the intonation sometimes goes up. Then read the dialogue and write a–j against the numbers 1–4 in the box below. The first one has been done as an example.

1 *a* (five *Yes/No* questions)

2 _____ (one question tag where the speaker is not sure of the answer)

3 _____ (three sentences which are a list of instructions about how to do something)

4 _____ (one unfinished statement)

A special washing machine

MRS MARSH: (a) Does this shop sell <u>wash</u>ing machines?

MR SHAW: Yes. This is the latest washing machine.

MRS MARSH: (b) Is it <u>Swe</u>dish?

MR SHAW: No, madam. It's English.

MRS MARSH: (c) Could you show me how it <u>wash</u>es?

MR SHAW: (d) Shall I give you a demon<u>stra</u>tion? This one is our special demonstration machine. It's so simple. (e) You take some sheets and <u>shirts</u>. (f) You put them in the ma<u>chine</u>. (g) You shut this <u>door</u>. And you push this button.

MRS MARSH: (h) The machine shouldn't shake like that, <u>should</u> it?

MR SHAW: Washing machines always shake, madam … Ah! It's finished now.

MRS MARSH: (i) But the sheets have <u>shrunk</u>, and so have the shirts.

MR SHAW: (j) Do you wish to <u>buy</u> this machine, madam?

MRS MARSH: … I'm not sure.

C36 **c** First check your answers by listening to the dialogue again. Then check in the key.

Practise reading the dialogue aloud. Record your voice to compare your production of the intonation with the recording.

4 Joining /ʃ/ sounds

a /ʃ/ sounds are joined between words.

EXAMPLE English‿sheep

Rewrite these phrases following the example in 1.
1 shops in England _English shops_
2 ships made in Denmark _____
3 sheep in Scotland _____
4 shampoo from Sweden _____
5 champagne from France _____
6 sheets from Ireland _____
7 shirts made in Poland _____
8 shorts from Finland _____
9 sugar from Turkey _____
10 shoes made in Spain _____

C37 **b** Listen and check your answers.
c Read the phrases aloud, joining the /ʃ/ sounds.
EXAMPLE English‿shops

5 Spelling

Look back over this unit at words with the target sound, and write what you noticed about how to spell the sound /ʃ/.

UNIT 33 /ʒ/ television

– Dad, what rhymes with explosion?
– Erosion.
– What about conclusion?
– Confusion.
– And television?
– Decision ... revision ... precision ...
– Stop, Dad! That's enough! Thank you.
– My pleasure. Any time.

1 Target sound /ʒ/

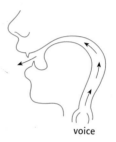

C38a **a** First practise the sound /ʃ/ (see page 114). Listen and repeat.

C38b **b** Use your voice to make the target sound /ʒ/. Listen and repeat.

C38c **c** Listen and repeat both sounds. /ʃ/ is unvoiced. /ʒ/ is voiced.

voice

2 Sound /ʒ/

/ʒ/

casual
Michelle has a job in a shop selling casual shoes.

massage
She also has a casual job doing sports massage

occasionally
She does sports massage occasionally, not every day.

collision
Yesterday Michelle saw a collision outside the shoe shop.

measure
She was measuring a shoe for a customer.

casualty
An ambulance took two injured people to casualty.

(Note: Two meanings of *casual* in the first two sentences: 1 *casual shoes* = relaxed style or fashion [opposite: formal]; 2 *casual job* = not regular work [opposite: permanent].)

C39a **a** Listen and repeat the words.

C39b **b** Listen to the sentences.

C39a **c** Sentence stress

In spoken English, the most important words for the speaker are strongly stressed. So there is often more than one 'correct' way of stressing a sentence, as it depends on the speaker's meaning. Guess which words might be spoken with stronger stress in the sentences. Then listen to the sentences again and <u>underline</u> the sentence stress (on page 117).

EXAMPLE <u>Mi</u>chelle has a <u>job</u> in a <u>shop</u> selling <u>casual</u> <u>shoes</u>.

C39a **d** Listen and repeat the sentences.

3 Television programmes

a First practise the sound /ʒ/ in some of the words from this unit. Read the words aloud or visit the website to practise.

u**s**ually une**s**ual **pleas**ure

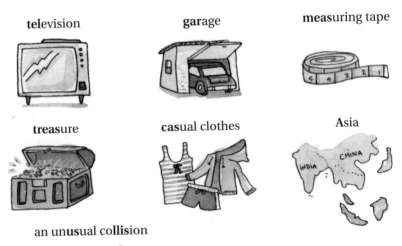

television   garage   mea**s**uring tape

treasure   casual clothes   Asia

an unusual collision

C40 b Listen.

Television Programmes: Channel 5	Sharon	Shaun	Charlotte	Mrs Marsh
7.00 – Children's film: *Treasure Island*	✓			
7.15 – News update: *An Unusual Collision*		✓		
7.30 – Fashion show: *Casual Clothes*				
7.45 – Travel film: *Crossing Asia*			✓	
8.15 – Do-it-yourself show: *How to Measure* *a New Garage*	✓			✓
8.30 – Variety show: *It's a Pleasure*		✓		

c Make as many sentences as you can about who's watching what on TV tonight.

EXAMPLE At 8.30, Shaun's watching a variety show called *It's a Pleasure*.

d Practise with a partner. Talk about which of the television programmes above you would like to watch. Also ask each other about what shows you usually watch.

EXAMPLES What do you usually watch on Thursdays?
Would you like to watch the fashion show *Casual Clothes*?

4 Intonation in thanks/responses

We usually say thank you and reply to thank you with intonation going down at the end. When somebody says 'Thank you' for doing something, we sometimes reply, 'It's a pleasure', or 'My pleasure.' Some other responses to thanks are: 'You're welcome', 'That's all right,' 'That's OK.'

C41 Practise ways of saying thank you and responses to thanks with intonation going down on the last strong stress. First listen and repeat the possible responses.

It's a pleasure.   My pleasure.   You're welcome.
That's all right.   That's OK.

EXAMPLE A: Thank you for lending me your television.
              B: It's a pleasure.

1 Thank you for mending my television.
2 Here's your measuring tape. Thank you so much.
3 I finished 'Treasure Island'. Thanks.
4 It was great to use your garage. Thanks a lot.
5 Thanks for the massage. It was great.

5 Spelling

Look back over this unit at words with the target sound, and write what you noticed about how to spell the sound /ʒ/.

UNIT 34 /tʃ/ chip

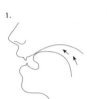

– Lovely little **ch**apel for a **ch**ur**ch** wedding bells … **ch**iming …
– Do you think they're a good ma**tch**?
– Good que**st**ion. They're like **ch**alk and **ch**eese. She's a **ch**eckout **ch**ick;
  he's the **ch**airman of a television **ch**annel. He's ri**ch**, **ch**arming …
– But she *is* the national **ch**ess **ch**ampion.
– Ah! … mm … a perfect ma**tch**, I imagine.

(Note: *They're like chalk and cheese* = idiom meaning they're very different.)

1 Target sound /tʃ/

C42a **a** First practise the sounds /t/ and /ʃ/ (see pages 89 and 114). Listen and repeat.

C42b **b** To make the target sound /tʃ/, begin to make /t/. Then slowly move your tongue from the roof of your mouth. Do it again more quickly. Don't use your voice. Listen and repeat: /tʃ/.

1.   2.

2 Minimal pairs

Sound 1 /ʃ/	Sound 2 /tʃ/
ship We like ships.	**chip** We like chips.
sheep This is a sheep farm.	**cheap** This is a cheap farm.
sherry It's a sherry trifle.	**cherry** It's a cherry trifle.
shop I'll buy this shop.	**chop** I'll buy this chop.
cash I couldn't cash it.	**catch** I couldn't catch it.
wash He's washing the television.	**watch** He's watching the television.

Minimal pair words

C43a a Listen and repeat the words.

C43b b You will hear five words from each minimal pair. For each word, write *1*
for /ʃ/ (sound 1) or *2* for /tʃ/ (sound 2).

EXAMPLE Pair 1: 2, 2, 1, 2, 1

Minimal pair sentences

C44a c Listen to the minimal pair sentences.

C44b d Listen to six of the sentences and write *1* for /ʃ/ (sound 1) or 2 for /tʃ/
(sound 2).

C44a e **Sentence stress**

First read the minimal pair sentences and guess which two words will be
strongly stressed in each sentence. Notice which words are nouns,
adjectives or main verbs. These are often important for the speaker's
meaning, so they are often (but not always) the stressed words. Then
listen to each sentence and <u>underline</u> the two strongly stressed words
(on page 120).

EXAMPLE He's <u>watch</u>ing the <u>television</u>.

C45 f Tick the words a) or b) that you hear in the sentences.

1 a) shop ☐   b) chop ☐

2 a) sherry ☐   b) cherry ☐

3 a) washing ☐   b) watching ☐

4 a) ships ☐   b) chips ☐

5 a) shin ☐   b) chin ☐

6 a) shoes ☐   b) choose ☐

3 Dialogue

a First practise the target sound /tʃ/ in words from the dialogue. Read the
words aloud or visit the website to practise.

choose   chops   Charles   much   lunch   Church
butcher   chicken   children   cheaper   **cheerful   charming
Cheshire   chump** chops

C46 b **Sentence stress**

Listen to the dialogue, paying attention to the target sound. Then read
the dialogue and guess which words are strongly stressed in each
sentence. The number in brackets tells you how many words will be
strongly stressed by the speaker in that line. The first line has been done
as an example. Then listen to the dialogue as many times as necessary
before deciding on your answers.

At the butcher's shop

(5) *(Charles Cheshire is a very cheerful, charming butcher.)*

CHARLES: (2) Good morning, Mrs Church.

MRS CHURCH: (5) Good morning, Charles. I'd like some chops for the children's lunch.

CHARLES: (2) Chump chops or shoulder chops, Mrs Church?

MRS CHURCH: (4) I'll have four shoulder chops, and I want a small chicken.

CHARLES: (3) Would you like to choose a chicken, Mrs Church?

MRS CHURCH: (2) Which one is cheaper?

CHARLES: (4) This one's the cheapest. It's a delicious chicken.

MRS CHURCH: (8) How much is all that? I haven't got cash. Can I pay by credit card?

CHARLES: (2) Of course, Mrs Church.

C46 c Check your answers by listening to the dialogue again. Then check in the key.

d Practise reading the dialogue aloud. Record your voice to compare your production of the target sound with the recording.

4 Intonation in a list

C47 a Listen to the recording of someone listing the ingredients in the recipe below. Notice how intonation keeps going up on each item of the list, but comes down at the end.

Recipe – Cheese-topped chops

Ingredients:

a <u>dash</u> of soy <u>sauce</u>

<u>four</u> <u>chops</u>

<u>Cheddar</u> <u>cheese</u>

<u>one</u> fresh <u>chilli</u> or a <u>pinch</u> of <u>chilli</u> powder

<u>cherries</u>

<u>mushrooms</u>

<u>shallots</u>

Practise reading this list aloud. Record your voice to compare your intonation with the recording.

C48 b Instructions

Listen to someone giving instructions about how to make cheese-topped chops. Notice how intonation can keep going up when giving instructions about how to do something, but comes down at the end.

1 <u>Pour</u> a little soy <u>sauce</u> over the <u>chops</u>.

2 <u>Chop</u> the <u>mush</u>rooms, <u>cheese</u> and <u>shallots</u>.

3 <u>Mix</u> the <u>mush</u>rooms, <u>cheese</u>, shallots and <u>chi</u>lli with a <u>dash</u> of soy <u>sauce</u>.

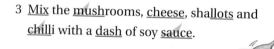

4 <u>Grill</u> the <u>chops</u>.

5 <u>Spread</u> the <u>mix</u>ture <u>o</u>ver the <u>chops</u>.

6 <u>Grill</u> the <u>chops</u> and <u>mix</u>ture for a few <u>mi</u>nutes.

7 Put the <u>chops</u> on a <u>dish</u> and <u>decorate</u> <u>each</u> <u>chop</u> with a <u>cherry</u>.

8 <u>Serve</u> the chops with <u>fresh</u> <u>French</u> <u>salad</u> and <u>chips</u>.

Practise reading these instructions aloud. Record your voice to compare your stress and intonation with the recording.

5 Spelling

Look back over this unit at words with the target sound, and write what you noticed about how to spell the sound /tʃ/.

UNIT 35 /dʒ/ January

> – Good morning. My name is Chas Jazz. I want to arrange to send an item of my luggage on to Japan.
> – Just one moment, Mr Jazz … *(on phone)* Hello. Could you hold on for just a moment, please?
> – Just in case there's any damage to this baggage, the Jumbojetset Company in Jamestown has …
> – I'm sorry Mr Jazz, but this is not the Jumbojetset Company. Their office is just round the corner.

1 Target sound /dʒ/

C49a **a** First practise the sound /tʃ/ (see page 120). Listen and repeat.

C49b **b** Use your voice to make the target sound /dʒ/. Listen and repeat.

C49c **c** Listen and repeat both sounds together. /tʃ/ is unvoiced. /dʒ/ is voiced.

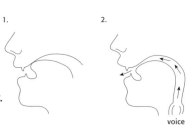

2 Minimal pairs

	Sound 1 /tʃ/	Sound 2 /dʒ/	
	cheap It's a cheap type of car.	**jeep** It's a jeep type of car.	
	choke Are you choking?	**joke** Are you joking?	
	riches A land full of riches.	**ridges** A land full of ridges.	
	cherries Do you like cherries?	**Jerry's** Do you like Jerry's?	
	larch I want a larch tree.	**large** I want a large tree.	
	H Do I write 'H' here?	**age** Do I write age here?	

Minimal pair words

C50a **a** Listen and repeat the words.

C50b **b** You will hear five words from each minimal pair. For each word, write *1* for /tʃ/ (sound 1) or *2* for /dʒ/ (sound 2).

EXAMPLE Pair 1:   2, 2, 1, 2, 1

Minimal pair sentences

C51a **c** Listen to the minimal pair sentences.

C51b **d** Listen to six of the sentences and write *1* for /tʃ/ (sound 1) or *2* for /dʒ/ (sound 2).

C51a **e** Sentence stress

First imagine how the minimal pair sentences will be spoken if the pair word is the most important word for the speaker's meaning. <u>Underline</u> this word (on page 124). Then listen to the sentences again and mark if the voice begins to go up or down on this word.

EXAMPLE It's a <u>cheap</u> type of car.

C52 **f** Tick the words a) or b) that you hear in the sentences.

1 a) choke	☐	b) joke	☐	
2 a) larch	☐	b) large	☐	
3 a) cheap	☐	b) jeep	☐	
4 a) chain	☐	b) Jane	☐	
5 a) chilly	☐	b) Jilly	☐	
6 a) cheered	☐	b) jeered	☐	

3 Dialogue

a First practise the target sound /dʒ/ in words from the dialogue. Read the words aloud or visit the website to practise.

jeep   jail   John   just   George   edge   **Je**rry   **lar**ger   **in**jured **dan**gerous   **a**gency   **tra**vel agency   jokes   bridge   **vill**age **dam**aged   **man**ager   **pass**enger   **Jan**uary   **dan**gerously

C53 b Read the dialogue below and fill the gaps (1–8) with the correct words from the box below. Then listen and check your answers.

jokes	bridge	village	damaged
manager	passenger	January	dangerously

A dangerous bridge

JERRY: Just outside this 1_____ there's a very dangerous bridge.

JOHN: Yes. Charles told me two jeeps crashed on it in 2_____ .
What happened?

JERRY: Well, George Churchill was the driver of the larger jeep, and he was driving very 3_____ .

JOHN: George Churchill? Do I know George Churchill?

JERRY: Yes. That ginger-haired chap. He's the 4_____ of the travel agency in Chester.

JOHN: Oh, yes. I remember George. He's always telling jokes. Well, was anybody injured?

JERRY: Oh, yes. The other jeep went over the edge of the 5_____ , and two children and another 6_____ were badly injured.

JOHN: Oh dear! Were both the jeeps 7_____ ?

JERRY: Oh, yes.

JOHN: And what happened to George?

JERRY: George? He's telling 8_____ in jail now, I suppose!

c Practise reading the dialogue aloud. Record your voice to compare your production of the target sound with the recording.

4 /tʃ/ and /dʒ/ sounds

C54 a Joining sounds
Notice that when two sounds /tʃ/ or /dʒ/ come together, we usually say both sounds.

EXAMPLE large (/dʒ/ /tʃ/) cherries

Listen and repeat.

large <u>ch</u>erries	<u>o</u>range juice	How much <u>ch</u>eese
which <u>j</u>ob	village <u>j</u>ail	wat<u>ch</u> chain
rich <u>ch</u>ild	teach <u>G</u>erman	large <u>g</u>entleman
which <u>ch</u>air	college <u>ch</u>ess	huge <u>j</u>umbo jet

b Crossword

Every answer has the sound /tʃ/ or /dʒ/.

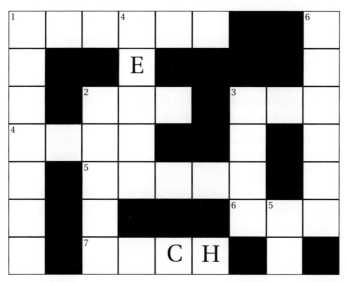

Clues

Across:

1 Some people get married in a ....
2 We eat bread, butter and ....
3 We buy jam in a ....
4 You'll get fat if you eat too much ......olate.
5 A game for two people.
6 You can see in the dark with a ......ch.
7 This isn't ...... a difficult puzzle.

Down:

1 A young hen is a ....
2 This book belongs to Jock. It's ......'. book.
3 The dangerous bridge is ...... outside the village.
4 HRCAE are the letters of this word. It means to arrive.
5 Tell me a j......e.
6 George's jeep was ...... than the other jeep.

5 Spelling

Look back over this unit at words with the target sound, and write what you noticed about how to spell the sound /dʒ/.

UNIT 36 REVIEW

Card game: Pick up unvoiced consonants: /p/, /t/, /k/, /ʃ/, /tʃ/

Photocopy and cut out cards from minimal pairs in Units 32, 34, 35 and add the cards from Units 24, 26 and 28.

Shuffle the cards and deal them face down all over the table.

Turn over any two cards and read their sentences aloud. If they both have any unvoiced consonants in the pair words, you keep them and you continue playing.

If they don't, turn them both face down again and the next person plays.

Collect as many cards as you can in a time limit, e.g. ten minutes.

TEST

You can use a dictionary if you wish, but you don't have to understand every word to do this test.

C55 1 For each line (1, 2, 3, 4, 5), first listen to the whole line, then circle the one word (or part of a word) that is said twice. Note that meaning is not important in this exercise. The purpose is to review the sounds by hearing them in contrast. One word is rarely used in everyday English, and this is marked by an asterisk *. Incomplete words have the rest of the word written in brackets, e.g. *chea(p)*.

	/s/	/z/	/ʃ/	/ʒ/	/tʃ/	/dʒ/
1	sue	zoo	shoe	–	chew	Jew(ish)
2	Sam	(e)xam	sham	–	cham(pion)	jam
3	so	zo(ne)	show	–	cho(sen)	Joe
4	C	Z	she	–	chea(p)	Gee!
5	sap	zap	chap(erone)*–		chap	Jap(anese)

Score ☐ / 5

2 Circle the words with the same consonant cluster as 1–3.

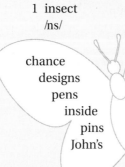

1 insect
/ns/

chance
designs
pens
inside
pins
John's

answer
televisions
instructions
ancestors

2 orange
/ndʒ/

range
sponge   lunch
stranger   much
ringer   French
exchange   bingo
lounge

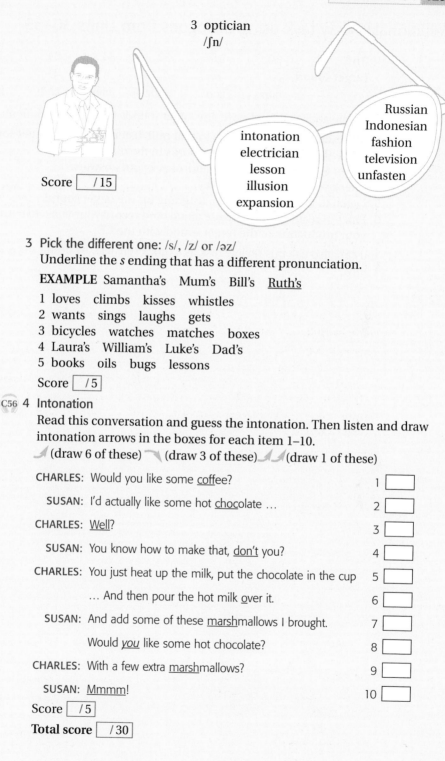

3 optician
/ʃn/

intonation
electrician
lesson
illusion
expansion

Russian
Indonesian
fashion
television
unfasten

Score [/ 15]

3 **Pick the different one:** /s/, /z/ or /əz/
Underline the *s* ending that has a different pronunciation.

EXAMPLE Samantha's Mum's Bill's <u>Ruth's</u>

1 loves climbs kisses whistles
2 wants sings laughs gets
3 bicycles watches matches boxes
4 Laura's William's Luke's Dad's
5 books oils bugs lessons

Score [/ 5]

C56 4 **Intonation**

Read this conversation and guess the intonation. Then listen and draw
intonation arrows in the boxes for each item 1–10.
◢ (draw 6 of these) ◥ (draw 3 of these) ◢◢ (draw 1 of these)

CHARLES: Would you like some <u>cof</u>fee?	1	[ ]
SUSAN: I'd actually like some hot <u>choc</u>olate …	2	[ ]
CHARLES: <u>Well</u>?	3	[ ]
SUSAN: You know how to make that, <u>don't</u> you?	4	[ ]
CHARLES: You just heat up the milk, put the chocolate in the cup	5	[ ]
… And then pour the hot milk <u>ov</u>er it.	6	[ ]
SUSAN: And add some of these <u>marsh</u>mallows I brought.	7	[ ]
Would *you* like some hot chocolate?	8	[ ]
CHARLES: With a few extra <u>marsh</u>mallows?	9	[ ]
SUSAN: <u>Mmmm</u>!	10	[ ]

Score [/ 5]

Total score [/ 30]

Additional review task using dialogues from Units 30–35

Unit	30	31	32	33	34	35
Target sound	/s/	/z/	/ʃ/	/ʒ/	/tʃ/	/dʒ/
	sun	zoo	shoe	television	chip	January

From the above table, choose any target sounds that you had difficulty with.

1 Listen again to the dialogue in that unit, listening for the target sound.
2 Circle the target sound in any words in the dialogue.
3 Listen to the dialogue again and check your answers.
4 Check your answers in the key.
5 Listen to the dialogue again, listening for the target sound.
6 Practise reading the dialogue aloud, and record your voice to compare your production of the target sound with the CD.

You can also use this review task as a quick self-test, by doing steps 2 and 4 only.

UNIT 37 /f/ fan

– I'm off, Ms Fox.
– It's only four. We finish at five, Mr Foot.
– I've had enough of this office for one day.
 Too much hiring and firing. I'm off.
– Well, just put those files on the floor, Mr Foot.
 Drive carefully. And don't forget the flowers for
 your wife.

(Note: *hiring and firing* = idiom meaning employing and dismissing workers.)

1 Target sound /f/

C57 To make the target sound /f/, touch
 your top teeth with your bottom lip.
 Blow out air between your lip and
 your teeth. Don't use your voice.
 Listen and repeat: /f/.

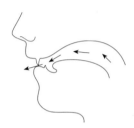

2 Minimal pairs A

	Sound 1 /p/	Sound 2 /f/	
	pin It's a sharp pin	**fin** It's a sharp fin.	
	peel Peel this orange.	**feel** Feel this orange.	
	pork There's no pork here.	**fork** There's no fork here.	
	pull The sign said 'Pull'.	**full** The sign said 'Full'.	
	snip Snip these flowers.	**sniff** Sniff these flowers.	
	palm He showed me his palm.	**farm** He showed me his farm.	

Minimal pair words

C58a a Listen and repeat the words.

C58b b You will hear five words from each minimal pair. For each word, write *1* for /p/ (sound 1) or *2* for /f/ (sound 2).

EXAMPLE Pair 1: 2, 1, 2, 1, 2

Minimal pair sentences

C59a c Listen to the minimal pair sentences.

C59b d Listen to six of the sentences and write *1* for /p/ (sound 1) or *2* for /f/ (sound 2).

C59a e **Sentence stress**

Listen to the minimal pair sentences again and <u>underline</u> the strongly stressed words (on page 131).

EXAMPLE He <u>showed</u> me his <u>palm</u>.

Minimal pairs B

	Sound 1	**Sound 2**	
	/h/	/f/	
	hold	**fold**	
	Hold this paper.	Fold this paper.	
	heat	**feet**	
	I like heat on the back.	I like feet on the back.	
	hill	**fill**	
	That sign said 'Hill'.	That sign said 'Fill'.	
	heel	**feel**	
	This heel's different.	This feels different.	
	honey	**funny**	
	This is honey.	This is funny.	
	hole	**foal**	
	It's got a little hole.	It's got a little foal.	

Minimal pair words

C60a a Listen and repeat the words.

C60b b You will hear five words from each minimal pair. For each word, write *1* for /h/ (sound 1) or *2* for /f/ (sound 2).

EXAMPLE Pair 1: 1, 1, 1, 2, 2

Minimal pair sentences

C61a c Listen to the minimal pair sentences.

C61b d Listen to six of the sentences and write *1* for /h/ (sound 1) or *2* for /f/ (sound 2).

C61a e Sentence stress
Listen to the minimal pair sentences again and <u>underline</u> the strongly stressed words (on page 132).

EXAMPLE <u>Fol</u>d this <u>pa</u>per.

C62 f Tick the words a), b) or c) that you hear in the sentences.

1 a) pin	☐	b) fin	☐	
2 a) peel	☐	b) feel	☐	
3 a) snipping	☐	b) sniffing	☐	
4 a) heel	☐	b) feel	☐	
5 a) harm	☐	b) farm	☐	
6 a) pole	☐	b) hole	☐	c) foal ☐

3 Dialogue

Intonation in requests can be down at the end but it usually sounds more polite going up.

a Practise these six requests from the dialogue with the intonation going up. Read the sentences aloud or visit the website to practise.

1 Please phone my office after five <u>days</u>, Mrs <u>Phil</u>lips.

2 Please give a friendly <u>laugh</u>.

3 Please use this felt-tipped <u>pen</u>, Mrs <u>Phil</u>lips.

4 Please look … er … soft and <u>beau</u>tiful.

5 Please sit on this <u>so</u>fa.

6 Please fill in this <u>form</u>.

C63 b First listen to the dialogue, paying attention to the target sound. Then read the dialogue and fill the gaps (a–f) with the requests (1–6) above. The first gap has been done as an example.

C63 Listen to the dialogue again and check your answers. Then check in the key.

A funny photographer

PHOTOGRAPHER: Good afternoon. How can I help you?

FRED: I'm Fred Phillips. I want a photograph of myself and my wife Phillippa.

PHOTOGRAPHER: Certainly, Mr Phillips. a) ***Please fill in this form***.

PHILLIPPA: I'll fill it in, Fred.

PHOTOGRAPHER: b)_____ Mr Phillips, do you prefer a full front photograph or a profile?

FRED: A full front, don't you think, Phillippa?

PHILLIPPA: Yes. A full front photograph.

FRED: Full front.

PHILLIPPA: *(hands in the form)* It's finished.

PHOTOGRAPHER: Thank you, Mrs Phillips. c)_____ Is it comfortable?

PHILLIPPA: Yes. It feels fine.

PHOTOGRAPHER: Mr Phillips, d)_____

FRED: That's difficult. If you say something funny I can laugh.

PHOTOGRAPHER: And, Mrs Phillips, e)_____

FRED: *(laughs)*

PHOTOGRAPHER: That's it finished.

FRED: Finished?

PHOTOGRAPHER: Finished, Mr Phillips.

PHILLIPPA: Will the photograph be ready for the fifth of February?

PHOTOGRAPHER: Yes. f)_____

c Practise reading the dialogue aloud. Record your voice to compare your production of the target sound and the intonation with the recording.

4 Intonation in *if* sentences

Match the beginning of these *if* sentences (1–7) with the endings (a–g).

1 If Fred laughs,   a he gets frightened.
2 If Grandfather flies,   b they can speak French.
3 If you want to eat fish,   c you're first.
4 If you telephone information, d it gets full of fat.
5 If you fry food,   e they're helpful.
6 If they're from France,   f he looks funny.
7 If you finish before the others, g you need a knife and fork.

C64 Listen to check and repeat. Notice how the intonation goes up and then down.

EXAMPLE

If Fred <u>laughs</u>, he looks <u>fun</u>ny.

5 Spelling

Look back over this unit at words with the target sound, and write what you noticed about how to spell the sound /f/.

UNIT 38 /v/ van

– Have you ever been to Venice?
– No, never. But I've heard you've just come back
  from Venice, haven't you?
– Best holiday I've ever had. The food was fabulous.
– Did you buy anything in Venice?
– Yes – this vest.
– Ah ... Yes ... A berry-coloured Venetian vest!
  ... Very fashionable!

1 Target sound /v/

C65a a First practise the sound /f/ (see page
131). This is an unvoiced sound.
Listen and repeat.

C65b b Use your voice to make the target
sound /v/. Listen and repeat.

C65c c Listen and repeat both sounds: /f/
and /v/.

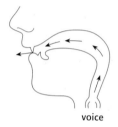

voice

2 Minimal pairs A

	Sound 1	**Sound 2**	
	/f/	/v/	
	safe	**save**	
	Safe here?	Save here?	
	fine	**vine**	
	Fine in the garden?	Vine in the garden?	
	fail	**veil**	
	It's a fail?	It's a veil?	
	few	**view**	
	This room has a few?	This room has a view?	
	fast	**vast**	
	They need a fast ship?	They need a vast ship?	
	ferry	**very**	
	Ferry late?	Very late?	

Minimal pair words

C66a a Listen and repeat the words.

C66b b You will hear five words from each minimal pair. For each word, write *1* for /f/ (sound 1) or *2* for /v/ (sound 2).

EXAMPLE Pair 1: 2, 1, 2, 2, 1

Minimal pair sentences

C67a c Listen to the minimal pair sentences. (Note: These are statements used as questions, so the intonation goes up.)

C67b d Listen to six of the sentences and write *1* for /f/ (sound 1) or *2* for /v/ (sound 2).

C67a e **Sentence stress**

Native speakers of English only sometimes use statements as questions. Listen to the minimal pair sentences again and notice how the speaker's voice begins to go up on the most important word for the speaker's meaning. This word is spoken with the strongest stress. Underline this word and any other strongly stressed words you hear in each sentence (on page 135).

EXAMPLE This <u>room</u> has a <u>view</u>?

Minimal pairs B

	Sound 1 /b/	Sound 2 /v/	
	bet They're good bets.	**vet** They're good vets.	
	best He wore his best.	**vest** He wore his vest.	
	ban Can they lift that ban?	**van** Can they lift that van?	
	bolt We need more bolts.	**volt** We need more volts.	
	boat Jones won the boat.	**vote** Jones won the vote.	
	berry It's a berry red colour.	**very** It's a very red colour.	

Minimal pair words

C68a a Listen and repeat the words. Then listen and repeat.

C68b b You will hear five words from each minimal pair. For each word, write *1* for /b/ (sound 1) or *2* for /v/ (sound 2).

EXAMPLE Pair 1:   1, 2, 1, 2, 1

Minimal pair sentences

C69a c Listen to the minimal pair sentences.

C69b d Listen to six of the sentences and write *1* for /b/ (sound 1) or *2* for /v/ (sound 2).

C69a e Sentence stress

Listen to the minimal pair sentences again and <u>underline</u> the two strongly stressed words in each sentence (on page 136).

C70 f Tick the words a), b) or c) that you hear in the sentences.

1 a) lift ☐   b) lived ☐
2 a) half ☐   b) halve ☐
3 a) fast ☐   b) vast ☐
4 a) boat ☐   b) vote ☐
5 a) bolts ☐   b) volts ☐
6 a) safe ☐   b) save ☐

3 Dialogue

a First practise the target sound /v/ in some of the words from the dialogue. Read the words aloud or visit the website to practise.

view   lived   five   of   have   love   vil**l**age   **valley**   **very**   **Vander** **lovely**   **Vic**tor   **living**   **arrived**   Vivienne

C71 b Intonation in statements

Intonation usually goes down at the end of a statement. Listen to the intonation in this dialogue. Then practise reading it aloud. Record your voice to compare your intonation and production of the target sound with the recording.

A fine view

VIVIENNE: Has the Vander family lived here for very long, Victor?

VICTOR: Five and a half years, Vivienne. We arrived on the first of February.

VIVIENNE: What a lovely view you have!

VICTOR: Yes. It's fabulous.

VIVIENNE: Look! You can see the village down in the valley

VICTOR: Yes. We just love living here because of the view.

4 Stress and intonation

C72 **a** Listen to this description and draw a down arrow on the last strong stress in each sentence. Check your answers and then practise reading the description aloud. Record your voice to compare your production of the target sound with the recording.

This is a photograph of a fat farmer arriving at a village.

The village is in a valley.

The farmer's driving a van.

It's the seventeenth of November.

It's a fine day but it's very cold.

Some of the leaves have fallen from the vine in the foreground of the photograph.

b Remember that intonation often goes down at the end of statements, short answers, *WH* questions, questions with 'or'.

Match these questions and answers, and draw down arrows on the last strong stress.

EXAMPLE What <u>month</u> is it in this <u>pho</u>tograph? No<u>vem</u>ber

1 Who's <u>driving</u> the <u>van</u>?	A <u>vine</u>.
2 How many <u>leaves</u> have fallen from the <u>vine</u>?	Ar<u>riving</u>.
3 <u>Where</u> do the <u>villagers</u> live?	<u>Five</u>.
4 Is the van <u>leaving</u> or a<u>rriving</u>?	In the <u>valley</u>.
5 In the <u>foreground</u> of the <u>photograph</u>, is it a <u>vine</u> or a <u>fir</u> tree?	<u>Four</u>.
6 Near the <u>village</u> are there <u>four</u> or <u>five</u> fir trees?	The <u>farmer</u>.

C73 Listen to check your answers, then practise saying the questions and answers.

5 Spelling

Look back over this unit at words with the target sound, and write what you noticed about how to spell the sound /v/.

UNIT 39 /w/ window

> – What do you want for your birthday?
> – Whatever you want to give me.
> – A watch? A wallet? ... um ... A wig? A wetsuit? A welcome
>   mat? ... er ... A woolly vest? Some wine? A grape vine?
> – Whatever.

1 Target sound /w/

D2a a First practise the sound /v/ (see page 135). Listen and repeat.

D2b b Make your lips round and hard to make the short target sound /w/. Listen and repeat.

D2c c Listen and repeat the two sounds: /v/ and /w/.

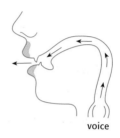

voice

2 Minimal pairs

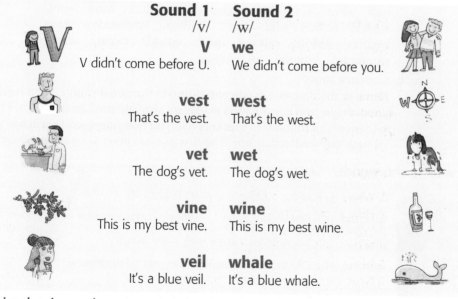

Sound 1 /v/	Sound 2 /w/
V	**we**
V didn't come before U.	We didn't come before you.
vest	**west**
That's the vest.	That's the west.
vet	**wet**
The dog's vet.	The dog's wet.
vine	**wine**
This is my best vine.	This is my best wine.
veil	**whale**
It's a blue veil.	It's a blue whale.

Minimal pair words

D3a a Listen and repeat the words.

D3b b You will hear five words from each minimal pair. For each word, write *1* for /v/ (sound 1) or 2 for /w/ (sound 2).

EXAMPLE Pair 1: 1, 1, 1, 2, 2

Minimal pair sentences

D4a **c** Listen to the minimal pair sentences.

D4b **d** Listen to five of the sentences and write *1* for /v/ (sound 1) or *2* for /w/ (sound 2).

D4a **e** Sentence stress

Listen to the minimal pair sentences again and <u>underline</u> the two strongly stressed words in each sentence (on page 139).

EXAMPLE   This is my <u>best</u> <u>vine</u>.

D5 **f** Tick the words a) or b) that you hear in the sentences.

1 a) vine	☐	b) wine	☐
2 a) V	☐	b) we	☐
3 a) veal	☐	b) wheel	☐
4 a) verse	☐	b) worse	☐
5 a) veils	☐	b) whales	☐
6 a) vet	☐	b) wet	☐

3 Dialogue

a First practise the target sound /w/ in words from the dialogue below. Read the words aloud or visit the website to practise.

well   what   wet   walk   warm   with   white   wine   went walked   woods   wild   sweet   **Wil**liam   **Wednes**day   wasn't **wear**ing   **wal**nut   **rail**way   **qui**et   **quick**ly   **twen**ty   **squir**rels **won**derful   Wi**no**na   **afterwards**

D6 **b** Sentence stress

Listen to the dialogue, paying attention to the target sound. Then read the dialogue and guess which words are strongly stressed in each sentence. The number in brackets tells you how many words will be strongly stressed in that line. The first line has been done as an example.

A walk in the woods.

VIRGINIA: (2) I saw … <u>Wil</u>liam again on <u>Wednes</u>day, Winona.

WINONA: (4) Oh? William again … *(Winona laughs.)* … Well, what happened?

VIRGINIA: (4) We went for a lovely walk in the woods.

WINONA: (6) Oh? In the wet? Wasn't it very wet on Wednesday?

VIRGINIA: (6) It *was* very cold and wet. But we were wearing very warm clothes
(4) and we walked quickly to keep warm.

WINONA: (6) Is that the woods next to the railway? It's not very quiet.

VIRGINIA: (6) Yes. But further away from the railway it was very quiet
(4) and there were wild squirrels everywhere. We counted
(2) twenty squirrels.

WINONA: (5) Twenty squirrels? And what did you do for lunch?
(2) A picnic with the squirrels?

VIRGINIA: (5) It was too wet. Afterwards we went to a restaurant. It was
(6) twelve o'clock. We had walnut cake and sweet white wine.
(1) It was wonderful.

WINONA: (3) So? William again … Well … ?

VIRGINIA: (1) Well? *(Virginia and Winona laugh.)*

D6 c Check your answers by listening to the dialogue again. Then check in the key.

d Practise reading the dialogue aloud. Record your voice to compare your production of the sentence stress and the target sound with the recording.

4 Stress and intonation

a Intonation usually goes down at the end of *WH* questions and short answers.

EXAMPLE

<u>Where</u> was it <u>quiet</u>?   In the <u>woods</u>.

D7 Match the answers (a–h) to the questions (1–8) about the dialogue. Then listen to check and repeat.

1 Where was it quiet?
2 What did they watch?
3 What did they drink?
4 Where were the squirrels?
5 Why did they walk quickly?
6 What did they eat for lunch?
7 What time did they have lunch?
8 What did William and Virginia do on Wednesday?

a The squirrels.
b Everywhere.
c To keep warm.
d In the woods.
e Twelve o'clock.
f Went for a walk.
g Walnut cake.
h Sweet white wine.

Practise reading the questions and answers aloud. Record your voice to compare your production of the intonation with the recording

b Intonation: old information/new information
Notice that intonation in *WH* questions can change when we are talking about old information, e.g. the first time we ask somebody's name, we ask: '<u>What's</u> your **name**?' This is new information. But if I then forget the name and ask again, I ask: '**What's** your <u>name</u>?' because I am asking about old information that has already been given. The intonation goes up to show that this is something we have already shared.

D8a Listen to Winona, later in the day, asking Virginia some questions about information they had shared.

<u>Where</u> were the squirrels ex<u>act</u>ly?

What <u>time</u> did you say you had <u>lunch</u>?

<u>Why</u> did you walk <u>quick</u>ly?

This is all old information that Virginia and Winona had already shared, so the intonation goes up.

 Now listen to Winona asking for new information.

What did you both talk about?

When did you arrange the meeting?

 Listen and mark whether these questions are old information or new information. The first two have been done as examples.

1 What did you say you drank? *old information*
2 What colour did you wear? *new information*
3 What did Victor say? _____
4 Why did you walk quickly? _____
5 What did Victor wear? _____
6 Where did you go with Victor? _____

  D9 c Linking /w/

The sound /w/ is used in rapid spoken English to link other sounds. The sound /w/ links words ending in /u/ or /ʊ/, e.g. *who, you, how, go, hello,* when the next word begins with a vowel. Listen to the examples then listen to six short interactions where this linking happens. Mark where you could hear linking /w/ in 1–6 below.

	/w/	/w/	/w/
EXAMPLES	Who‿is?	You‿are.	Go‿away!

1 A: Hello, everybody! How are you?   B: Hello, Emma. Oh I'm OK now, I had the flu and felt terrible.

2 A: Who isn't here?   B: Joe isn't. A few others aren't.

3 A: Is Sue OK? Anybody know about Sue?   B: I don't know if Sue is off with the flu as well.

4 A: How do I get to a garage?   B: You go under a bridge and through a village.

5 A: Do you understand?   B: No, I don't really.

6 A: Oh, it's so unfair! You always get two ice creams!   B: Grow up!

 Check your answers in the key. Then practise the interactions with a partner. Record your voices to compare your production of linking /w/ with the recording.

5 Spelling

Look back over this unit at words with the target sound, and write what you noticed about how to spell the sound /w/.

UNIT 40 /j/ yellow

> – Did you use to use a computer when you
>   were younger?
> – No. When I was young there didn't use to be any
>   computers. I just used to play with a yo-yo … um …
>   I haven't played with a yo-yo for years … er …
>   Have *you* got a yo-yo?
> – No, just a computer.

1 Target sound /j/

D10a **a** First practise the sound /iː/ (see page 3). Listen and repeat.

D10b **b** To make the target sound /j/, begin to make the sound /iː/ but very quickly move your tongue to make the next sound. Do not touch the roof of your mouth with your tongue or you will make another sound like /dʒ/ (see page 124). Listen and repeat.

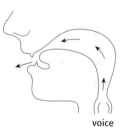

voice

D10c **c** Listen and repeat both sounds: /dʒ/ and /j/.

2 Minimal pairs

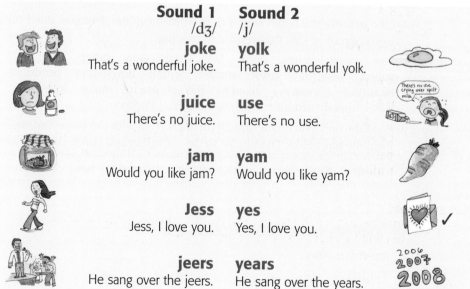

Sound 1	Sound 2
/dʒ/	/j/
joke	**yolk**
That's a wonderful joke.	That's a wonderful yolk.
juice	**use**
There's no juice.	There's no use.
jam	**yam**
Would you like jam?	Would you like yam?
Jess	**yes**
Jess, I love you.	Yes, I love you.
jeers	**years**
He sang over the jeers.	He sang over the years.

Minimal pair words

D11a a Listen and repeat the words.

D11b b You will hear five words from each minimal pair. For each word, write *1* for /dʒ/ (sound 1) or 2 for /j/ (sound 2).

EXAMPLE Pair 1:   2, 1, 2, 1, 1

Minimal pair sentences

D12a c Listen to the minimal pair sentences.

D12b d Listen to five of the sentences and write *1* for /dʒ/ (sound 1) or *2* for /j/ (sound 2).

D12a e **Sentence stress**
Listen to the minimal pair sentences again and <u>underline</u> the strongly stressed words (on page 143). Stressed syllables are **LOUD**er and s l o w er. Unstressed syllables are quieter and quicker. This gives English its rhythm.

EXAMPLE Would you <u>like jam?</u>

D13 f Tick the words a) or b) that you hear in the sentences.

1 a) joke	☐	b) yolk	☐
2 a) jam	☐	b) yam	☐
3 a) Jess	☐	b) yes	☐
4 a) jeers	☐	b) years	☐
5 a) juice	☐	b) use	☐
6 a) jet	☐	b) yet	☐

3 Dialogue

a First practise the target sound /j/ in words from the dialogue. Read the words aloud or visit the website to practise.

York years Young news few Hugh stew tunes huge
yellow **yes**terday **tu**tor **stu**dent **on**ion **news**paper pro**du**ces
beautiful ex**cuse** me **used** to did you **use** to **mu**sic knew
New tubes **stu**pid uni**ver**sity **tu**ba **Eu**rope

D14 b Read the dialogue below and fill the gaps (1–8) with the correct words from the box below. Then listen to the recording and check your answers.

music   knew   New   tubes   **stu**pid   uni**ver**sity   **tu**ba   **Eu**rope

Not so stupid

JOHN YEE: Excuse me. Did you use to live in York?

JOE YOUNG: Yes.

JOHN YEE: Did you use to be a tutor at the 1_____ ?

JOE YOUNG: Yes. For a few years.

JOHN YEE: Do you remember Hugh Yip? He was a 2_____ student.

JOE YOUNG: Hugh Yip? Did he use to have a huge yellow jeep?

JOHN YEE: Yes. And he used to play beautiful tunes on the 3_____ .

JOE YOUNG: Yes, I 4_____ Hugh. He used to be a very stupid student. Do you have any news of Hugh?

JOHN YEE: Yes. He's a millionaire now in 5_____ York.

JOE YOUNG: A millionaire? Playing the tuba?

JOHN YEE: Oh, no. He produces jam in 6_____ , and tins of onion stew, and sells them in 7_____ . I read about Hugh in the newspaper yesterday.

JOE YOUNG: Oh! Well, he wasn't so 8_____ .

c Practise reading the dialogue aloud. Record your voice to compare your production of the target sound with the recording.

4 Stress and intonation: highlighting a word

D15a a Notice that the speaker can choose to make any word the most important one for the meaning of a sentence, and to make that word more strongly stressed than the other words. The meaning of the sentence changes slightly. Listen to one of the questions from the dialogue said with five different meanings because each time a different word is given this stronger stress.

1 <u>Did</u> you use to live in York? Suggests the meaning: (There are different opinions about this. What's the truth?)

2 Did <u>you</u> use to live in York? Suggests: (I did. Or somebody else did What about you?)

3 Did you <u>use</u> to live in York? Suggests: (But not now.)

4 Did you use to <u>live</u> in York? Suggests: (But maybe you worked somewhere else.)

5 Did you use to live in <u>York</u>? Suggests: (Not some other city.)

D15b Now listen to another sentence said with five different meanings. Match each sentence (1–5) with the correct suggested meaning (a–e).

1 <u>He</u> had a yellow jeep.   a) (But not any more. Not now.)

2 He <u>had</u> a yellow jeep.   b) (But nobody else did.)

3 He had <u>a</u> yellow jeep.   c) (Not a car or any other kind of vehicle.)

4 He had a <u>yell</u>ow jeep   d) (Just one. Not several of them.)

5 He had a yellow <u>jeep</u>.   e) (Not a red one or any other colour.)

D16 **b** Linking /j/

The sound /j/ is used in rapid spoken English to link other sounds. The sound /j/ links words ending in /iː/ or /ɪ/, e.g. *she, he, I, we, my, boy, say, they*, when the next word, begins with a vowel. Listen to the examples then listen to six short interactions where this linking happens. Mark where you could hear linking /j/ in 1–6 below.

	/j/	/j/	/j/
EXAMPLES	I‿agree.	He‿is here.	The way‿out.

1 A: Let's play a card game.   B: OK, I'll deal.

2 A: That boy is very rude.   B: Yes, he ought to be more polite.

3 A: Are those printouts of my emails?   B: Yes, they are.

4 A: He always feels sad when he's alone.   B: I understand. I often do too.

5 A: Say it again, please.   B: I said today is my eightieth birthday.

6 A: They all had a good cry at the funeral.   B: There wasn't a dry eye in the church.

Check your answers in the key. Then practise the interactions with a partner. Record your voices to compare your production of linking /j/ with the recording.

c About you

Read these answers and answer T (True) or F (False) or D (Don't know).
1 When you were three you used to dress yourself. (   )
2 When you were six months old you used to feed yourself. (   )
3 When you were a baby you used to be beautiful. (   )
4 When you were first at school you used to be stupid. (   )
5 When you were younger you used to really like music. (   )

Choose one of the statements, or make up a similar one, and ask somebody about it.

EXAMPLE When you were (ten) years old, did you use to like (cycling)?

5 Spelling

Look back over this unit at words with the target sound, and write what you noticed about how to spell the sound /j/.

UNIT 41 /h/ hat

– Have you ever been to a hospital?
– Yes. I wasn't actually ill. But I used to play hockey, and I injured my hand. I had to go to Hill End Hospital.
– How did it happen?
– Oh, somebody just hit my hand very hard with a hockey stick.

1 Target sound /h/

D17 To make the target sound /h/, push a lot of air out very quickly. Do *not* touch the roof of your mouth with your tongue. Listen and repeat: /h/.

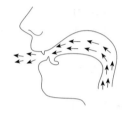

2 Minimal pairs

	Sound 1 (no sound)	Sound 2 /h/	
	ill Is Tom ill in hospital?	**hill** Is Tom Hill in hospital?	
	eel That's a beautiful eel.	**heel** That's a beautiful heel.	
	and Put your head *and* heart into it.	**hand** Put your head, hand, heart into it.	
	old Old Mrs Smith's hand.	**hold** Hold Mrs Smith's hand.	
	ear She's lost her earring.	**hear** She's lost her hearing.	
	islands I love the islands.	**highlands** I love the highlands.	

Minimal pair words

D18a a Listen and repeat the words.

D18b b You will hear five words from each minimal pair. For each word, write *1* for no sound (sound 1) or 2 for /h/ (sound 2).

EXAMPLE Pair 1: 2, 2, 1, 2, 1

Minimal pair sentences

D19a c Listen to the minimal pair sentences.

D19b d Listen to six of the sentences and write *1* for no sound (sound 1) or *2* for /h/ (sound 2).

D19a e Sentence stress
Listen to the minimal pair sentences again. Notice that the speaker can choose to make any word the most important one for the meaning of a sentence, and to make that word more strongly stressed than the other words. When you are reading English books or newspapers a word that is much more strongly stressed than the others in a sentence is printed in *italics* or in ***bold italics***. Notice this in the sound 1 sentence in Pair 3: Put your head ***and*** heart into it. The speaker does this to suggest the meaning: 'not just your head but also your heart', so the pronunciation of *and* changes. Here it is pronounced /ænd/ when it is strongly stressed. It is usually weakly stressed, and pronounced /ənd/.

D20 f Tick the words a) or b) that you hear in the sentences.

1 a) eels ☐ b) heels ☐
2 a) and ☐ b) hand ☐
3 a) eye ☐ b) high ☐
4 a) art ☐ b) heart ☐
5 a) ow ☐ b) how ☐
6 a) air ☐ b) hair ☐

3 Dialogue

a First practise the target sound /h/ in words from the dialogue. Read the words aloud or visit the website to practice.

Hi he how has had have hit heard hope house
horse **Holly** **hus**band **happ**ened be**hind** per**haps**
un**happy** **hos**pital **horr**ible **Hel**ena

b Read the dialogue and fill in the gaps. After each number there are two gaps. The first gap is a word starting with /h/. The second gap is a word starting with a vowel. Choose words from the box below. Number 1 has been done as an example.

| having ambulance all **hospital** heard **accident** how |
| he unhappy hit **Helena** ice-**cream** injured operation |

A horrible accident

EMMA: Hi, Holly.

HOLLY: Emma, have you 1 _heard_ ? There's been a horrible _accident_ .

EMMA: Oh, dear! What's happened?

HOLLY: Helena's husband has had an accident on his horse.

EMMA: 2_____ awful! Is he _____ ?

HOLLY: Yes. He's been taken to 3_____ in an _____ .

EMMA: How did it happen?

HOLLY: He was 4_____ by an _____ van. It was on the crossing just behind his house.

EMMA: How horrible!

HOLLY: He's 5_____ an emergency _____ in hospital now. Poor 6_____ ! She's so _____ .

EMMA: Perhaps 7_____ 'll be _____ right, Holly.

HOLLY: I hope so.

D21 **c** Check your answers by listening to the dialogue, then practise reading the dialogue aloud. Record your voice to compare your production of the target sound with the recording.

4 Intonation

D22 **a** Exclamation

Listen and repeat.

Oh <u>dear</u>?   How <u>ho</u>rrible!

How <u>aw</u>ful!   How <u>te</u>rrible!

Practise responding to these statements with an exclamation.

EXAMPLE A: Hamish has had an accident.
              B: How awful!

1 A helicopter has hit Adrian's house.

2 Harry's holiday hotel was hit by the hurricane.

3 Andrew spent all his holiday in hospital.

4 Haley hit herself with a heavy hammer.

5 Ellen's husband is ill in hospital.

6 I've hurt my hand and I can't hold anything.

b Word linking with /h/

Notice that in rapid spoken English, words are sometimes linked by the disappearance of the sound /h/. The sound /h/ often disappears in the weak forms of: *he, him, his, her, has, had, have*. Like the word *and* in 2e, the pronunciation of these words changes with strong or weak stress in a sentence.

	Strong stress	Weak stress	
he	/hiː/	/hɪ/ or /ɪ/	Where <u>is</u> he?
him	/hɪm/	/ɪm/	I <u>told</u> him.
his	/hɪz/	/ɪz/	She's his <u>wife</u>.
her	/hɜ/	/ə/	I <u>told</u> her.
has	/hæz/	/əz/	<u>What</u> has happened?
had	/hæd/	/əd/	They had <u>seen</u> it.
have	/hæv/	/əv/	They have <u>gone</u>.

Now listen and mark the disappearing /h/ sound in the questions below while you read silently.

EXAMPLE 1 Who found (h)im?

Detective at work: disappearing /h/

1 Who found him?

2 What's his name? Harry?

3 Who else have you spoken to? She's his wife?

4 What's her phone number? She hasn't a phone? Has she got a mobile?

5 What has the neighbour said about him?

6 What had he eaten?

 Check your answers in the key. Then practise the questions. Record your voice to compare your production of these weakly stressed 'h' words with the recording.

5 Spelling

 Look back over this unit at words with the target sound, and write what you noticed about how to spell the sound /h/.

UNIT 42 /θ/ thin

– What did you **th**ink of the new **th**eatre?
– I **th**ought it would have been better. It cost
 thousands to rebuild. But I **th**ought it was
 no**th**ing special. What did you **th**ink?
– I **th**ought it was really some**th**ing!

1 Target sound /θ/

D24 To make the target sound /θ/, put your
tongue between your teeth. Blow out
air between your tongue and your top
teeth. *Do not* use your voice. Listen
and repeat: /θ/.

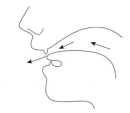

2 Minimal pairs A

	Sound 1 /s/	**Sound 2** /θ/	
	mouse What a sweet little mouse!	**mouth** What a sweet little mouth!	
65+10=100	**sum** Is this sum OK?	**thumb** Is this thumb OK?	
	sick It's very sick.	**thick** It's very thick.	
	sink He's sinking.	**think** He's thinking.	
	pass There's a mountain pass.	**path** There's a mountain path.	

Minimal pair words

D25a **a** Listen and repeat the words.

D25b **b** You will hear five words from each minimal pair. For each word, write *1*
for /s/ (sound 1) or 2 for /θ/ (sound 2).

EXAMPLE Pair 1: 1, 2, 1, 2, 1

Minimal pair sentences

D26a **c** Listen to the minimal pair sentences.

D26b **d** Listen to five of the sentences and write *1* for /s/ (sound 1) or *2* for /θ/
(sound 2).

D26a **e** Sentence stress

Listen to the minimal pair sentences again and <u>underline</u> the sentence stress (on page 151).

EXAMPLE Is this <u>sum</u> OK?

Minimal pairs B

	Sound 1 /f/	Sound 2 /θ/
	first He's got a first.	**thirst** He's got a thirst.
	fin A fin soup, please.	**thin** A thin soup, please.
	half I'd like a half.	**hearth** I'd like a hearth.

Minimal pair words

D27a **a** Listen and repeat the words.

D27b **b** You will hear five words from each minimal pair. For each word, write *1* for /f/ (sound 1) or 2 for /θ/ (sound 2).

EXAMPLE Pair 1: 2, 1, 1, 1, 2

Minimal pair sentences

D28a **c** Listen to the minimal pair sentences.

D28b **d** Listen to three of the sentences and write *1* for /f/ (sound 1) or *2* for /θ/ (sound 2).

D28a **e** Sentence stress

Listen to the minimal pair sentences and <u>underline</u> the sentence stress.

EXAMPLE He's got a <u>first</u>.

Minimal pairs C

	Sound 1 /t/	Sound 2 /θ/
	tree It's a big tree.	**three** It's a big three.
	tanks The President sends his tanks.	**thanks** The President sends his thanks.
	sheet The knife was hidden in a sheet.	**sheath** The knife was hidden in a sheath.

Minimal pair words

D29a a Listen and repeat the words.

D29b b You will hear five words from each minimal pair. For each word, write *1* for /t/ (sound 1) or 2 for /θ/ (sound 2).

EXAMPLE Pair 1: 1, 2, 1, 1, 2

Minimal pair sentences

D30a c Listen to the minimal pair sentences.

D30b d Listen to three of the sentences and write *1* for /t/ (sound 1) or *2* for /θ/ (sound 2).

D30a e Sentence stress

Listen to the minimal pair sentences and <u>underline</u> the sentence stress (on page 52).

EXAMPLE It's a <u>big tree</u>.

D31 f Tick the words a) or b) that you hear in the sentences.

1 a) sink	☐	b) think	☐
2 a) mouse	☐	b) mouth	☐
3 a) tin	☐	b) thin	☐
4 a) taught	☐	b) thought	☐
5 a) moss	☐	b) moth	☐
6 a) fought	☐	b) thought	☐

3 Dialogue

a First practise the target sound /θ/ in words from the dialogue below. Read the words aloud or visit the website to practise.

three   **thir**sty   **thank** you   **thous**and   **Thurs**day   **author** **Cath**erine   Sa**man**tha   **noth**ing   **some**thing   mathema**ti**cian Ruth   Roth   worth   month   moth   moths

b In this dialogue, each numbered line has a word that is especially important because of Ruth's strong response to what Catherine says. Read the dialogue and <u>underline</u> the most important word in each numbered line. Number 1 has been done as an example.

Gossips

CATHERINE: Samantha Roth is only thirty.

RUTH: (1) Is she? I thought she was thirty-<u>three</u>.

CATHERINE: Samantha's birthday was last Thursday.

RUTH: (2) Was it? I thought it was last month.

CATHERINE: The Roths' house is worth six hundred thousand.

RUTH: (3) Is it? I thought it was worth three hundred thousand.

CATHERINE: Ross Roth is the author of a book about moths.

RUTH: (4) Is he? I thought he was a mathematician.

CATHERINE: I'm so thirsty.

RUTH: (5) Are you? I thought you drank something at the Roths'.

CATHERINE: No. Samantha gave me nothing to drink.

RUTH: (6) Shall I buy you a drink?

CATHERINE: Thank you.

D32 c Check your answers by listening to the dialogue. Notice that the especially important words are much **LOUD**er and s l o w er, and the intonation goes up.

d Practise reading the dialogue aloud. Record your voice to compare your production of the intonation and the target sound with the recording.

4 Intonation

In the dialogue Ruth expresses surprise with intonation going up.

D33 a Listen and repeat.

<u>Is</u> she? <u>Was</u> he? <u>Is</u> it? <u>Are</u> you?

b Match the statements below in A (1–7) with the correct responses in B (a–g).

A

1 Catherine is at the theatre.

2 Ross Roth is thirty-three.

3 It's Samantha's birthday today.

4 I'm so thirsty.

5 The Roths' house is north of here.

6 Mrs Roth is thirty.

7 The Roths' house is worth 600,000.

B

a Are you? I thought you drank something.

b Is she? I thought she was at the Roths'.

c Is he? I thought he was thirty.

d Is she? I thought she was thirty-three.

e Is it? I thought it was last month.

f Is it? I thought it was worth 300,000.

g Is it? I thought it was south.

D34 Check your answers by listening to the recording. Listen to each statement and respond.

Practise with a partner.

5 Spelling

Look back over this unit at words with the target sound, and write what you noticed about how to spell the sound /θ/.

UNIT 43 /ð/ the feather

– Did *these people* talk about their neighbours?
– Well, yes they talked a bit ... er ... about ... this and that.
– That's what I hate about those people. They're there at
their windows just watching everybody in the street,
and then they gossip about it for the next week.
– Everybody talks about other people. I mean here *you*
are talking about *them*!

1 Target sound /ð/

D35a a First practise the sound /θ/ (see page
151). Listen and repeat.

D35b b Use your voice to make the target
sound /ð/. Listen and repeat: /ð/.

D35c c Listen and repeat both sounds:
/θ/ is unvoiced. /ð/ is voiced.

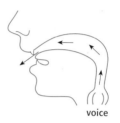

voice

2 Minimal pairs A

	Sound 1 /d/	Sound 2 /ð/	
	Dan Smith is bigger, Dan Jones.	**than** Smith is bigger than Jones.	
	day Day arrived.	**they** *They* arrived.	
	dare Jim dares his friend.	**there** Jim there's his friend.	
	doze Doze after lunch.	**those** Those after lunch.	
	Ida I don't know her sister, Ida.	**either** I don't know her sister either.	

Minimal pair words

D36a a Listen and repeat the words.

D36b b You will hear five words from each minimal pair. For each word, write *1* for /d/ (sound 1) or *2* for /ð/ (sound 2).

EXAMPLE Pair 1: 1, 1, 2, 1, 2

Minimal pair sentences

D37a c Listen to the minimal pair sentences.

D37b d Listen to five of the sentences and write *1* for /d/ (sound 1) or *2* for /ð/ (sound 2).

D37a e Sentence stress

Listen to the minimal pair sentences again and <u>underline</u> the sentence stress (on page 155).

EXAMPLE <u>Doze</u> after <u>lunch</u>.

Minimal pairs B

	Sound 1 /z/	Sound 2 /ð/	
	close The shop sign said 'Closing'.	**clothe** The shop sign said 'Clothing'.	
	breeze Breeze means air moving.	**breathe** Breathe means air moving.	
	boos The boos echoed loudly.	**booth** The booth echoed loudly.	
	size That's a large size.	**scythe** That's a large scythe.	

Minimal pair words

D38a a Listen and repeat the words.

D38b b You will hear five words from each minimal pair. For each word, write *1* for /z/ (sound 1) or *2* for /ð/ (sound 2).

EXAMPLE Pair 1: 2, 1, 1, 2, 1

Minimal pair sentences

D39a c Listen to the minimal pair sentences.

D39b d Listen to four of the sentences and write *1* for /z/ (sound 1) or *2* for /ð/ (sound 2).

D39a e Sentence stress

Listen to the minimal pair sentences again and <u>underline</u> the sentence stress (above).

EXAMPLE <u>That's</u> a large <u>size</u>.

D40 f Tick the words a) or b) that you hear in the sentences.

1 a) Ida ☐ b) either ☐
2 a) day ☐ b) they ☐
3 a) dares ☐ b) there's ☐
4 a) size ☐ b) scythe ☐
5 a) bays ☐ b) bathe ☐
6 a) boos ☐ b) booth ☐

3 Dialogue

a First practise the target sound /ð/ in words from the dialogue. Read the words aloud or visit the website to practise.

the this that than there **other** **another** **rather** toge**th**er
leather **feathers** **Brothers** smoo**th**er **ei**ther with clo**th**es

D41 b Listen to the dialogue, paying attention to the target sound.

The hat in the window

MISS BROTHERS: I want to buy the hat in the window.

ASSISTANT: There are three hats together in the window, madam. Do you want the one with the feathers?

MISS BROTHERS: No. The other one.

ASSISTANT: The small one for three hundred and three euros?

MISS BROTHERS: No. Not that one either. The one over there. The leather one.

ASSISTANT: Ah! The leather one. Now this is another leather hat, madam. It's better than the one in the window. It's a smoother leather.

MISS BROTHERS: But I'd rather have the one in the window. It goes with my clothes.

ASSISTANT: Certainly, madam. But we don't take anything out of the window until three o'clock on Thursday.

c Practise reading the dialogue aloud. Record your voice to compare your production of the target sound with the recording.

4 Sentence stress

D42 a Talk about the three hats using the words from the box below.
A: <u>Which</u> <u>hat</u> do <u>you</u> think is _____ than the <u>others</u>?

B: The one with the <u>feathers</u>.
C: The <u>leather</u> hat.
D: The one for <u>three</u> hundred and <u>three</u> euros.

better	more **fashionable**
cheaper	more **stupid**
prettier	more **comfortable**
uglier	more **expensive**

D43 **b Intonation**

Match the *WH* questions (1–7) with the statements (a–g). Listen and respond.

1 What's <u>th</u>is?

a These are <u>z</u>ips.

2 What are <u>those</u>?

b That's <u>Z</u>ack.

3 What's that <u>an</u>imal?

c This is <u>Z</u>.

4 What's this <u>le</u>tter?

d This is the <u>z</u>oo.

5 What's that <u>num</u>ber?

e Those are <u>ze</u>bras.

6 What are <u>these</u>?

f That's a <u>ze</u>ro.

7 Who's <u>that</u>?

g That's a <u>ze</u>bu.

5 Spelling

Look back over this unit at words with the target sound, and write what you noticed about how to spell the sound /ð/.

UNIT 44 REVIEW

Card game: Pick up voiced consonants:
/z/ (zoo), /ʒ/ (television), /dʒ/ (January), /v/ (van),
/w/ (window), /j/ (yellow), /h/ (hat), /ð/ (the feather)

Photocopy and cut out cards from Units 31–43.

Shuffle the cards and deal them face down all over the table.

Turn over any two cards and read their sentences aloud. If they both have any voiced consonants in the minimal pair words, you keep them and you continue playing.

If they don't, turn them face down again and the next person plays.

Collect as many cards as you can in a time limit, e.g. ten minutes.

TEST

You can use a dictionary if you wish, but you don't have to understand every word to do this test.

D44 1 For each line (1, 2, 3, 4, 5), first listen to the whole line, then circle the one word (or part of a word) that is said twice. Meaning is not important in this exercise. The purpose is to review the sounds by hearing them in contrast. Some words are rarely used in everyday English, and this is shown by an asterisk *. Incomplete words have the rest of the word written in brackets, e.g. *fou(nd)*.

/f/	/v/	/w/	/j/	/h/	/θ/	/ð/
1 fee	V	we	ye*	he	the(sis)	thee*
2 fou(nd)	vow	Wow!	yow(l)	how	thou(sand)	thou*
3 foe*	vo(te)	woe*	yo(ga)	hoe	tho(le)*	though
4 fie*	vie	why	–	high	thigh	thy*
5 fis(t)	vis(cose)	whis(per)	–	his(tory)	this(tle)	this

Score ☐ /5

2 Circle the words with the same consonant cluster as 1–3.

1 gift
/ft/

coughed arrived
laughed kissed wished
loved lofty soft
fifth lift

2 moths
/θs/

months
clothes
paths lengths
Judith's
naturopaths

Thursday
tablecloths
smooths
three

3 swan
/sw/

sword
Swedish enquire
sweeten swum
square swear suite
suitable swift

Score [/ 15]

D45 **3 Word linking**

Listen and add the sound /j/ (yellow) or /w/ as in the example.

EXAMPLE Well, who⌣is the boss? I⌣am.

/w/   /j/
Well, who⌣is the boss? I⌣am.

YASMIN: I⌣asked you⌣a question, Wesley.

WESLEY: Oh⌣I'm sorry⌣I didn't hear you, Yasmin.

YASMIN: You⌣often do that, and I⌣always get annoyed.

WESLEY: Oh⌣is that so? Why⌣is that, Yasmin?

YASMIN: It's just annoying! Why⌣are you doing it, Wesley?

WESLEY: Just to⌣annoy you, Yasmin.

Score [/ 5]

4 Word stress

Underline the stressed syllable in these words. (Score half a mark per item.)

valley village beautiful railway Europe perhaps
hospital mathematician author leather

Score [/ 5]

Total score [/ 30]

Additional review task using dialogues from Units 37–43

Unit	37	38	39	40	41	42	43
Target sound	/f/	/v/	/w/	/j/	/h/	/θ/	/ð/
	fan	van	window	yellow	hat	thin	the feather

From the above table, choose any target sounds that you had difficulty with.

1 Listen again to the dialogue in that unit, listening for the target sound.

2 Circle the target sound in any word in the dialogue.

3 Listen to the dialogue again and check your answers.

4 Check your answers in the key.

5 Listen to the dialogue again, listening for the target sound.

6 Practise reading the dialogue aloud, and record your voice to compare your production of the target sound with the recording.

You can also use this review task as a quick self-test, by doing steps 2 and 4 only.

UNIT 45 /m/ mouth

– I'm thinking of moving.

– Oh. Where to?

– mm … I'm not sure. I might move to Manchester
  … mm … or I may go to Cambridge … Sometimes
  I'm … imagining myself moving to … Munich …
  or Rome or … maybe Marseille or …

– Well don't call the removers until you make up
  your mind.

1 Target sound /m/

D46 To make the target sound /m/, close
your lips. Use your voice. /m/ comes
through your nose. Listen and repeat: /m/.

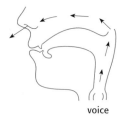
voice

2 Sound /m/

/m/

mile
The mile is very old.

mine
This is mine.

mummy
He loves his mummy.

comb
I want a comb.

name
He's proud of his name.

D47a **a** Listen and repeat the words

D47b **b** Listen to the sentences.

D47b **c** Sentence stress
Listen to the sentences again and <u>underline</u> the sentence stress (above).
Stressed syllables are **LOUD**er and s l o w er. Unstressed syllables are
quieter and quicker. This gives English its rhythm.

EXAMPLE This is <u>mine</u>.

D47b **d** Listen and repeat the sentences.

3 Dialogue

 a First practise the target sound /m/ in words from the dialogue below. Read the words aloud or visit the website to practise.

summer **family charm**ing small smart **muffins Cam**bridge Tim some from **Malcolm Mich**am **MacCall**um time Mum met come make home **may**be **mann**ers tomorrow **remem**ber

b Read the dialogue and guess the missing words with the sound /m/. The first one has been done. The missing words are all in the box below.

> time Mum met come make home **may**be **mann**ers tomorrow remember

Mum's muffins

MALCOLM: Mum, may Tim Mitcham come 1 _home_ with me for tea tomorrow?

MRS MACCALLUM: Of course, Malcolm. Have I 2_____ Tim before?

MALCOLM: You met him in the summer. He's very small.

MRS MACCALLUM: Oh, yes. I 3_____ Tim. He's very smart. And he has charming 4_____ . Does his family 5_____ from Cambridge?

MALCOLM: Yes. And … Oh, Mum! … Will you 6_____ some home-made muffins, tomorrow?

MRS MACCALLUM: Mm. 7_____ . If I have 8_____ .

MALCOLM: I told Tim about your muffins, 9_____ . That's why he's coming for tea 10_____ .

D48 c Check your answers by listening to the dialogue. Then practise reading the dialogue aloud. Record your voice to compare your production of the target sound with the recording.

4 Intonation

'Mm' has many meanings, depending on the intonation.

D49 a Listen to four dialogues with different meanings of 'Mm'.

1 Mmm means 'What did you say?'

2 Mm means 'yes'

3 Mmmmm means 'How nice!'

4 Mmm … means ' I'm thinking about what to say.'

b Read this conversation and guess which intonation and meaning 'Mm' will have in B's answers.

> A: Would you like some home-made muffins?
>
> B: (1) Mm?
>
> A: Would you like some muffins?
>
> B: (2) Mm …
>
> A: Well, make up your mind.
>
> B: (3) Mm.
>
> A: Here you are.
>
> B: (4) *(eating)* Mm!
>
> A: I'm glad you like them. I made them myself. Would you like to try them with marmalade?
>
> B: (5) Mm?
>
> A: Marmalade. They're marvellous with marmalade. Would you like some?
>
> B: (6) Mm.
>
> A: Here you are.
>
> B: (7) *(eating)* Mm!

D50 c Listen to the conversation and check your answers.

d Practise reading the conversation aloud. Record your voice to compare your production of the target sound and the intonation with the recording.

Practise in pairs, taking turns to be A and B.

5 Spelling

Look back over this unit at words with the target sound, and write what you noticed about how to spell the sound /m/.

UNIT 46 /n/ nose

– Hello … Oh! … No, never … Nothing … No. Nobody … No, we didn't … I'm not interested … No, definitely not … No. I didn't phone you … No, I did not send you an email … No. Not in the least … Can't you take no for an answer? … No, I don't want to make a donation to anything. I haven't any money. And please don't phone me again.

1 Target sound /n/

D51 To make the target sound /n/, don't close your lips. Put your tongue on the roof of your mouth. Touch your side teeth with the sides of your tongue. Use your voice. /n/ comes through your nose. Listen and repeat: /n/.

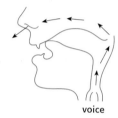

voice

2 Minimal pairs

	Sound 1 /m/	Sound 2 /n/	
	mile The mile is very old.	**Nile** The Nile is very old.	
	mine This is mine.	**nine** This is nine.	
	mummy He loves mummy.	**money** He loves money.	
	comb I want a comb.	**cone** I want a cone.	
	name He's proud of this name.	**mane** He's proud of this mane.	

Minimal pair words

D52a a Listen and repeat the words.

D52b b You will hear five words from each minimal pair. For each word, write *1* for /m/ (sound 1) or *2* for /n/ (sound 2).

EXAMPLE Pair 1: 1, 1, 1, 2, 2

Minimal pair sentences

D53a **c** Listen to the minimal pair sentences.

D53b **d** Listen to five of the sentences and write *1* for /m/ (sound 1) or *2* for /n/ (sound 2)

D53a **e** Sentence stress

Listen to the minimal pair sentences again and match each pair with the stress patterns (a–e) below. The big circles are the strongly stressed words in the sentence and the small circles are the weakly stressed words.

EXAMPLE a) oooO Pair 4: I want a <u>comb</u>. / I want a <u>cone</u>.

a) **oooO**   b) **ooO**   c) **oOoooO**
d) **oOooO**   e) **ooOo**

Notice that the weakly stressed words are said more quickly, and that the pronunciation of some words changes if they are weakly stressed, e.g. *of* /ɒv/ becomes /əv/, *is* /ɪz/ becomes /z/ or /əz/, *a* is pronounced /ə/.

D54 **f** Tick the words a) or b) that you hear in the sentences.

1 a) combs ☐   b) cones ☐

2 a) mine ☐   b) nine ☐

3 a) name ☐   b) mane ☐

4 a) some ☐   b) sun ☐

5 a) warm ☐   b) warn ☐

6 a) money ☐   b) mummy ☐

3 Dialogue

a First practise the target sound /n/ in words from the dialogue. Read the words aloud or visit the website to practise.

no   not   near   name   noise   **Nott**ing **Hill**   **mor**ning   **man**ager   **av**enue   **fur**nished   **un**furnished   don't   want   rent   month   friends   pounds   **even**ing   North**end**   a**part**ment   **cen**tral   in**ex**pensive   one   can   than   down   fif**teen**   **Lon**don   **Mar**tin   Syllabic /n/

In the following words /n/ is usually a syllable.

often   **sta**tion   **ov**en   **kitch**en   accommo**da**tion   **pris**on   e**lev**en   for**bidd**en   tele**vis**ion   **cer**tainly   **thous**and   **Nel**son   **gar**den   **agen**cy

D55 **b** First listen to the dialogue, paying attention to the target sound. Then read the dialogue and fill the gaps (1–8) by choosing eight words from the list above (syllabic /n/).

At an accommodation agency

MARTIN: Good morning. My name is Martin Nelson. Are you the manager?

MANAGER: Yes, I am. How can I help you, Mr 1_____ ?

MARTIN: I want an apartment in central London.

MANAGER: 2_____ , Mr Nelson. How much rent do you want to pay?

MARTIN: No more than £1,000 a month.

MANAGER: £1,000 a month? We don't often have apartments as inexpensive as that. Not in central London. We have one apartment for £2,179 a month in Notting Hill. It's down near the 3_____ in Northend Avenue.

MARTIN: Is it furnished?

MANAGER: No. It's unfurnished. The kitchen has no 4_____ . It's forbidden to use the 5_____ . No friends in the apartment after 6_____ in the evening. No noise and no 7_____ after 11.15 p.m. No . . .

MARTIN: No thank you! I want an apartment, not a 8_____ !

D55 c Listen to the dialogue again and check your answers.

d Practise reading the dialogue aloud. Record your voice to compare your production of the target sound with the recording.

4 Mini bingo game

D56 a Practise saying these numbers. Listen and repeat, paying attention to the sound /n/.

1	7	11	9	10	13	17	15	18	19
20	21	22	23	24	25	26	27	28	29
70	71	72	73	74	75	76	77	78	79
90	91	92	93	94	95	96	97	98	99

b Play in a group of five people. (A student studying alone can record the numbers, and then choose two of the boxes below.)

One person calls out the numbers above in any order. Take turns to call the numbers.

The others each choose one of the boxes A, B, C or D below.

Cross out each number in your box as it is called (or put a small piece of paper on top of each number as it is called).

The first person to cross out all their numbers wins.

A

9	20	99
15	79	71
97	19	10

B

1	79	11
13	9	7
99	27	10

C

77	79	99
18	19	97
11	91	29

D

1	79	9
17	19	18
99	21	70

5 Spelling

Look back over this unit at words with the target sound, and write what you noticed about how to spell the sound /n/.

UNIT 47 /ŋ/ ring

- What are you doing in the holidays?
- I'm thinking about going somewhere near Naples.
- Naples! How interesting! What are you planning to do there?
- Nothing much ... swimming ... lying in the sun ... having a good time.....eating ... drinking ... just relaxing.
- Ah! How charming!

1 Target sound /ŋ/

D57 To make the target sound /ŋ/, touch the back of the roof of your mouth with the back of your tongue. Use your voice. /ŋ/ comes through your nose. Listen and repeat: /ŋ/.

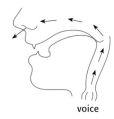

voice

2 Minimal pairs A

	Sound 1 /n/	Sound 2 /ŋ/	
	win What a win!	**wing** What a wing!	
	thin Why this thin?	**thing** Why this thing?	
	ban Ban the book.	**bang** Bang the book.	
	ran They ran for an hour.	**rang** They rang for an hour.	
	run She has never run before.	**rung** She has never rung before.	
	Ron Is it Ron?	**wrong** Is it wrong?	

Minimal pair words

D58a a Listen and repeat the words.

D58b b You will hear five words from each minimal pair. For each word, write *1* for /n/ (sound 1) or *2* for /ŋ/ (sound 2).

EXAMPLE Pair 1: 2, 1, 1, 2, 1

Minimal pair sentences

D59a c Listen to the minimal pair sentences.

D59b d Listen to six of the sentences and write *1* for /n/ (sound 1) or *2* for /ŋ/ (sound 2)

D59a e Sentence stress

Listen to the minimal pair sentences again and <u>underline</u> the sentence stress (on page 168).

EXAMPLE <u>What</u> a <u>win</u>!

Minimal pairs B

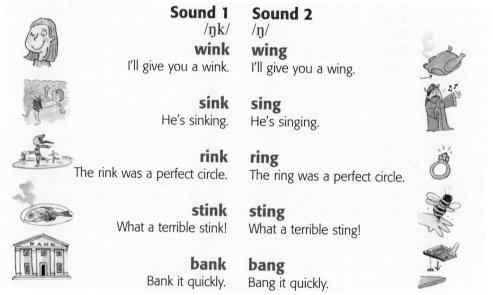

	Sound 1	**Sound 2**
	/ŋk/	/ŋ/
	wink	**wing**
	I'll give you a wink.	I'll give you a wing.
	sink	**sing**
	He's sinking.	He's singing.
	rink	**ring**
	The rink was a perfect circle.	The ring was a perfect circle.
	stink	**sting**
	What a terrible stink!	What a terrible sting!
	bank	**bang**
	Bank it quickly.	Bang it quickly.

Minimal pair words

D60a a Listen and repeat the words.

D60b b You will hear five words from each minimal pair. For each word, write *1* for /ŋk/ (sound 1) or *2* for /ŋ/ (sound 2).

EXAMPLE Pair 1: 2, 2, 1, 1, 2

Minimal pair sentences

D61a c Listen to the minimal pair sentences.

D61b d Listen to five of the sentences and write *1* for /ŋk/ (sound 1) or *2* for /ŋ/ (sound 2)

Sentence stress

D61a e Listen to the minimal pair sentences again and <u>underline</u> the sentence stress (on page 169).

EXAMPLE I'll <u>give</u> you a <u>wing</u>.

D62 f Tick the words a), b) or c) that you hear in the sentences.

1 a) Ron ☐ b) wrong ☐

2 a) ran ☐ b) rang ☐

3 a) sinks ☐ b) sings ☐

4 a) win ☐ b) wink ☐ c) wing ☐

5 a) ban ☐ b) bank ☐ c) bang ☐

6 a) sinners ☐ b) sinkers ☐ c) singers ☐

3 Dialogue

a First practise the target sound /ŋ/ in words from the dialogue. Read the words aloud or visit the website to practise.

ring strong string King Lang **mor**ning evening **some**thing **in**teresting

/ŋk/: pink drink **think**ing **Dun**can

/ŋg/: **fing**ers **An**gus

verb + ing: **hang**ing **ring**ing **sing**ing **bang**ing **bring**ing **put**ting **talk**ing **whisper**ing **shout**ing **stand**ing **say**ing **go**ing **do**ing **hold**ing **help**ing **walk**ing **get**ting **sleep**ing **run**ning **happ**ening.

D63 b **Correction**

There are nine items to change in the dialogue. First listen to the dialogue, paying attention to the target sound. Then read the dialogue and listen at the same time. Make the words the same as the recording.

Noisy neighbours

(Duncan King is lying in bed trying to sleep. Sharon King is standing near the window watching the neighbours, Angus and Susan Lang.)

DUNCAN KING: *(angrily).* Bang! Bang! Bang! Sharon! What are the Langs doing at nine o'clock on Sunday morning?

SHARON KING: Well, Angus Lang is talking, Duncan.

DUNCAN KING: Yes, but what's the banging noise, Sharon?

SHARON KING: *(looking out of the window)* Angus is standing on a ladder and banging some nails into the wall with a hammer. Now he's hanging some strong string on the nails.

DUNCAN KING: And what's Susan Lang doing?

SHARON KING: Susan's bringing something interesting for Angus to drink. Now she's putting it under the ladder, and … Ohh!

DUNCAN KING: What's happening?

SHARON KING: The ladder's going …

DUNCAN KING: What's Angus doing?

SHARON KING: He's holding the string in his fingers and he's shouting to Susan.

DUNCAN KING: And is Susan helping him?

SHARON KING: No. She's running to our house. Now she's ringing our bell.

BELL: RING! RING! RING!

DUNCAN KING: I'm not going to answer it. I'm sleeping.

c Practise reading the corrected dialogue aloud. Record your voice to compare your production of the target sound with the recording.

4 Intonation

D64 a Practise these *WH* questions and statements with the intonation going down. Talk about the pictures. Listen and respond, like the example.

EXAMPLE

A: What's Sharon <u>King</u> doing?

B: She's looking out of the <u>win</u>dow.

Sharon <u>King</u>

1

Angus Lang

2

Angus

3

Susan Lang

4

Mr Lang

5

Mrs Lang

6

Duncan King

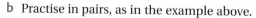

b Practise in pairs, as in the example above.

5 Spelling

Look back over this unit at words with the target sound, and write what you noticed about how to spell the sound /ŋ/.

UNIT 48 /l/ letter

- Do you like marshmallows?
- Yes, they're lovely. But I also like lollipops. How about you?
- I like lollipops too. But what I really like is chocolate and vanilla ice cream.
- Mmm!

1 Target sound /l/

D65a a First practise the sound /n/ (see page 165). Listen and repeat.

D65b b To make the target sound /l/, the air goes over the sides of your tongue and out of your mouth. Listen: /l/.

D65c c Listen and repeat both sounds: /n/ and /l/.

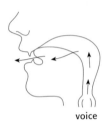

voice

2 Minimal pairs

	Sound 1 /n/	Sound 2 /l/	
	no We need no tables.	**low** We need low tables.	
	night It's a bright night.	**light** It's a bright light.	
	nine That nine is too long.	**line** That line is too long.	
	Jenny I love Jenny.	**jelly** I love jelly.	
	snap That's a snapping noise.	**slap** That's a slapping noise.	

Minimal pair words

D66a a Listen and repeat the words.

 D66b b You will hear five words from each minimal pair. For each word, write *1* for /n/ (sound 1) or *2* for /l/ (sound 2).

EXAMPLE Pair 1: 2, 1, 2, 1, 2

Minimal pair sentences

D67a c Listen to the minimal pair sentences.

D67b d Listen to five of the sentences and write *1* for /n/ (sound 1) or *2* for /l/ (sound 2)

D67a e Sentence stress

Listen to the minimal pair sentences again and <u>underline</u> the sentence stress (on page 172).

EXAMPLE We need <u>no</u> tables.

D68 f Tick the words a) or b) that you hear in the sentences.

1 a) night	☐	b) light	☐
2 a) no	☐	b) low	☐
3 a) bin	☐	b) bill	☐
4 a) knot	☐	b) lot	☐
5 a) snow	☐	b) slow	☐
6 a) snacks	☐	b) slacks	☐

3 Dialogue

a First practise the target sound /l/ in words from the dialogue. Read the words aloud or visit the website to practise.

leg lunch like love **later** **lettuce** **love**ly **Lily** lemonade
hello eleven **melon** **nearly** usually **yellow** Mrs Carpe**llo**
please plate black **Lesley** glass left lamb slice o'**clock**
early sa**lad** **really** **jelly** olives

D69 b First listen to the dialogue, paying attention to the target sound. Then read the dialogue and fill the gaps (1–10) by choosing the correct words from the box below.

> glass left lamb slice o'clock **early** **salad** **really**
> **jelly** olives

Early for lunch at the office canteen

(Lesley is the cook. Lily Carpello is nearly always early for lunch.)

LILY : Hello, Lesley.

LESLEY: Hello, Mrs Carpello. You're very 1_____ for lunch. It's only eleven 2_____ .

LILY: When I come later there's usually nothing 3_____ .

LESLEY: What would you like, Mrs Carpello?

LILY: Leg of 4_____ , please.

LESLEY: And would you like a plate of 5_____ ? It's lettuce with black 6_____ .

LILY: Mm. Lovely. I 7_____ like olives.

LESLEY: A 8_____ of lemonade?

LILY: Yes, please. I'd like that. And I'd love a 9_____ of melon and some of that yellow 10_____ .

D69 c Check your answers by listening to the dialogue again. Then practise reading the dialogue aloud. Record your voice to compare your production of the target sound with the recording.

4 Final /l/ and /l/ before a consonant: /l/ ball

– Tell me about your Uncle Phil, Carol.
– Well, he's small. And he's old and wrinkled …
and he smiles … and he travels all round the
world with his twelve animals. And he sells
beautiful jewellery.
– What a very unusual uncle!

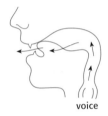

D70 a Notice that /l/ sounds a little different when it comes at the end of a word or before a consonant. To make this /l/ sound, move the back of the tongue up towards the roof of the mouth. Listen: /l/ ball. Listen and repeat: /l/ ball.

voice

b Dialogue
First practise this /l/ sound in words from the dialogue. Read the words aloud or visit the website to practise.

/l/ at the end of a word
Bill tell I'll Paul fall pull small

/l/ before a consonant
help **difficult** fault spoilt child **holding** **salesman** my**self**
always

Syllabic /l/ – each /l/ sound is a syllable
litt**le** **uncle** **careful** spe**cial** **bicycle** sen**sible** **beautiful**
gentleman

D71 c Read the dialogue and fill the gaps (1–6) by choosing the correct words from the list above (syllabic /l/). Then listen to the dialogue and check your answers.

A spoilt little boy in a bicycle shop

PAUL: What a 1_____ bicycle!

UNCLE BILL: Paul! Be 2_____ !

SALESMAN: Excuse me, sir. This child is too small to ride this bicycle. It's a very difficult bicycle to …

UNCLE BILL: Be careful, Paul!

PAUL: You always tell me to be careful. Don't help me. I won't fall.

SALESMAN: But, sir. This is a very 3_____ bicycle. It's …

PAUL: Don't pull the bicycle, Uncle Bill. I'll do it myself.

UNCLE BILL: Be 4_____ , Paul. This 5_____ says it's a …

(Paul falls)

PAUL: It was Uncle Bill's fault. He was holding the 6_____ .

d Practise reading the dialogue aloud. Record your voice to compare your production of the target sound with the recording.

D72 e Intonation in exclamations

Practise exclamations about the pictures below. Listen and respond, like the example.

EXAMPLE What a <u>tall</u> gentleman!

gentleman

| tall | small | little | horrible | miserable |

| beautiful | wonderful | comfortable | unusual | uncomfortable |

gentleman / needle / candle / apple / child

bottle / table / hospital / pencil / bicycle

5 Spelling

Look back over this unit at words with the target sound, and write what you noticed about how to spell the sound /l/.

UNIT 49 /r/ rain

- Would you like to come rowing with me and Caroline on Friday?
- Yes, but I'm terribly busy writing, Rachel …
- Oh come on, Blake, take a break! You need to relax. Remember the last time we went rowing. 'Row, row, row your boat gently down the stream. Merrily, merrily, merrily, merrily, life is but a dream.'
- Oh, all right. 'Row, row, row your …'

1 Target sound /r/

D73 To make the target sound /r/, turn the tip of your tongue up as in the picture. *Do not* touch the roof of your mouth with your tongue. The sides of your tongue should touch your top back teeth. Listen and repeat: /r/.

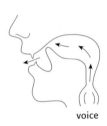

voice

2 Minimal pairs

	Sound 1 /l/	Sound 2 /r/	
	long It's the long road.	**wrong** It's the wrong road.	
	light Is it light?	**right** Is it right?	
	load It's a long load.	**road** It's a long road.	
	jelly Do you like jelly?	**Jerry** Do you like Jerry?	
	fly I'd like to fly it.	**fry** I'd like to fry it.	
	glass There's some glass.	**grass** There's some grass.	

Minimal pair words

D74a **a** Listen and repeat the words.

D74b **b** You will hear five words from each minimal pair. For each word, write *1* for /l/ (sound 1) or *2* for /r/ (sound 2).

EXAMPLE Pair 1:   1, 1, 2, 2, 2

Minimal pair sentences

D75a **c** Listen to the minimal pair sentences.

D75b **d** Listen to six of the sentences and write *1* for /l/ (sound 1) or *2* for /r/ (sound 2)

D75a **e** Sentence stress

Listen to the minimal pair sentences again and match each pair with one of the stress patterns (a–f) below. The big circles are the strongly stressed words in the sentence and the small circles are the weakly stressed words (or syllables).

EXAMPLE a) ooOO (Pair 1) It's the <u>long road</u>. / It's the <u>wrong road</u>.

a) **ooOO**   b) **OoO**   c) **ooO**   d) **ooOO**   e) **oOooOo**   f) **ooooOo**

Notice that the weakly stressed words are said more quickly, and this changes the pronunciation, e.g. *to* and *do* are pronounced /tə/ and /də/.

D76 **f** Tick the words a) or b) that you hear in the sentences.

1 a) long	☐	b) wrong	☐
2 a) jelly	☐	b) Jerry	☐
3 a) glass	☐	b) grass	☐
4 a) collect	☐	b) correct	☐
5 a) lane	☐	b) rain	☐
6 a) flea	☐	b) free	☐

3 Dialogue

a First practise the target sound /r/ in words from the dialogue. Read the words aloud or visit the website to practise.

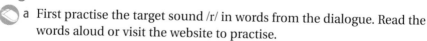

Rose Ruth **Ru**by **real**ly **Ru**ssia **rail**way **Ro**land **ve**ry **Je**rry
parent **La**ra **lo**rry **ma**rried **Eu**rope **cle**verest A**me**rica proud
pretty **li**brary li**bra**rian **wai**tress **cen**tral **res**taurant **coun**tries
Austria Aus**tra**lia **in**teresting elec**tri**cian **chil**dren drive
secretary grown **up** Greece France **eve**rywhere

D77 b Listen to the dialogue, paying attention to the target sound.

A proud parent

LARA: Are all the children grown up now, Ruth?

RUTH: Oh, yes, Lara. Ruby is the cleverest one. She's a librarian in the public library.

LARA: Very interesting. And what about Laura?

RUTH: She's a secretary at the central railway station.

LARA: And what about Rose? She was always a very pretty child.

RUTH: Rose is a waitress in a restaurant in Paris. She's married to an electrician.

LARA: And what about Jerry and Roland?

RUTH: Jerry drives a lorry. He drives everywhere in Europe.

LARA: Really? Which countries does he drive to?

RUTH: France and Austria and Greece and Russia.

LARA: And does Roland drive a lorry too?

RUTH: Oh, no. Roland is a pilot, Lara.

LARA: Really? Which countries does he fly to?

RUTH: Australia and America.

c Practise reading the dialogue aloud. Record your voice to compare your production of the target sound with the recording.

4 Intonation

D78 a Finish these sentences about Mrs Reed's children. Find the answers in the dialogue above. Practise intonation going up in the unfinished part of the sentence, and down when the sentence finishes.

EXAMPLE Ruby isn't a train driver – she's a librarian.

1 Jerry isn't an electrician – _____

2 Rose isn't a secretary – _____

3 Roland isn't a photographer – _____

4 Laura isn't a waitress – _____

5 Ruby isn't a lorry driver – _____

b Silent /r/

When there is no vowel following it, /r/ is silent. This 'rule' only applies to some speakers of English, e.g. in south-east England, South Africa, Australia. But many native speakers always pronounce /r/, e.g. in south-west England, Scotland, America. So you may choose to omit this exercise if you are learning a variety of English where /r/ is always pronounced.

Listen to this conversation while reading it silently. Notice that every letter 'r' is silent. Then practise reading the conversation aloud.

In the airport

ANNOUNCER: R.T. Airways flight number four four seven to New York will depart later this afternoon at 16.40 hours.

DR DARLING: Wonderful! I'm going to the bar to order some more German beer.

MR MARTIN: Where's the bar?

DR DARLING: It's upstairs. There's a bookshop too. And a supermarket. This is a marvellous airport!

MR MARTIN: Oh dear! I wanted to get to New York earlier.
Ah! Here's an air hostess.
Excuse me. I don't understand. Has there been an emergency?

AIR HOSTESS: Oh, no, sir. There's just a storm, and the weather forecast says it will get worse. So the plane will leave a little later this afternoon.

MR MARTIN: Are you sure?

AIR HOSTESS: Oh, yes, sir. Our departure time is at 4.40 this afternoon.

5 Spelling

 Look back over this unit at words with the target sound, and write what you noticed about how to spell the sound /r/.

UNIT 50 REVIEW

Card game: Pick up pairs

Photocopy and cut out cards from all minimal pairs in units 45–49.

Shuffle the cards and deal them face down all over the table.

Turn over any two cards and read their sentences aloud. If they are minimal pairs, you keep them and you continue playing.

If these two cards aren't minimal pairs, turn them face down again and the next person plays.

Collect as many minimal pairs as you can in a time limit, e.g. 10 minutes.

TEST

You can use a dictionary if you wish, but you don't need to understand every word to do this test.

D80 1 For each line (1, 2, 3, 4, 5), first listen to the whole line, then circle the one word (or part of a word) that is said twice. Meaning is not important in this exercise. The purpose is to review the sounds by hearing them in contrast. Some of the words are rarely used in everyday English, and this is shown by an asterisk *. Incomplete words have the rest of the word written in brackets, e.g. *par(agraph)*.

	/m/	/n/	/ŋ/	/l/	/r/
1	Pam	pan	pang*	pal	par(agraph)
2	Mum	Mon(day)	mung*	mull	Murr(ay)
3	some	sun	sung	sull(y)*	Surr(ey)
4	Tim	tin	ting*	till	tyr(anny)
5	my	nigh*	–	lie	rye

Score ☐ / 5

2 Circle the words with the same consonant clusters as 1–2.

1 bread
/br/

2 wings
/ŋz/

blend   spring
bridge   umbrella
brush   spread
embrace   bled   bride

wrongs
winks   kings
whims   springs   shrinks
songs   thongs   wins
thinks

Score ☐ / 10

3 Sound maze

All the words in this maze can be pronounced with a syllabic consonant, e.g. *table(l), station(n), Adam(m)*. You can only cross to a square that has syllabic /n/.

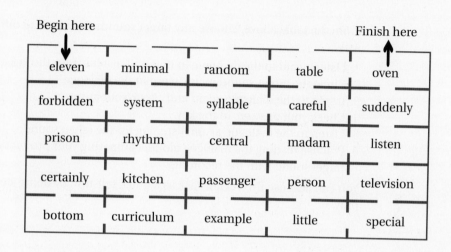

Begin here

Finish here

eleven	minimal	random	table	oven
forbidden	system	syllable	careful	suddenly
prison	rhythm	central	madam	listen
certainly	kitchen	passenger	person	television
bottom	curriculum	example	little	special

Score ☐ / 10

4 Syllabic /l/ and /m/

From the maze in 3 above, list five words with syllabic /l/ and five words with syllabic /m/. (Score half a mark per item.)

Syllabic /l/ _____, _____, _____, _____,

_____

Syllabic /m/ _____, _____, _____, _____,

_____

Score ☐ / 5

Total score ☐ / 30

Additional review task using dialogues from Units 45–49

Unit	44	45	46	47	48
Target sound	/m/	/n/	/ŋ/	/l/	/r/
	mouth	nose	ring	letter	rain
				ball	

From the table above, choose any target sounds that you had difficulty with.

1 Listen again to the dialogue in that unit, listening for the target sound.
2 Circle the target sound in any word in the dialogue.
3 Listen to the dialogue again and check your answers.
4 Check your answers in the key.
5 Listen to the dialogue again, listening for the target sound.
6 Practise reading the dialogue aloud, comparing your production of the target sound with the recording.

You can also use this review task as a quick self-test, by doing steps 2 and 4 only.

OVERVIEW

Card game: Overview minimal pairs snap

Photocopy and cut out cards from all minimal pairs in Units 1–49, or from units you have had difficulty with.

Shuffle the cards and deal them face down to make a pile of cards in front of each player.

Take turns to quickly turn your top card face up on top of a new pile in the centre of the table. When you see two cards appear that are a minimal pair, quickly say 'Snap!' and put your hand on the pile. Then you can add all those cards to your pile.

Collect all the cards you can in a time limit, e.g. ten minutes.

TEST

D81 1 For each line (1, 2, 3, 4, 5, 6, 7), first listen to the whole line, then circle the one word that is said twice. Meaning is not important in this exercise. The purpose is to review the sounds by hearing them in contrast. Some of the words are rarely used in everyday English. This is shown by an asterisk*. Incomplete words have the rest of the word written in brackets, e.g. *fou(nd)*.

	/iː/	/ɪ/	/e/	/æ/	/ʌ/	/ɑː/	
1	beat	bit	bet	bat	but	Bart	
	/ɒ/	/ɔː/	/ʊ/	/uː/	/ɜː/		
2	cod	cord	could	cooed	curd		
	/eɪ/	/aɪ/	/ɔɪ/	/aʊ/	/eʊ/	/ɪə/	/eə/
3	A	I	Oy!	Ow!	Oh!	ear	air
	/p/	/b/	/t/	/d/	/k/	/g/	
4	P	B	T	D	key	ghee*	
	/s/	/z/	/ʃ/	/ʒ/	/tʃ/	/dʒ/	
5	so	zo(ne)	show	–	cho(sen)	Joe	
	/f/	/v/	/w/	/j/	/h/	/θ/	/ð/
6	fee	V	we	ye*	he	the(sis)	thee*
	/m/	/n/	/ŋ/	/l/	/r/		
7	Pam	pan	pang*	pal	par(agraph)		

2 Intonation

Draw the correct intonation arrow (↗ or ↘) in each box.

1 ☐ end of statement / *WH* question / command / 'agreement' tag / less friendly / new information

2 ☐ *Yes/No* question / unfinished statement / surprised / 'unsure' tag / friendly / old information

3 English sounds

The purpose of this exercise is not to teach you how to make English sounds, but to give you an overview from a different perspective of how English sounds are made.

Match the sounds in A (1–7) with the descriptions in B (a–g) of how to make the sounds. The first has been done as an example.

A

Vowels

1 /iː/ /ɜː/ /ɑː/ /uː/ /ɔː/

2 /ɪ/ /e/ /ʊ/ /ə/ /æ/ /ʌ/ /ɒ/

3 /ɪə/ /ʊə/ /eə/ /eɪ/ /ɔɪ/ /aɪ/

Consonants

4 /p/ /b/ /t/ /d/ /k/ /g/
  /tʃ/ /dʒ/

5 /f/ /v/ /θ/ /ð/ /s/ /z/ /ʃ/ /ʒ/ /h/

6 /r/ /j/ /w/

7 /m/ /n/ /ŋ/
  /l/

B

a) 'diphthongs' – made of two vowel sounds

b) 'long vowels' – a longer sound

c) 'short vowels' – a shorter sound

d) 'nasals' – air coming through the nose

  'lateral' – air coming around the sides of the tongue

e) 'approximants' – air moving between two parts of the mouth which are not so close to each other

f) 'fricatives' – air moving between two parts of the mouth which are very close to each other

g) 'plosives' or 'stops' – air released suddenly

  'affricates' – air released slowly

MASK

You can use this mask to just look at the minimal pair pictures and really listen to the sounds first.

You can also revise difficult sounds using the mask.

(e.g. 1 Mask on – listen and repeat. 2 Mask off – read aloud. 3 Mask on – remember and say aloud. 4 Mask off – read aloud to check.)

Cut along the dotted line

Diagnostic Test A: Answers and interpretation

Section 1   On the Result sheet (page xii) place a cross against any items that were incorrect or had a question mark or no answer was written. This indicates work on these sounds may be needed.

Check in the *List of likely errors* on the website (http://www.cambridge.org/elt/elt_projectpage.asp?id=2500905).

Same (1a, 5c, 8b, 9b, 12b, 15b, 17b, 18b, 19b, 24a)

Different (all other items)

Section 2   1 up   2 down   3 down   4 up

5 up   6 up   7 down   8 down

9 up   10 down

Errors in this section indicate that work on intonation may be needed. Check for this aspect of pronunciation in the *List of likely errors*.

Section 3   1 mis**take**   2 **English**   3 a**way**   4 lemon**ade**

5 conver**sation**

Errors in this section indicate that work on word stress may be needed. Check for this aspect of pronunciation in the *List of likely errors*.

Section A Vowels

Making English sounds

1   1 The first sound is a diphthong. All the others are short vowels.

2 The second sound is a short vowel. All the others are diphthongs.

3 The first sound is a short vowel. All the others are long vowels.

2   1 b   2 c   3 d   4 a

3   1 b   2 a   3 d   4 e   5 c   6 g   7 f   8 i   9 h

UNIT 1 /iː/ sheep

3c 1 Peter 2 cheese 3 beef 4 please
5 beef 6 eat 7 tea 8 me
9 teas 10 three

4c China – Chinese, Bali – Balinese, Malta – Maltese, Portugal – Portuguese, Lebanon – Lebanese, Japan – Japanese, Nepal – Nepalese, Vietnam – Vietnamese

4d Yes, it's Chi<u>nese</u>. It's <u>Chi</u>nese tea.

Yes, it's Japa<u>nese</u>. It's <u>Ja</u>panese seaweed.

Yes, it's Bali<u>nese</u>. It's <u>Bali</u>nese ice cream.

Yes, it's Vietna<u>mese</u>. It's <u>Viet</u>namese rice.

5 The sound /iː/ is usually written with the letters 'ee' (three, sweet), 'ea' (eat, speak), 'e' (be, these). Some other spellings: 'i' (policeman), 'eo' (people), 'ei' (ceiling), 'ie' (piece).

UNIT 2 /ɪ/ ship

2b Pair 2: 2, 2, 1, 2, 2
Pair 3: 1, 1, 2, 1, 2
Pair 4: 1, 2, 2, 1, 1
Pair 5: 2, 2, 1, 1, 1
Pair 6: 2, 2, 1, 2, 1

2d 1 (2) 2 (1) 3 (2) 4 (1) 5 (2) 6 (2)

2e Pair 1: Look <u>out</u> for that <u>sheep</u>!/Look <u>out</u> for that <u>ship</u>!

Pair 2: <u>Stop</u> it <u>leak</u>ing!/<u>Stop</u> it <u>lick</u>ing!

Pair 3: What <u>love</u>ly <u>cheeks</u>!/What <u>love</u>ly <u>chicks</u>!

Pair 4: This <u>peel's</u> got vitamin <u>C</u> in it./This <u>pill's</u> got vitamin <u>C</u> in it.

Pair 5: Throw <u>out</u> that <u>bean</u>./Throw <u>out</u> that <u>bin</u>.

Pair 6: He's <u>going</u> to <u>leave</u>./He's <u>going</u> to <u>live</u>.

2f 1 a – He wants a sheep for his birthday.

2 b – That's a very small bin.

3 b – Look at these chicks.

4 a – That's a cheap machine.

5 a – What a high heel!

6 b – Don't eat that pill.

3c 1 festival 2 prize-winning 3 interesting 4 chimpanzees
5 gymnastics 6 History 7 terrific 8 beginning

4c	1 No, not **for**ty – four**teen**.
	2 No, not **nine**ty – nine**teen**.
	3 No, not **six**ty – six**teen**.
	4 No, not **eigh**ty – eigh**teen**.
	5 No, not **thir**ty – thir**teen**.
5	The sound /ɪ/ is usually written with the letter 'i' (finish, window), and with the letter 'y' at the end of a word (very, study).
	Some other spellings: 'e' (example, because), 'u' (minute), 'ee' (coffee), 'ay' (Monday).

UNIT 3 /e/ pen

2b	Pair 2: 1, 2, 2, 1, 2
	Pair 3: 2, 1, 1, 2, 2
	Pair 4: 1, 1, 1, 2, 2
	Pair 5: 2, 1, 1, 2, 1
	Pair 6: 1, 1, 2, 2, 1
2d	1 (1) 2 (1) 3 (2) 4 (2) 5 (2) 6 (1)
2e	Pair 1: I need a <u>pin</u>./I need a <u>pen</u>.
	Pair 2: That's my <u>bin</u>./That's my <u>Ben</u>.
	Pair 3: It's a big <u>tin</u>./It's a big <u>ten</u>.
	Pair 4: Where's the <u>pig</u>?/Where's the <u>peg</u>?
	Pair 5: There's the <u>bill</u>./There's the <u>bell</u>.
	Pair 6: She wants a <u>chick</u>./She wants a <u>cheque</u>.
2f	1 a – Give me another pin, please.
	2 b – There's a peg over there.
	3 a – I buy them in tins.
	4 a – I'll just sit the alarm clock on this shelf.
	5 b – He needs a new desk.
	6 b – She'll just peck at her food.
3a	jealous (2) help (1) everybody (4) any (2) bench (1) Kevin (2)
	America (4) Mexican (3) Emily (3) Ben (1) very (2) bread (1)
	Eddie (2)
3c	1 d 2 b 3 f 4 a 5 g 6 e 7 c
4d	ex'cept 'exercise ex'pect expe'dition ex'pel ex'periment
	ex'penditure 'expert ex'pression ex'tend 'extra 'extrovert
5	The sound /e/ is usually written with the letter 'e' (pen, hotel).
	Some other spellings: 'ea' (heavy, ready), 'a' (any, many), 'ie' (friend), 'ai' (again).

UNIT 4 /æ/ man

2b	Pair 2: 1, 2, 2, 1, 1
	Pair 3: 1, 1, 2, 2, 2
	Pair 4: 2, 1, 1, 2, 2
	Pair 5: 1, 1, 1, 2, 2
	Pair 6: 2, 1, 1, 2, 1

2d   1 (2)   2 (1)   3 (1)   4 (2)   5 (2)   6 (1)

2e   <u>Look</u> at the <u>men</u>./<u>Look</u> at the <u>man</u>.

I'm <u>send</u>ing the <u>table</u>./I'm <u>sand</u>ing the <u>table</u>.

It's a <u>lovely gem</u>./It's a <u>lovely jam</u>.

We had <u>bread</u> for <u>lunch</u>./We had <u>Brad</u> for <u>lunch</u>.

2f   1 b – I've bought a new pan.

2 a – Did you see the men?

3 b – Did you say 'and'?

4 b – I like the fatter cheese.

5 a – Don't pet the dog.

6 a – These are bedclothes.

3a   1 c   2 a   3 b

1 b   2 c   3 a

3b   2 Amsterdam   3 Allen   4 anchovy, salad sandwich

5 had, map, Africa, had, Saturday   6 bad, absent

7 passenger, Salvador, animals, antelope, alligator

8 crashed, back, advertising, angry   9 contracts, cancelled, management

10 have, back, travel, sacked

4c   1 b   2 c   3 a

5   The sound /æ/ is always written with the letter 'a' (angry, taxi).

UNIT 5 /ʌ/ cup

2b	Pair 2: 1, 1, 2, 1, 2
	Pair 3: 1, 2, 1, 2, 1
	Pair 4: 2, 2, 1, 2, 1
	Pair 5. 1, 2, 2, 1, 2
	Pair 6: 2, 1, 1, 2, 2

2d   1 (2)   2 (1)   3 (1)   4 (2)   5 (1)   6 (2)

2e   Pair 2: d) **ooOooOo**   There's a <u>hat</u> in the <u>gar</u>den./There's a <u>hut</u> in the garden.

Pair 3: c) **ooOooO**   See the <u>tracks</u> on the <u>road</u>./ See the <u>trucks</u> on the road.

Pair 4: b) **ooOoo**   There's a <u>ban</u> on it./There's a <u>bun</u> on it.

Pair 5: a) **oooO**   She's got a <u>bag</u>./She's got a <u>bug</u>.

Pair 6: e) **oOooOo**   My <u>an</u>kle was <u>in</u>jured./My <u>un</u>cle was <u>in</u>jured.

2f   1 a – What a dirty cap!

2 b – This hut is too small.

3 b – There's a black bug on the table.

4 a – They live in a mad house.

5 a – I hang my coat on the door.

6 b – The children run quickly.

3c
1 nothing	2 honey	3 brother	4 other
5 lovely	6 does	7 month	8 worry
9 company	10 wonderful		

4a   1 N   2 A   3 A   4 N   5 A;   words for statement: strong, down

5   The sound /ʌ/ is usually written with the letter 'u'.

Some other spellings: 'oe' (does), 'ou' (cousin), 'o' (many common words with the sound /ʌ/ have this spelling, e.g. words in 3c above; others: love, above, onion, monkey, comfortable, gloves, coloured, London, money)

UNIT 6 /ɑː/ heart

Minimal pairs A

2b   Pair 2:   1, 2, 2, 1, 2

Pair 3:   1, 1, 2, 2, 1

Pair 4:   2, 1, 2, 2, 1

Pair 5:   1, 1, 1, 2, 2

2d   1 (2)   2 (1)   3 (1)   4 (2)   5 (1)

2e   Pair 1: What a <u>love</u>ly <u>cap</u>!/What a <u>love</u>ly <u>carp</u>!

Pair 2: He <u>touched</u> his <u>hat</u>./He <u>touched</u> his <u>heart</u>.

Pair 3: It's a <u>farm</u> <u>cat</u>./It's a <u>farm</u> <u>cart</u>.

Pair 4: There's a <u>ban</u> on it./There's a <u>barn</u> on it.

Pair 5: I'll <u>pack</u> the <u>car</u>./I'll <u>park</u> the <u>car</u>.

Minimal pairs B

2b   Pair 2:   2, 2, 1, 2, 1

Pair 3:   2, 1, 2, 2, 1

Pair 4:   1, 1, 2, 2, 1

Pair 5:   2, 1, 2, 1, 1

2d   1 (1)   2 (1)   3 (2)   4 (1)   5 (2)

2e   Pair 1: What a <u>beau</u>tiful <u>cup</u>!/What a <u>beau</u>tiful <u>carp</u>!

Pair 2: There's a <u>prob</u>lem with my <u>hut</u>./There's a <u>prob</u>lem with my <u>heart</u>.

Pair 3: He <u>cov</u>ered his <u>cut</u>./He <u>cov</u>ered his <u>cart</u>.

Pair 4: <u>What's</u> in that <u>bun</u>?/<u>What's</u> in that <u>barn</u>?

Pair 5: '<u>Come down</u>', she said./'<u>Calm down</u>', she said.

2f   1 c – He's broken my heart.

2 b – That's a bad cut.

3 a – I gave him a cap.

4 b – There's a mouse in this barn.

5 a – Why don't you come down?

6 a – I don't like Patty's.

3c   1 marvellous   2 fantastic   3 smart   4 fabulous   5 attractive

5   The sound /aː/ is usually written with the letter 'a' (father, ask).

Some other spellings: 'au' (aunt), 'al' (half), 'ear' (heart), 'ar' (star).

UNIT 7 Review

1   1 ban   2 bet   3 bud   4 peak   5 party

2   1 done, doesn't, does, come, us

2 half, arm, are, aren't, can't

3 people, piece, these, she, need

3   2 f   3 d   4 b   5 a   6 e

4   <u>ad</u>vertising   under<u>stand</u>   <u>Leb</u>anon   lemo<u>nade</u>   <u>sand</u>wich   ex<u>pen</u>sive   <u>sun</u>glasses   fan<u>tas</u>tic   <u>pho</u>tograph   gui<u>tar</u>

Additional review task

Unit 1   cheaper, cheapest, eat, Marguerite's, cheese, please, beef, tea, teas, me, three, Christina, Peter, Janine

Unit 2   interesting, films, evening, Mrs /mɪsɪz/, is, Kim, in, coming, cinema, it's, Children's, film, festival, ill, Bill, we've (weak form of *we*), tickets, prize-winning, children, listen, is it, gorillas, chimpanzees, Africa, six, Olympic, gymnastics, competitions, big, History, English, Cricket, terrific, pity, miss, kids, begins, fifty, minutes, quick, beginning.

Unit 3   friends, Emma, Ben, hello /heləʊ/ or /hələʊ/, Emily, Eddie, everybody, except, Adele, again /əgen/ or /əgeɪn/, Kevin, Red, Peppers, terribly, yes, better, said, help, yourself, Mexican, bench, French, bread, shelf, get, lemonade, met, yet, very, friendly, spend, America, best, Kerrie, well, jealous, expensive, spent, everything, any, left

Unit 4   Aaron, Ajax Travel, Amsterdam, Mrs Allen, anchovy, salad, sandwich, contact, Anthony, map, Africa, had, Saturday, bad, habit, absent, passenger, San Salvador, animals, anteater, antelope, alligator, crashed, backup, advertising, programmes, angry, contracts, cancelled, management, have, come back, sacked

Strong forms: He had to …; He hadn't done the …; He doesn't have to …

Unit 5   doesn't, love, honey, Duncan, nothing, unhappy, understand, much,
          untrue, cousin, Justin, brother, Dudley, funny, one, other, Hunter, lovely,
          unattractive, utter rubbish, does, just once, month, lunch, mustn't, worry,
          company, just, shut up, wonderful
          Note: *but* is usually pronounced with the weak form /bət/.

Unit 6   party, bar, laughing, garden, after dark, marvellous, Margaret, glass, Alana,
          Tara Darling, Markus Marsh, dancing, grass, stars, Bart, guitar, she can't
          dance, dancer, photograph, Martin
          Note: Strong forms: They are. Here you are.

UNIT 8 /ɒ/ clock

2b   Pair 2:   1, 1, 2, 1, 2
      Pair 3:   2, 2, 1, 1, 2
      Pair 4:   1, 2, 2, 2, 1
      Pair 5:   1, 2, 1, 2, 2
      Pair 6:   2, 2, 1, 2, 1

2d   1 (2)   2 (1)   3 (1)   4 (2)   5 (1)   6 (1)

2e   Pair 2: b) oooOO   He's got a <u>white</u> <u>cat</u>./He's got a <u>white</u> <u>cot</u>.

      Pair 3: a) OooO   <u>Look</u> for the <u>fax</u>./<u>Look</u> for the <u>fox</u>.

      Pair 4: e) OoooO   <u>Put</u> it in a <u>sack</u>./<u>Put</u> it in a <u>sock</u>.

      Pair 5: d) OoOOo   <u>Turn</u> that <u>tap</u> <u>slowly</u>./<u>Turn</u> that <u>top</u> <u>slowly</u>.

      Pair 6: c) ooOoO   I can <u>see</u> their <u>backs</u>./I can <u>see</u> their <u>box</u>.

2f   1 b – What a pretty little cot!

      2 a – He tried to put his head in a sack.

      3 b – The top was made of metal.

      4 a – Which Pat do you want?

      5 a – I liked the baddie in that film.

      6 b – Write in block letters.

3c   1 horrible   2 soft   3 strong   4 hot   5 long   6 popular

4b   2 box (command)
      3 hot, Mrs Wong (suggestion)
      4 washing machine, Robin (suggestion)
      5 office (command)
      6 shops, Oscar (suggestion)
      7 doctor, Bronwen (suggestion)

5   The sound /ɒ/ is written with the letter 'o' (on, stop).
      Some other spellings: 'a' (want, what), 'au' (because).

UNIT 9 /ɔː/ ball

2b   Pair 2:   2, 2, 1, 1, 1

             Pair 3:   1, 1, 2, 1, 2

             Pair 4:   1, 2, 1, 2, 1

             Pair 5:   2, 2, 2, 1, 1

             Pair 6:   2, 1, 1, 2, 1

2d   1(2)   2 (2)   3 (1)   4 (2)   5 (1)   6 (1)

2e   Pair 1: Is your name <u>Don</u>?/Is your name <u>Dawn</u>?

             Pair 2: This <u>cod</u> was in the <u>sea</u>./This <u>cord</u> was in the <u>sea</u>.

             Pair 3: He was <u>shot</u>./He was <u>short</u>.

             Pair 4: It's a <u>small pot</u>./It's a <u>small port</u>.

             Pair 5: <u>Look</u> for the <u>fox</u>./<u>Look</u> for the <u>forks</u>.

             Pair 6: I <u>don't</u> like these <u>spots</u>./I <u>don't</u> like these <u>sports</u>.

2f   1 b – My doctor doesn't like these sports.

             2 a – These pots are very dirty.

             3 b – Look at that white cord on the water.

             4 a – Mr Smith was shot.

             5 a – The lion walked towards Tom and Rod.

             6 a – I said, 'What a dog!'

4b   1   In the <u>drawer</u>?   2   It's too <u>warm</u>?

             3   <u>Georgia</u>?   4   Forty-five <u>forks</u>?

             5   A <u>horse</u>?   6   At <u>four</u> in the <u>morning</u>?

             7   <u>Orlando</u>? In New <u>York</u>?   8   <u>My</u> fault?

5   The sound /ɔː/ is written with the letter 'aw' (Dawn), 'or' (cord), 'a' (ball), 'augh' (daughter).

UNIT 10 /ʊ/ book

2b   Pair 2:   1, 2, 2, 1, 1

             Pair 3:   2, 2, 2, 1, 1

             Pair 4:   2, 1, 2, 1, 1

             Pair 5:   1, 1, 2, 1, 2

2d   1 (1)   2 (2)   3 (1)   4 (2)   5 (2)

2e   Pair 2:   you

             Pair 3:   I'll

             Pair 4:   ar<u>ou</u>nd

             Pair 5:   me

2f	1 b – That cook is very noisy.
	2 a – Lock it up carefully.
	3 a – He's my godfather.
	4 a – How do you spell 'cod'?
5	The sound /ʊ/ is usually written with the letters 'oo' (foot, good) or 'u' (push, put).
	Other spelling: 'o' (woman).

UNIT 11 /uː/ boot

2b	Pair 2: 1, 1, 1, 2, 2
	Pair 3: 2, 1, 1, 2, 1
	Pair 4: 2, 2, 1, 2, 1
	Pair 5: 2, 1, 1, 2, 1
2d	1 (2) 2 (1) 3 (1) 4 (1) 5 (1)
2e	<u>water</u>proof <u>boots</u>
	a <u>wind</u>-proof <u>jacket</u>
	<u>child</u>proof con<u>tai</u>ners
	an <u>oven</u>proof <u>dish</u>
	a <u>water</u>proof <u>coat</u>
	a <u>bullet</u>-proof <u>vest</u>
2f	1 a – Look, I want you to come here.
	2 a – That's full.
	3 a – Did you say 'Pull'?
	4 b – That's a foolish skirt.
	5 b – He wooed Mary.
3c	GIRLS: (2) <u>noon</u>, <u>Luke</u>
	MISS LUKE: (4) <u>noon</u>, <u>learn</u>, <u>cook</u>, <u>soup</u>
	(5) <u>turn</u>, <u>pu</u>, <u>look</u>, <u>un</u>, <u>two</u>
	LUCY: (2) <u>cuse</u>, <u>Luke</u>
	MISS LUKE: (1) <u>Yes</u>
	LUCY: (2) chew, shoe
	MISS LUKE: (5) who, chew, floor, you, Lu
	LUCY: (2) <u>No</u>, <u>Su</u>
	MISS LUKE: (1) <u>Who</u>
	LUCY: (2) <u>Su</u>, <u>Duke</u>
	SUSAN: (3) <u>me</u>, <u>stu</u>, <u>lu</u>
	JULIE: (1) <u>you</u>
	SUSAN: (8) <u>was</u>, <u>me</u>, <u>my</u>, <u>mouth's</u>, <u>full</u>, <u>chew</u>, <u>Look</u>, <u>Luke</u>

JULIE: (4) <u>Stop</u>, <u>hair</u>, <u>Su</u>, <u>you</u>

SUSAN: (1) <u>YOU</u>

JULIE: (1) <u>YOU</u>

MISS LUKE: (11) <u>use</u>, <u>me</u>, <u>you</u>, <u>two</u>, <u>tin</u>, <u>rude</u>, <u>stay</u>, <u>school</u>, <u>stead</u>, <u>go</u>, <u>pool</u>

5   The sound /uː/ is usually written with the letters 'u' (music) or 'oo' (food). Some other spellings: 'o' (do), 'ou' (you), 'ui' (fruit), 'oe' (shoe), 'ew' (new), 'wo' (two), 'ough' (through).

UNIT 12 /ɜː/ girl

Minimal pairs A

2b   Pair 2: 1, 2, 2, 2, 1

      Pair 3: 1, 1, 2, 2, 1

      Pair 4: 1, 2, 2, 1, 2

2d   1 (1)   2 (2)   3 (1)   4 (1)

2e   Pair 1: She's got <u>four</u>./She's got <u>fur</u>.

      Pair 2: It's a <u>torn</u> <u>sign</u>./It's a <u>turn</u> <u>sign</u>.

      Pair 3: I <u>would</u>n't like <u>warm</u> soup./I <u>would</u>n't like <u>worm</u> soup.

      Pair 4: He's a <u>fast</u> <u>walk</u>er./He's a <u>fast</u> <u>work</u>er.

Minimal pairs B

2b   Pair 2: 1, 1, 2, 1, 2

      Pair 3: 1, 1, 1, 2, 2

      Pair 4: 2, 2, 1, 2, 1

2d   1 (1)   2 (2)   3 (1)   4 (2)

2e   Pair 1: The <u>sign</u> says <u>ten</u>./The <u>sign</u> says <u>turn</u>.

      Pair 2: <u>Look</u> at it, <u>Ben</u>./<u>Look</u> at it <u>burn</u>.

      Pair 3: It's a <u>colour</u>ful <u>bed</u>./It's a <u>colour</u>ful <u>bird</u>.

      Pair 4: It's the <u>west</u> <u>wind</u>./It's the <u>worst</u> <u>wind</u>.

Minimal pairs C

2b   Pair 2: 2, 2, 1, 2, 1

      Pair 3: 1, 1, 2, 1, 2

      Pair 4: 1, 1, 2, 2, 2

2d   1 (1)   2 (2)   3 (2)   4 (1)

2e   Pair 1: <u>Fabulous</u> <u>fun</u>./<u>Fabulous</u> <u>fern</u>.

      Pair 2: <u>Look</u> at that <u>bun</u>./<u>Look</u> at that <u>burn</u>.

      Pair 3: That's a <u>tin</u>y little <u>bud</u>./That's a tiny little <u>bird</u>.

      Pair 4: There's a <u>gull</u> on the <u>beach</u>./There's a <u>girl</u> on the <u>beach</u>.

2f   1 a – That's a very small bed.

2 b – He's got a lot of buns.

3 a – That's a very long ward.

4 a – Why don't you walk faster?

5 b – She always wears shirt dresses.

6 b – His name's John … er … Thomas, I think.

4b   2 ⟋ not sure

3 ⟍ expects agreement

4 ⟋ not sure

5 ⟍ expects agreement

6 ⟍ expects agreement

5   The sound /ɜː/ is usually written with the letters 'ur' (turn), 'or' (worm), 'ir' (bird) or 'er' (fern).

UNIT 13 /ə/ a camera

3c   1 a   2 b   3 b   4 b   5 a   6 b

4b   A: I'm going tə thə librəry.

B: Cən yə buy səmething fə me ət the newsagənt's?

A: Bət the newsagənt's is ə mile frəm thə librəry

B: No. Not that newsagənt's. Not thə one thət's next tə thə fish ənd chip shop. I mean thə one thət's near thə butchərs.

A: Oh, yes. Well, what də yə want?

B: Səme chocolətes ənd ə tin əf sweets ənd ən əddress book.

5   The sound /ə/ is usually written with the letters 'a' (again, woman), 'o' (today, police), 'e' (open, quiet), 'er' (water, mother).

Some words have the sound /ə/ when they are weakly stressed in a sentence, and are written with 'a' (am, a, an, and, as, at, shall), 'o' (for, from, of, to) and 'e' (the, them).

UNIT 14 REVIEW

1   1 pull   2 fall   3 could   4 word

2   1 were, burn, early, shirt, worst

2 torn, water, all, four, talk

3 shoe, two, through, super, do

4 full, cook, would, look, good

3   1 ⟍   2 ⟋   3 ⟍   4 ⟋   5 ⟋   6 ⟍

Additional review task

Unit 8   Onwash, wrong, Mrs Bloggs, want, holiday, horrible, job, washing, socks, bottle, soft, strong, lots, hot, long, often, sorry, got, wants, popular

Unit 9   sports, report, four, morning, Roarers, football, York, Laura Short, reporter, airport, all, footballers, walking, towards, George Ball, awful, score, forty-four, fault

/fɔːlt/ or /fɒlt/, forwards, always, falling, ball

Unit 10 book, Mr Cook, could, put, bookshelf, full, cookery, shouldn't (*should* here is the weak form /ʃəd/), look, took, foot, good

Note: room, bedroom can also be pronounced /ruːm/.

Unit 11 two, rudest, students, school, afternoon, Miss Luke, soup, computers, unit, twenty-two, excuse me, Lucy, chewing gum, shoe, who (strong form), threw, you (strong form), Susan Duke, Julie, excuse, continue, rudeness, pool

Unit 12 worst, nurse, thirsty, hurts, dirty, shirts, work, early, er, Turner, weren't (strong form), were (strong form), Thursday, Sherman, Sir Herbert, Colonel Burton, world

Unit 13 See Key for 4b on page 196.

UNIT 15 /eɪ/ male

2b   Pair 2:   1, 1, 1, 2, 1

Pair 3:   2, 1, 1, 2, 1

Pair 4:   1, 2, 1, 2, 1

Pair 5:   2, 2, 1, 1, 2

Pair 6:   1, 1, 2, 2, 1

2d   1 (2)   2 (1)   3 (2)   4 (2)   5 (1)   6 (1)

2e   Pair 1: What an <u>awful</u> <u>pen</u>!/What an <u>awful</u> <u>pain</u>!

Pair 2: The <u>dog's</u> in the <u>shed</u>./The <u>dog's</u> in the <u>shade</u>.

Pair 3: It's a <u>difficult</u> <u>edge</u>./It's a <u>difficult</u> <u>age</u>.

Pair 4: Just <u>wet</u>./Just <u>wait</u>.

Pair 5: <u>Test</u> this <u>food</u>./<u>Taste</u> this <u>food</u>.

Pair 6: That's <u>too</u> much <u>pepper</u>./That's <u>too</u> much <u>paper</u>.

2f   1 a – This student has a very bad pen.

2 a – Let's sit in the shed.

3 a – Please give me some more pepper.

4 b – The children were late out from school.

5 a – Her letter writing is very good.

6 a – Open the door and get ready to leave.

4b   2 Today?

3 Eighty-eight

4 Going away?

5 By plane?

6 To Spain?

7 Me?

5   The sound /eɪ/ is usually written with the letters 'a' (take), 'ay' (day) or 'ai' (wait).

Some other spellings: 'ey' (grey), 'ea' (break), 'eigh' (eight).

UNIT 16 /aɪ/ fine

2b   Pair 2: 2, 2, 1, 2, 1

Pair 3: 1, 1, 2, 2, 1

Pair 4: 2, 1, 2, 1, 2

Pair 5: 1, 1, 2, 1, 2

Pair 6: 1, 2, 2, 1, 2

2d   1 (2)   2 (1)   3 (1)   4 (2)   5 (2)   6 (1)

2e   Pair 1: That was a <u>good</u> <u>bar</u>./That was a <u>good</u> <u>buy</u>.

Pair 2: What a <u>noisy</u> <u>bark</u>./What a <u>noisy</u> <u>bike</u>.

Pair 3: He <u>loves</u> his <u>Pa</u>./He <u>loves</u> his <u>pie</u>.

Pair 4: It's got <u>two</u> <u>R's</u>./It's got <u>two</u> <u>eyes</u>.

Pair 5: It's a <u>cart</u>./It's a <u>kite</u>.

Pair 6: <u>Check</u> the <u>heart</u>./<u>Check</u> the <u>height</u>.

2f   1 a – I want a new cart.

2 b – The old lady was dining.

3 a – What a big star!

4 b – She has a good life.

5 a – This leather's hard.

6 b – Do you like pie?

3c   1 nice   2 iced   3 type   4 bike   5 mobile   6 library   7 tonight
8 Friday   9 climbing   10 spider

5   The sound /aɪ/ is usually written with the letters 'i' (time) or 'y' (sky).

Some other spellings: 'igh' (high), 'ey' (eye), 'ie' (lie), 'uy' (buy).

UNIT 17 /ɔɪ/ boy

2b   Pair 2: 2, 1, 2, 2, 2

Pair 3: 1, 1, 2, 1, 2

Pair 4: 2, 2, 2, 1, 1

Pair 5: 1, 2, 2, 1, 1

2d   1 (2)   2 (1)   3 (2)   4 (1)   5 (2)

2e   Pair 1: It's <u>all</u> there./It's <u>oil</u> there.

Pair 2: It's a <u>ball</u> on his <u>head</u>./It's a <u>boil</u> on his <u>head</u>.

Pair 3: <u>Look</u> at that <u>golden</u> <u>corn</u>./<u>Look</u> at that <u>golden</u> <u>coin</u>.

Pair 4: The <u>paper</u> <u>tore</u>./The <u>paper</u> <u>toy</u>.

Pair 5: <u>Hear</u> the <u>engine</u> <u>roar</u>./<u>Hear</u> the <u>engine</u>, <u>Roy</u>.

2f	1 b – I found this coin in the garden.
	2 b – The little boy was boiling with anger.
	3 a – Look! It's all on the floor.
	4 a – Aw! You've broken that glass.
	5 b – He's a terrible boy.
	6 a – Did you put all of it in the salad?

4a

annoying	unem**ploy**ment	**oy**ster
em**ploy**er	ap**point**ment	en**joy**
poisonous	des**troy**er	**oint**ment
moist	em**broi**dery	**toi**let
disa**ppoint**ed	**join**	

4b *Disappointed* /ˌdɪsəˈpɔɪntɪd/ and *unemployment* /ˌʌnɪmˈplɔɪmənt/ have secondary stress on the first syllable. The main strong stress is on the third syllable.

5 The sound /ɔɪ/ is written with the letters 'oi' (noise) or 'oy' (boy).

UNIT 18 /aʊ/ house

2b	Pair 2:	1, 1, 2, 2, 1
	Pair 3:	1, 2, 1, 2, 1
	Pair 4:	2, 1, 2, 1, 1
	Pair 5:	1, 1, 2, 1, 2

2d 1 (2)   2 (2)   3 (1)   4 (1)   5 (1)

2e Pair 1: It's the <u>best</u> <u>car</u>./It's the <u>best</u> <u>cow</u>.

Pair 2: It was a <u>long</u> <u>bar</u>./It was a <u>long</u> <u>bow</u>.

Pair 3: Her <u>bra</u> was <u>wrinkled</u>./Her <u>brow</u> was <u>wrinkled</u>.

Pair 4: There's <u>beautiful</u> <u>grass</u> here./There's <u>beautiful</u> <u>grouse</u> here.

Pair 5: '<u>Arch</u>!' he said <u>loudly</u>./'<u>Ouch</u>!' he said <u>loudly</u>.

2f	1 a – The bus drove into the car.
	2 a – There's a lot of grass near the farm.
	3 b – Her brow was white.
	4 a – 'Ha!' he said loudly.
	5 b – 'Ow!' he said, 'You hit me.'
	6 b – Near the mountain there is a little town.

3b ~~pronouncing~~ shouting; ~~Calm~~ Sit; ~~town~~ brown; ~~down~~ out; ~~Now?~~ How?; ~~on the mountain~~ in the town

4b 1 c   2 a   3 b   4 f   5 d   6 e

4d 1 e   2 c   3 b   4 a   5 d

5 The sound /aʊ/ is written with the letters 'ou' (about) or 'ow' (down).

UNIT 19 /əʊ/ phone

Minimal pairs A

2b   Pair 2:   1, 1, 2, 1, 2

Pair 3:   2, 1, 1, 2, 2

Pair 4:   1, 1, 1, 2, 2

Pair 5:   1, 2, 2, 1, 2

Pair 6:   2, 2, 1, 1, 2

2d   1 (2)   2 (1)   3 (2)   4 (1)   5 (2)

2e   Pair 1: It's a large <u>burn</u>./It's a large <u>bone</u>.

Pair 2: It's a green <u>fern</u>./It's a green <u>phone</u>.

Pair 3: That's my <u>Bert</u>./That's my <u>boat</u>.

Pair 4: I <u>work</u> early./I <u>woke</u> early.

Pair 5: He likes <u>flir</u>ting./He likes <u>floa</u>ting.

Minimal pairs B

2b   Pair 2:   1, 1, 2, 2, 2

Pair 3:   1, 2, 1, 2, 2

Pair 4:   2, 2, 1, 1, 1

Pair 5:   1, 1, 2, 2, 2

2d   1 (1)   2 (2)   3 (2)   4 (1)   5 (1)

2e   Pair 1: Gino's <u>caught</u>./Gino's <u>coat</u>.

Pair 2: It's a <u>nought</u>./It's a <u>note</u>.

Pair 3: We had a <u>bought</u> picnic./We had a <u>boat</u> picnic.

Pair 4: It's my <u>jaw</u>./It's my <u>Joe</u>.

Pair 5: Give me the <u>ball</u>./Give me the <u>bowl</u>.

2f   1 a – They have a nice green fern in the hall.

2 a – You can have coffee. Or do you want tea?

3 b – It's a very heavy bowl.

4 a – Don't burn the chicken.

5 a – I walk early in the morning.

4a   old: cold, sold, hold, told, gold
      hole: bowl, stole

4b   Across: 1 lonely   2 won't   3 no   4 go   5 pillow
      Down: 1 low   2 on   3 no   4 go   5 yellow

5   The sound /əʊ/ is usually written with the letters 'o' (go, old), 'oa' (boat) or 'ow' (know).

UNIT 20 /ɪə/ year

2b Pair 2: 1, 2, 2, 2, 1

Pair 3: 2, 1, 2, 1, 2

Pair 4: 1, 1, 2, 1, 1

Pair 5: 2, 1, 1, 2, 2

2d 1 (1) 2 (1) 3 (2) 4 (2) 5 (1)

2e Pair 1: That <u>E's</u> too big./That <u>ear's</u> too big.

Pair 2: It's a small <u>bee</u>./It's a small <u>beer</u>.

Pair 3: This <u>tea</u> tastes salty./This <u>tear</u> tastes salty.

Pair 4: It's an old <u>pea</u>./It's an old <u>pier</u>.

Pair 5: He has a black <u>bead</u>./He has a black <u>beard</u>.

2f 1 b – I've just swallowed a beer.

2 a – The tea fell on the floor.

3 a – What a funny bead!

4 b – That's a very unusual pier.

5 a – There should be two 'E's and you've only got one.

6 b – How are you, dear?

3c 1 beer   2 year   3 clear   4 mountaineer   5 beard   6 beer   7 hear
8 Cheers

4b He can hear‿us too.

Dear‿old Mrs Lear‿is here‿in the kitchen.

This mountaineer‿always spends some time each year‿in the mountains.

5 The sound /ɪə/ is usually written with the letters 'ea' (dear, ear).

Other spellings: 'ere' (here).

UNIT 21 /eə/ chair

2b Pair 2: 1, 2, 2, 2, 1

Pair 3: 2, 2, 1, 1, 2

Pair 4: 2, 1, 2, 1, 2

Pair 5: 1, 1, 1, 1, 2

Pair 6: 2, 1, 1, 2, 2

2d 1 (1) 2 (2) 3 (2) 4 (2) 5 (1) 6 (1)

2e Pair 1: The <u>ear</u> isn't <u>good</u>./The <u>air</u> isn't <u>good</u>.

Pair 2: It's a <u>sweet</u> <u>beer</u>./It's a <u>sweet</u> <u>bear</u>.

Pair 3: That's an <u>old</u> <u>pier</u>./That's an <u>old</u> <u>pear</u>.

Pair 4: <u>How</u> do you spell '<u>hear</u>'?/<u>How</u> do you spell '<u>hair</u>'?

Pair 5: That's a <u>tear</u>./That's a <u>tear</u>.

Pair 6: '<u>Three</u> <u>cheers!</u>' he said./'<u>Three</u> <u>chairs!</u>' he said.

2f	1 a – 'Three cheers', he said.
	2 b – There was a small bear on the table.
	3 a – That's a very big pier.
	4 a – Look! It's here.
	5 a – Can I borrow your pen, please, Dan, dear?
	6 b – He said her name but it wasn't Claire.
4b	There‿it is.
	They're‿under‿a table.
	I've looked everywhere‿in the house.
5	The sound /eə/ is usually written with the letters 'are' (square) or 'ere' (where).
	Other spellings: 'eir' (their), 'ear' (wear).

UNIT 22 REVIEW

1	1 buy b here c air d weigh e toe
2	1 page, weight, pain
	2 shy, frightened, sigh
	3 how's, owl, found
	4 home, snow, though
	5 their, they're, stare
3	1 We're looking for‿a builder‿or‿an architect, Adler‿and Anderson.
	2 Where‿are their‿offices?
	3 They're‿over there, aren't they?
	4 Are you an engineer‿or‿an architect, Mr‿Adler?
	5 I'm a structural engineer‿and this is Blair‿Anderson, our‿architect.
4	<u>ti</u>me<u>ta</u>ble to<u>day</u> <u>cy</u>cling <u>horse</u> <u>ri</u>ding a<u>ppoint</u>ment <u>snow</u>ball <u>at</u>mosphere <u>no</u>where <u>work</u> it <u>out</u> <u>turn</u> it <u>down</u>

Additional review task

Unit 15	railway, station, Mr Grey, waiting, train, late, ages, eight eighteen, Baker, afraid, made, mistake, timetable, changed, April, May, today, say
Unit 16	Heidi, Caroline, Nigel, typing, smiling, Hi, nice, silence, like, iced, ninety-nine, type, mind, Friday, bike, riding, sometimes, mobile, Riley, five, library, nineteen, High, bye, tonight, drive, climbing, Miles, right, behind, spider
Unit 17	Joyce Royal, Rolls Royce, noisy, employed, boy, Roy Coyne, noise, annoying, oil, pointing, boiling, spoilt, destroyed, disappointing,voice, toy, appointment
Unit 18	mouse, house, shouting, loudly, found, ow, down , frown, brown , round, around, lounge, ground, couch, now, out, how, upside down, somehow, town, Mrs Brown
	Note: our, ours are also pronounced /aː/, /aːz/.

Unit 19   snow, October, Joe Jones, woke, ago, hello, oh, Joanna, window, no, closed, going, go, don't, over, joking, OK, coat, snowball, throw, nose

Unit 20   bearded, mountaineer, Mr Lear, Austria, beer, here, dear, idea, year, atmosphere, clear, windier, beard, nearly, disappeared, hear, cheers

Unit 21   pair, hairclips, Claire, they're, carefully, everywhere, nowhere, anywhere, upstairs, downstairs, there, square, Mary, wearing, hair, where's, chair.

Section B Consonants

Making English sounds

1	1 unv.	2 unv.	3 v.	4 unv.
	5 v.	6 unv.	7 v.	8 v.
	9 unv.	10 v.	11 unv.	

2   1 d   2 i   3 l   4 a   5 c   6 k   7 e   8 g   9 b   10 h   11 j   12 f

3   1 b   2 c   3 a   4 f   5 d   6 g   7 e

UNIT 23 /p/ pen

3c   2 pocket   3 potato   4 pepper   5 past   6 policeman
b stop   c cup   d help   e dropped   f upstairs

4a
a <u>p</u>in	a <u>p</u>encil	a paper <u>p</u>late
a <u>p</u>en	a <u>p</u>ostcard	a <u>pep</u>per pot
a <u>p</u>ear	a <u>p</u>icture	a <u>p</u>lastic <u>sp</u>ider
some <u>s</u>oap	a <u>c</u>arpet	a pi<u>a</u>no
a <u>p</u>ipe	a <u>pupp</u>y	an ex<u>pen</u>sive <u>p</u>resent for <u>P</u>oppy
a <u>sp</u>oon	an <u>a</u>pple	

5   The sound /p/ is written with the letters 'p' (paper, shop) or 'pp' (happy, shopping).

UNIT 24 /b/ baby

2b   Pair 2:   1, 1, 2, 1, 2
       Pair 3:   1, 1, 2, 2, 2
       Pair 4:   2, 2, 1, 1, 2
       Pair 5:   1, 2, 1, 1, 2
       Pair 6:   1, 2, 2, 1, 2

2d   1 (1)   2 (1)   3 (1)   4 (2)   5 (2)

2e   Pair 1: It's a <u>useful</u> <u>p</u>in./It's a <u>useful</u> <u>b</u>in.
       Pair 2: <u>P</u>en, please!/<u>B</u>en, please!
       Pair 3: <u>Look</u> at the <u>y</u>ellow <u>p</u>ear./<u>Look</u> at the <u>y</u>ellow <u>b</u>ear.
       Pair 4: It's an <u>old</u> <u>c</u>ap./It's an <u>old</u> <u>c</u>ab.
       Pair 5: What a <u>lively</u> <u>p</u>up!/What a <u>lively</u> <u>p</u>ub!
       Pair 6: Do you <u>like</u> <u>P</u>oppy?/Do you <u>like</u> <u>B</u>obby?

2f   1 b – That's a very small bin.
       2 a – My friend's name is Poppy.
       3 a – That pup is very noisy.
       4 a – It's a pig house.
       5 b – Put it on the horse's back.
       6 a – What a lovely peach!

3c	Bob job pub cab proverb

4b

1 handbag	2 football	3 ping pong ball	4 shopping bag
5 hairbrush	6 paintbrush	7 postcard	8 birthday card
9 policeman	10 postman		

4c

shopkeeper	pet shop,	hip pocket	blood bank
blackboard	beach ball	bookshop	bus stop
bathrobe	backpack	baseball	peppermint

5   The sound /b/ is written with the letters 'b' (cab) or 'bb' (cabbie).

UNIT 25 /t/ table

3a   travel agent (LQ)   twenty-two (QLL)   tonight (LQ)   student (LQ)
important (LQ)   department store (QQL)   tomatoes (LL)   toilet (LQ)
to (L)   skirts (Q)   basement (Q)   telephone (L)   cricket bat (QQ)
exactly (Q)   cafeteria (L)   tomatoes (LL)   fruit (Q)   tell (L)
top (L)   Thai (L)   time (L)   next (Q)

3b   2 Thai   3 tomatoes   4 tell   5 top   6 telephone   7 time

b fruit   c next   d basement   e restaurant   f cricket bat   g exactly

4c   1 Which floor is the <u>rest</u>aurant on?   new
2 <u>Which</u> floor is the restaurant?   old
3 <u>What's</u> on the next floor?   old
4 Where can I buy a <u>hat</u>?   new
5 <u>Where's</u> the sport's department?   old
6 <u>Which</u> floor is the toilet?   old
7 Where's the <u>trav</u>el agent's?   new
8 <u>Where's</u> the supermarket?   old

5   The sound /t/ is written with the letters 't' (sit) or 'tt' (sitting).
Other spelling: 'th' (Thai).

UNIT 26 /d/ door

2b   Pair 2:   1, 1, 2, 1, 2
Pair 3:   2, 2, 2, 1, 1
Pair 4:   1, 2, 1, 2, 2
Pair 5:   2, 2, 1, 1, 2
Pair 6:   2, 1, 2, 2, 1

2d   1 (2)   2 (1)   3 (2)   4 (1)   5 (2)   6 (1)

2e   Pair 1: You <u>too</u>?/You <u>do</u>?
Pair 2: You <u>sent</u> the <u>e</u>mails?/You <u>send</u> the <u>e</u>mails?
Pair 3: Is the <u>red cart</u> hers?/Is the <u>red card</u> hers?
Pair 4: Can he <u>write</u> well?/Can he <u>ride</u> well?
Pair 5: Does this <u>train</u> smell?/Does this <u>drain</u> smell?
Pair 6: Is there a <u>trunk</u> outside?/Is there a <u>drunk</u> outside?

2f	1 b – I don't like riding.
	2 a – That's a nice cart.
	3 a – He bought a bat, racquet and some balls.
	4 b – I send all the parcels by air mail.
	5 a – That's the worst sight.
	6 b – I want to dry this shirt
3a	The sound /d/ is louder here before a vowel.

nobody (L)   darling (L)   bad (Q)   cards (Q)   Daisy (L)
date (L)   played (Q)   dancing (L)   listened (Q)   don't (L)
phoned (Q)   tried (Q)   today (L)   rained (Q)

3b	2 darling 3 date 4 nobody 5 today 6 don't 7 dancing
	b bad c phoned d played e cards f listened g tried
5	The sound /d/ is written with the letters 'd' (day) or 'dd' (midday).

UNIT 27 /k/ key

2c	They are all statements. The intonation goes down. The first four sentences have an adjective and a noun. The most important word for the speaker's meaning is the last one.

It's a <u>hairy</u> <u>coat</u>.

He's got a <u>lovely</u> <u>curl</u>.

It's a <u>brilliant</u> <u>class</u>.

She's got a <u>strong</u> <u>back</u>.

It's <u>crowing</u>.

3a	/k/ is louder before a vowel and the two words join together.

1 /ks/   2 /kt/   3 /kw/   4 /kl/   5 /kr/

milk (Q)   cuckoo (LL)   like (Q)   next (Q)   Kate (L)   fork (Q)
make (Q)   American (L)   carved (L)   call (L)   coffee (L)
plastic (Q)   course (L)   cream (L)

3b	2 Call 3 Kate 4 cream 5 American 6 carved 7 course
	8 Cuckoo
	b milk c make d fork e next f plastic
4b	1 It's an electric cuckoo clock.
	2 It's a plastic key ring.
	3 It's a dirty egg whisk.
	4 It's a dirty cola bottle.
	5 It's an expensive cream cake.
	6 It's a comfortable car coat.
	7 It's a black address book.

5   The sound /k/ is written with the letters 'k' (ask), 'ke' (like), 'ck' (back), 'c' (can), 'qu' (question), 'x' (taxi).

Other spelling: 'sch' (school).

UNIT 28 /g/ girl

2b   Pair 2:   1, 2, 2, 1, 2

           Pair 3:   2, 2, 2, 1, 1

           Pair 4:   1, 1, 2, 2, 2

           Pair 5:   1, 2, 1, 2, 1

2d   1 (2)   2 (1)   3 (2)   4 (1)   5 (1)

2e   Pair 1: <u>It's</u> a <u>hairy coat</u>./<u>It's</u> a <u>hairy goat</u>.

           Pair 2: He's got a <u>lovely curl</u>./He's got a <u>lovely girl</u>.

           Pair 3: It's a <u>brilliant class</u>!/It's a <u>brilliant glass</u>!

           Pair 4: She's got a <u>strong back</u>./She's got a <u>strong bag</u>.

           Pair 5: It's <u>crowing</u>./It's <u>growing</u>.

2f   1 b – That man looks like a gold fish.

           2 a – There's a fly on your back.

           3 a – My grandmother bought a Dutch clock.

           4 a – What a beautiful curl!

           5 b – There's a green frog in the garden.

           6 b – The detective was looking for a good glue.

3a   The sound /g/ is louder before a vowel.

           computer   postcard   weekend   catch   cut   camp   couple
           Carol   Craig

3c   2 Glasgow, beginning, August   3 Carol, catch, gossip

           4 computer, games, girls   5 guess, weekend

           6 postcard, Portugal   7 Greece, camp, garden

           8 cut, grass

4   1 /gz/   2 /gl/   3 /gr/

5   The sound /g/ is written with the letters 'g' (big) or 'gg' (bigger).

UNIT 29 REVIEW

1   1 tore   2 Bill   3 pay   4 key   5 do

2   1 strong, retry, distrust, entrance, electric

      2 enclosed, class, clothes, chocolate, quickly

      3 appreciate, impressive, probably, present, prawn

3   1 emptied   2 filled   3 combed   4 pushed   5 shouted

4   <u>tele</u>phone   re<u>mem</u>ber   cafe<u>te</u>ria   pho<u>tog</u>rapher's   a po<u>lice</u>man
        a <u>post</u>card   a paper <u>plate</u>   A<u>mer</u>ican   <u>some</u>body   a green <u>coffee</u> cup

Additional review task

Unit 23   passports, please, Tupman, airport, plane, Paris, Poppy, stupid, put, pocket, pen, pencil, pipe, postcard, envelope, stamp, pin, stop, perhaps, plastic, newspaper, apple, pear, plastic, cup, spoon, paper, plates, piece, potato pie, pepper pot, pulling, Peter, people, impatient, help, dropped, past, upstairs, policeman

Unit 24   birthday, Barbara, Bob, somebody, blouse, beautiful, blue, butterflies, big, black, buttons, Ruby, buy, brother, book, birds, remember, terribly, been, busy, job, pub, cab, cabbie, about, but, remember, proverb, better

Unit 25   department store, customer, assistant, want, to, skirt, skirts, upstairs, next, get, Thai, cafeteria, first, fruit, next, counter, left, tins, tomatoes, try, supermarket, basement, tell, travel, agent's, it's, right, restaurant, cricket, bat, get, sports, equipment, take, lift, department, top, telephone, twelfth, opposite, photographer's, what's, time, exactly, twenty-two, minutes, ten

Unit 26   damaged, Daisy, David, darling, did, do, yesterday, date, didn't, rained, day, and, had, bad, cold, decided, phoned, nobody, answered, repaired, today, don't, Donald, Dianne, dancing, didn't, stayed, played, cards, Jordan, listened, radio, studied, told, tried

Unit 27   cuckoo, clock, like, cream, coffee, Kate Clark, call, Karen Cook, OK, thanks, milk, cream cakes, thank, make, take, cake fork, excuse, next, bookshelf, electric, American, plastic, carved, exactly, six, o'clock, quiet, course, look, fantastic, exciting, clever

Unit 28   Craig, Maggie, Greg, Glasgow, beginning, August, giggling, gossip, got together, games, girls, guess, Portugal, going, go, Greece, garden, grateful, grass

UNIT 30 /s/ sun

2c   That <u>S</u>ue was a<u>ma</u>zing.

It's pro<u>noun</u>ced /<u>si:</u>/.

<u>Sip</u> it <u>slow</u>ly.

I <u>heard</u> a <u>bus</u>.

I want the <u>big piece</u>.

<u>What's</u> the <u>price</u>?

4b   2 In winter let's_ski_in the snow.

3 Sam takes_such good photographs.

4 Sarah laughs_silently.

5 In summer let's_sail into the sunset.

6 Sue likes_some cats.

7 Lucas_sends lots of text messages.

8 Is Chris_such a cheapskate?

5   The sound /s/ is written with the letters 's' (bus), 'ss' (boss), 'x' (box), 'ce' (price).

UNIT 31 /z/ zoo

2b

Pair 2:   1, 2, 2, 2, 1

Pair 3:   2, 2, 1, 2, 1

Pair 4:   2, 1, 2, 1, 2

Pair 5:   1, 1, 2, 2, 2

Pair 6:   1, 2, 1, 2, 1

2d   1 (1)   2 (1)   3 (2)   4 (2)   5 (1)   6 (2)

2f   1 b – I heard a buzz.

2 a – Sip it slowly.

3 a – What's the price?

4 b – I only have a few pens.

5 b – 'Help, please!' he shouted.

6 a – He lived in a town called Sackville.

3a   1 /s/ /z/   2 /s/ /z/   3 /s/ /z/   4 /s/ /z/   5 /s/ /z/   6 /s/ /z/   7 /z/ /s/

8 /s/ /z/   9 /s/ /s/   10 /z/ /z/

4b   2 j (other possible answers are d and k)   3 k   4 h   5 g   6 i   7 l

8 a   9 d   10 c   11 b   12 e

5   The sound /z/ is written with the letters 'z' (zoo), 's' (dogs), 'x' (example).

UNIT 32 /ʃ/ shoe

2b

Pair 2:   1, 1, 2, 1, 2

Pair 3:   1, 2, 2, 1, 1

Pair 4:   1, 1, 1, 2, 1

Pair 5:   1, 2, 2, 1, 2

Pair 6:   2, 2, 1, 2, 1

2d   1 (2)   2 (2)   3 (1)   4 (2)   5 (1)   6 (1)

2e

Pair 1: C is third./She is third.

Pair 2: I like Sue's./I like shoes.

Pair 3: Sip it carefully./Ship it carefully.

Pair 4: Look at that ass./Look at that ash.

Pair 5: He won't sew it./He won't show it.

Pair 6: 'Puss!' he shouted./'Push!' he shouted.

2f   1 a – Those are Sue's.

2 b – Look at that dirty ash.

3 a – 'Puss!' he shouted.

4 b – The mice lived in a shack.

5 a – I'm going to buy some new seats.

6 a – Tom should save.

3c	1 a, b, c, d, j
	2 h
	3 e, f, g
	4 i
4b	2 Danish_ships
	3 Scottish_sheep
	4 Swedish_shampoo
	5 French_champagne
	6 Irish_sheets
	7 Polish_shirts
	8 Finnish_shorts
	9 Turkish_sugar
	10 Spanish_shoes
5	The sound /ʃ/ is written with the letters 'sh' (shop).
	Other spelling: 'ch' (champagne).

UNIT 33 /ʒ/ television

2c	She also has a casual job doing sports massage.
	She does sports massage occasionally, not every day.
	Yesterday Michelle saw a collision outside the shoe shop.
	She was measuring a shoe for a customer.
	An ambulance took two injured people to casualty.
5	The sound /ʒ/ is written with the letter 's' (usual, decision).
	Other spelling: 'g' (garage).

UNIT 34 /tʃ/ chip

2b	Pair 2: 1, 1, 2, 2, 1
	Pair 3: 2, 2, 2, 1, 1
	Pair 4: 2, 1, 2, 1, 2
	Pair 5: 1, 1, 1, 2, 2
	Pair 6: 2, 1, 2, 2, 1
2d	1 (1) 2 (2) 3 (1) 4 (1) 5 (2) 6 (2)
2e	Pair 1: We like ships./We like chips.
	Pair 2: This is a sheep farm./This is a cheap farm.
	Pair 3: It's a sherry trifle./It's a cherry trifle.
	Pair 4: I'll buy this shop./I'll buy this chop.
	Pair 5: I couldn't cash it./I couldn't catch it.
	Pair 6: He's washing the television./He's watching the television.

2f	1 b – That's a very expensive chop.
	2 b – Would you like cherry or orange?
	3 a – He's washing the television.
	4 a – There are too many ships here.
	5 a – I fell down and cut my shin.
	6 b – I want to choose, please.

3c (2) ... <u>mor</u> ... <u>Church</u>

(5) ... <u>mor</u> ... <u>Charles</u> ... <u>chops</u> ... <u>chil</u> ... <u>lunch</u>

(2) <u>Chump</u> ... <u>shoul</u>

(4) ... <u>four</u> ... <u>shou</u> ... <u>small</u> ... <u>chick</u>

(3) ... <u>like</u> ... <u>choose</u> ... <u>chick</u>

(2) <u>Which</u> ... <u>chea</u>

(4) <u>This</u> ... <u>chea</u> ... <u>lic</u> ... <u>chick</u>

(8) <u>How</u> ... <u>much</u> ... <u>that</u> ... <u>have</u> ... <u>cash</u> ... <u>pay</u> ... <u>cred</u> ... <u>card</u>

(2) ... <u>course</u> ... <u>Church</u>

5 The sound /tʃ/ is written with the letters 'ch' (church).

Other spelling: 'tch' (kitchen), 't' (question).

UNIT 35 /dʒ/ January

2b Pair 2: 1, 1, 2, 2, 2

Pair 3: 1, 2, 2, 2, 1

Pair 4: 2, 1, 2, 1, 1

Pair 5: 2, 2, 1, 2, 1

Pair 6: 1, 1, 2, 1, 2

2d 1 (2)   2 (1)   3 (2)   4 (1)   5 (1)   6 (2)

2e Pair 1: It's a <u>cheap</u> type of car./It's a <u>jeep</u> type of car.

Pair 2: Are you <u>choking</u>?/Are you <u>joking</u>?

Pair 3: A land full of <u>riches</u>./A land full of <u>ridges</u>.

Pair 4: Do you like <u>cherries</u>?/Do you like <u>Jerry's</u>?

Pair 5: I want a <u>larch</u> tree./I want a <u>large</u> tree.

Pair 6: Do I write '<u>H</u>' here?/Do I write <u>age</u> here?

2f 1 a – I don't want you to choke.

2 b – She planted a large tree in the garden.

3 a – I don't like those cheap kinds of cars.

4 b – This is my new watch, Jane.

5 a – It's chilly in the garden.

6 b – The crowed jeered when he finished speaking.

3b	1 village	2 January	3 dangerously	4 manager
	5 bridge	6 passenger	7 damaged	8 jokes

4b	Across: 1 church 2 jam 3 jar 4 choc 5 chess 6 tor 7 such
	Down: 1 chicken 2 Jock's 3 just 4 reach 5 ok 6 larger
5	The sound /dʒ/ is written with the letters 'j' (joke), ge (age), 'dge' (edge).

UNIT 36 REVIEW

1	1 zoo 2 jam 3 so 4 she 5 chap
2	1 chance, inside, answer, instructions (second and third letters but not the last two letters), ancestors
	2 range, sponge, stranger, exchange, lounge
	3 intonation, electrician, expansion, Russian, fashion
3	1 kisses 2 sings 3 bicycles 4 Luke's 5 books
4	1 ⤴ 2 ⤵ 3 ⤵ 4 ⤴ 5 ⤴⤴ 6 ⤵ 7 ⤵ 8 ⤴ 9 ⤴ 10 ⤵

Additional review task

Unit 30	it's, expensive, let's, seaside, Saturday, sweetie, yes, sailing, water-skiing, that's exciting, just, sit, sun, swimming, instead, stay, Six Star, spend, Sunday, sensible, Sue, sleep, outside, sand, smallest, possible, sum, Sam Smith, such, cheapskate
Unit 31	Zena, Susan, workers, busy, parcels, Susan's, smells, Lazarus, something's, does, says, contains, isn't, animals, noise, is, buzzing, buzzes, Zzzzzzzzzzzzzzzzz, those, bees, parcels, surprising, amazing, zoo
Unit 32	special, washing, machine, Mrs Marsh, Mr Shaw, shop, machines, Swedish, English, show, washes, shall, demonstration, sheets, shirts, shut , push, shouldn't, shake, should, finished, shrunk, wish, sure
Unit 33	television, treasure, unusual, collision, casual, Asia, measure, garage, pleasure
Unit 34	butcher's, Charles Cheshire, cheerful, charming, butcher, Mrs Church, chops, children's, lunch, chump, chicken, choose, which, cheaper, cheapest, much
Unit 35	dangerous, bridge, Jerry, John, Just, village, jeeps, January, George, larger, dangerously, ginger-haired, manager, agency, jokes, injured, edge, passenger, damaged, jail

UNIT 37 /f/ fan

Minimal pairs A

2b	Pair 2: 1, 1, 2, 2, 2
	Pair 3: 2, 1, 1, 2, 1
	Pair 4: 1, 1, 2, 1, 2
	Pair 5: 2, 2, 2, 1, 1
	Pair 6: 1, 1, 2, 1, 2
2d	1 (1) 2 (2) 3 (2) 4 (2) 5 (1) 6 (1)

2e Pair 1: It's a <u>sharp</u> <u>pin</u>./It's a <u>sharp</u> <u>fin</u>.

Pair 2: <u>Peel</u> this <u>orange</u>./<u>Feel</u> this <u>orange</u>.

Pair 3: There's <u>no</u> <u>pork</u> here./There's <u>no</u> <u>fork</u> here.

Pair 4: The <u>sign</u> said '<u>Pull</u>'./The <u>sign</u> said '<u>Full</u>'.

Pair 5: <u>Snip</u> these <u>flowers</u>./<u>Sniff</u> these <u>flowers</u>.

Pair 6: He <u>showed</u> me his <u>palm</u>./He <u>showed</u> me his <u>farm</u>.

Minimal pairs B

2b Pair 2: 2, 1, 2, 1, 2

Pair 3: 1, 1, 2, 2, 1

Pair 4: 2, 2, 1, 2, 1

Pair 5: 1, 1, 2, 1, 1

Pair 6: 1, 2, 2, 1, 2

2d 1 (1)   2 (2)   3 (2)   4 (1)   5 (2)   6 (1)

2e Pair 1: <u>Hold</u> this <u>paper</u>./<u>Fold</u> this <u>paper</u>.

Pair 2: I like <u>heat</u> on the <u>back</u>./I like <u>feet</u> on the <u>back</u>.

Pair 3: That <u>sign</u> said '<u>Hill</u>'./That <u>sign</u> said '<u>Fill</u>'.

Pair 4: This <u>heel's</u> <u>different</u>./This <u>feels</u> <u>different</u>.

Pair 5: This is <u>honey</u>./This is <u>funny</u>.

Pair 6: It's <u>got</u> a little <u>hole</u>./It's <u>got</u> a little <u>foal</u>.

2f 1 b – That's a long fin.

2 a – Peel this potato, please.

3 b – She walked round the garden sniffing flowers.

4 b – Please feel this shoe.

5 a – We don't harm these animals.

6 b – That's a very big hole.

3b b 3   c 5   d 2   e 4   f 1

4 1 f   2 a   3 g   4 e   5 d   6 b   7 c

5 The sound /f/ is written with the letters 'f' (fun) or 'ff' (fluffy).

Other spelling: 'ph' (photo), 'fe' (wife).

UNIT 38 /v/ van

Minimal pairs A

2b Pair 2: 2, 2, 1, 2, 1

Pair 3: 1, 1, 1, 2, 2

Pair 4: 1, 2, 1, 2, 1

Pair 5: 2, 2, 1, 1, 2

Pair 6: 1, 2, 1, 1, 2

2d 1 (2)   2 (1)   3 (1)   4 (2)   5 (2)   6 (1)

2e
　　　　Pair 1: <u>Safe</u> here?/<u>Save</u> here?

　　　　Pair 2: <u>Fine</u> in the garden?/<u>Vine</u> in the garden?

　　　　Pair 3: It's a <u>fail</u>?/It's a <u>veil</u>?

　　　　Pair 4: This <u>room</u> has a <u>few</u>?/This <u>room</u> has a <u>view</u>?

　　　　Pair 5: They <u>need</u> a <u>fast</u> ship?/They <u>need</u> a <u>vast</u> ship?

　　　　Pair 6: <u>Ferry</u> late?/<u>Very</u> late?

Minimal pairs B

2b
　　　　Pair 2:　1, 1, 1, 1, 2

　　　　Pair 3:　2, 1, 2, 1, 2

　　　　Pair 4:　1, 2, 2, 1, 2

　　　　Pair 5:　2, 2, 1, 2, 1

　　　　Pair 6:　1, 1, 1, 2, 2

2d
　　　　1 (2)　　2 (2)　　3 (1)　　4 (1)　　5 (1)　　6 (2)

2e
　　　　Pair 1: They're <u>good</u> <u>bets</u>./They're <u>good</u> <u>vets</u>.

　　　　Pair 2: He <u>wore</u> his <u>best</u>./He <u>wore</u> his <u>vest</u>.

　　　　Pair 3: Can they <u>lift</u> that <u>ban</u>?/Can they <u>lift</u> that <u>van</u>?

　　　　Pair 4: We <u>need</u> more <u>bolts</u>./We <u>need</u> more <u>volts</u>.

　　　　Pair 5: <u>Jones</u> won the <u>boat</u>./<u>Jones</u> won the <u>vote</u>.

　　　　Pair 6: It's a <u>berry</u> red <u>colour</u>./It's a <u>very</u> red <u>colour</u>.

2f
　　　　1 a – We always lift carefully.

　　　　2 b – Halve the apple.

　　　　3 a – New York is a fast city.

　　　　4 a – We've got the boat.

　　　　5 a – There should be fifty bolts.

　　　　6 a – Is safe an adjective or a verb?

4a
　　　　at a <u>vill</u>age./in a <u>vall</u>ey./driving a <u>van</u>./of No<u>vem</u>ber./very <u>cold</u>./of the <u>pho</u>tograph.

4b
　　　　1 <u>van</u> ... The <u>far</u>mer.　　　　2 <u>vine</u> .... <u>Four</u>.

　　　　3 <u>vill</u>agers ... In the <u>vall</u>ey.　　4 a<u>rri</u>ving ... A<u>rri</u>ving.

　　　　5 <u>fir</u> tree .... A <u>vine</u>.　　　　6 <u>five</u> fir trees? ... <u>Five</u>.

5
　　　　The sound /v/ is written with the letter 'v' (van).

　　　　Other spellings: 've' (have), 'f' (of).

UNIT 39 /w/ window

2b	Pair 2: 1, 2, 2, 2, 1
	Pair 3: 2, 2, 1, 1, 2
	Pair 4: 1, 2, 1, 2, 1
	Pair 5: 2, 2, 1, 1, 1
2d	1 (2) 2 (1) 3 (2) 4 (1) 5 (2) 6 (1)
2e	Pair 1: <u>V</u> didn't come before <u>U</u>./<u>We</u> didn't come before <u>you</u>.
	Pair 2: <u>That's</u> the <u>vest</u>./<u>That's</u> the <u>west</u>.
	Pair 3: The <u>dog's</u> <u>vet</u>./The <u>dog's</u> <u>wet</u>.
	Pair 4: This is my <u>best</u> <u>vine</u>./This is my <u>best</u> <u>wine</u>.
	Pair 5: It's a <u>blue</u> <u>veil</u>./It's a <u>blue</u> <u>whale</u>.
2f	1 a – What a beautiful vine!
	2 b – He wrote 'we' at the beginning of the sentence.
	3 a – Please change this veal.
	4 b – This book is worse.
	5 b – We were surprised to see some whales in the water.
	6 a – Give him the vet food.
3c	(4) <u>Oh</u> ... <u>Will</u> ... <u>Well</u> ... <u>happ</u>
	(4) ... <u>went</u> ... <u>love</u> ... <u>walk</u> ... <u>woods</u> ...
	(6) <u>Oh</u> ... <u>wet</u> ... <u>Was</u> ... <u>ver</u> ... <u>wet</u> ... <u>Wednes</u> ...
	(6) ... <u>was</u> ... <u>cold</u> ... <u>wet</u> ... <u>wear</u> ... <u>ver</u> ... <u>clothes</u>
	(4) ... <u>walked</u> ... <u>quick</u> ... <u>keep</u> ... <u>warm</u>
	(6) ... <u>that</u> ... <u>woods</u> ... <u>next</u> ... <u>rail</u> ... <u>not</u> ... <u>quiet</u> ...
	(6) <u>Yes</u> ... <u>fur</u> ... <u>way</u> ... <u>rail</u> ... <u>ver</u> ... <u>quiet</u>
	(4) ... <u>wild</u> ... <u>squir</u> ... <u>ev</u> ... <u>coun</u>
	(2) <u>twen</u> ... <u>squirr</u>
	(5) ... <u>twen</u> ... <u>squirr</u> ... <u>what</u> ... <u>do</u> ... <u>lunch</u>
	(2) ... <u>pic</u> ... <u>squirr</u>
	(5) ... <u>too</u> ... <u>wet</u> ... <u>Af</u> ... <u>went</u> ... <u>res</u> ...
	(6) <u>twelve</u> ... <u>clock</u> ... <u>wal</u> ... <u>cake</u> ... <u>sweet</u> ... <u>wine</u> ...
	(1) <u>won</u> ...
	(3) <u>So</u> ... <u>Will</u> ... <u>Well</u> ...
	(1) <u>Well</u> ...
4a	1 d 2 a 3 h 4 b 5 c 6 g 7 e 8 f
4b	3 <u>Vic</u>tor (new information) 4 <u>Why</u> (old information)
	5 <u>Vic</u>tor (new information) 6 <u>Where</u> (old information).

4c

1 A: Hello ʷ everybody. How ʷ are you?

B: Hello ʷ Emma. Oh ʷ I'm OK now ʷ I had the flu ʷ and felt terrible.

2 A: Who ʷ isn't here?

B: Joe ʷ isn't. A few ʷ others aren't.

3 A: Is Sue ʷ OK? Anybody know ʷ about Sue?

B: I don't know ʷ if Sue ʷ is off with the flu ʷ as well.

4 A: How do ʷ I get to ʷ a garage?

B: You go ʷ under a bridge and through ʷ a village.

5 A: Do you ʷ understand?

B: No ʷ I don't really.

6 A: Oh ʷ it's so ʷ unfair! You ʷ always get two ʷ ice creams.

B: Grow ʷ up!

5

The sound /w/ is usually written with the letter 'w' (well).

Other spellings: 'wh' (what), 'qu' (quick), 'o' (one).

UNIT 40 /j/ yellow

2b

Pair 2: 1, 1, 2, 1, 2

Pair 3: 1, 1, 1, 2, 2

Pair 4: 2, 2, 1, 2, 1

Pair 5: 2, 1, 2, 1, 2

2d

1 (1)   2 (1)   3 (2)   4 (2)   5 (2)

2e

Pair 1: That's a <u>wonderful joke</u>./That's a <u>wonderful yolk</u>.

Pair 2: There's <u>no juice</u>./There's <u>no use</u>.

Pair 3: <u>Would</u> you like <u>jam</u>?/<u>Would</u> you like <u>yam</u>?

Pair 4: <u>Jess</u>, I <u>love</u> you./<u>Yes</u>, I <u>love</u> you.

Pair 5: He <u>sang</u> over the <u>jeers</u>./He <u>sang</u> over the <u>years</u>.

2f

1 b – That's a bad yolk.

2 a – Let's eat jam.

3 a – Jess, let's go to the cinema.

4 b – These were terrible years for him.

5 a – What juice is that?

6 a – He hasn't flown by jet.

3b

1 university   2 music   3 tuba   4 knew   5 New   6 tubes
7 Europe   8 stupid

4a

1 b   2 a   3 d   4 e   5 c

4b

1 A: Let's play ʲ a card game.

B: OK ʲ I'll deal.

2 A: That boy ʲ is very rude.

B: Yes. He ʲ ought to be more polite.

3 A: Are those printouts of my ʲ emails?

B: Yes, they ʲ are.

4 A: He‿always feels sad when he's alone.
   B: I‿understand. I‿often do too.

5 A: Say‿it again, please.
   B: I said today‿is my‿eightieth birthday.

6 A: They‿all had a good cry‿at the funeral.
   B: There wasn't a dry‿eye‿in the church.

5   The sound /j/ is written with the letters 'y' (yes) or 'u' (student).
   Other spelling 'ew' (new).

UNIT 41 /h/ hat

2b   Pair 2:   1, 2, 2, 1, 1

         Pair 3:   2, 1, 1, 2, 1

         Pair 4:   1, 1, 2, 2, 2

         Pair 5:   2, 1, 2, 1, 2

         Pair 6:   2, 2, 1, 1, 2

2d   1 (1)   2 (2)   3 (2)   4 (1)   5 (2)   6 (1)

2f   1 a – I don't like these eels.

         2 a – He hurt his foot, leg and arm.

         3 b – These children have got beautiful high brows.

         4 b – Do you like heart?

         5 b – 'How!' he shouted loudly.

         6 a – What lovely air!

3c   2 how/injured   3 hospital/ambulance   4 hit/ice-cream
   5 having/operation   6 Helena/unhappy   7 he/all

4b   1 Who found (h)im?

         2 What's (h)is name? Harry?

         3 Who else (h)ave you spoken to? She's (h)is wife?

         4 What's (h)er phone number? She hasn't a phone? (H)as she got a mobile?

         5 What (h)as the neighbour said about (h)im?

         6 What (h)ad (h)e eaten?

5   The sound /h/ is written with the letter 'h' (hill).
   Other spelling: 'who' (who).

UNIT 42 /θ/ thin

Minimal pairs A

2b   Pair 2:   1, 1, 2, 2, 1

         Pair 3:   1, 2, 2, 2, 1

         Pair 4:   2, 2, 1, 2, 1

         Pair 5:   2, 2, 2, 1, 1

2d   1 (2)   2 (1)   3 (2)   4 (1)   5 (1)   6 (2)

2e   Pair 1: What a <u>sweet</u> little <u>mouse</u>!/What a <u>sweet</u> little <u>mouth</u>!

              Pair 2: Is this <u>sum</u> O<u>K</u>?/Is this <u>thumb</u> O<u>K</u>?

              Pair 3: It's very <u>sick</u>./It's very <u>thick</u>.

              Pair 4: He's <u>sin</u>king./He's <u>thin</u>king.

              Pair 5: There's a <u>moun</u>tain <u>pass</u>./There's a <u>moun</u>tain <u>path</u>.

Minimal pairs B

2b   Pair 2:   1, 1, 2, 2, 1

              Pair 3:   1, 1, 1, 2, 1

2d   1 (2)   2 (1)   3 (1)   4 (2)

2e   Pair 1: He's got a <u>first</u>./He's got a <u>thirst</u>.

              Pair 2: A <u>fin</u> <u>soup</u>, please./A <u>thin</u> <u>soup</u>, please.

              Pair 3: I'd like a <u>half</u>./I'd like a <u>hearth</u>.

Minimal pairs C

2b   Pair 2:   1, 2, 2, 1, 2

              Pair 3:   1, 1, 2, 2, 1

2d   1 (2)   2 (2)   3 (2)   4 (1)

2e   That's a big <u>tree</u>./That's a big <u>three</u>.

              The <u>Pres</u>ident sends his <u>tanks</u>./The <u>Pres</u>ident sends his <u>thanks</u>.

              The <u>knife</u> was hidden in a <u>sheet</u>./The <u>knife</u> was hidden in a <u>sheath</u>.

2f   1 a – I always sink in the bath.

              2 b – He's got a big mouth.

              3 a – Don't burn it. That saucepan is only tin.

              4 b – The teacher thought quickly.

              5 a – Look at that moss on that stone.

              6 a – The two men fought very hard.

3c   2 month   3 three   4 mathematician   5 Roth's   6 I

4b   2 c   3 e   4 a   5 g   6 d   7 f

5   The sound /θ/ is written with the letters 'th' (think).

UNIT 43 /ð/ the feather

Minimal pairs A

2b   Pair 2:   1, 1, 1, 2, 2

              Pair 3:   1, 2, 1, 2, 1

              Pair 4:   2, 2, 1, 1, 2

              Pair 5:   2, 1, 1, 2, 2

2d   1 (1)   2 (2)   3 (2)   4 (1)   5 (2)

2e	Pair 1: <u>Smith</u> is <u>bigger</u>, Dan <u>Jones</u>./<u>Smith</u> is <u>bigger</u> than <u>Jones</u>.
	Pair 2: <u>Day</u> <u>arrived</u>./<u>They</u> <u>arrived</u>.
	Pair 3: <u>Jim</u> <u>dares</u> his <u>friend</u>./<u>Jim</u> <u>there's</u> his <u>friend</u>.
	Pair 4: <u>Doze</u> after <u>lunch</u>./<u>Those</u> after <u>lunch</u>.
	Pair 5: I <u>don't</u> know her <u>sister</u>, <u>Ida</u>./I <u>don't</u> know her <u>sister</u> <u>either</u>.

Minimal pairs B

2b	Pair 2: 2, 1, 1, 2, 1
	Pair 3: 1, 1, 2, 2, 2
	Pair 4: 2, 2, 1, 1, 2
2d	1 (1) 2 (2) 3 (2) 4 (1)
2e	Pair 1: The <u>shop</u> sign said 'Closing'./The <u>shop</u> sign said 'Clothing'.
	Pair 2: <u>Breeze</u> means <u>air</u> <u>moving</u>./ <u>Breathe</u> means <u>air</u> <u>moving</u>.
	Pair 3: The <u>boos</u> echoed <u>loudly</u>./The <u>booth</u> echoed <u>loudly</u>.
	Pair 4: <u>That's</u> a large <u>size</u>./<u>That's</u> a large <u>scythe</u>.
2f	1 a – We don't like his wife, Ida.
	2 a – Day came later than in summer.
	3 a – Jim dares his friend.
	4 a – She needs a smaller size.
	5 b – Will they sea bathe?
	6 b – The booth sounded very bad.
4b	1 d 2 e 3 g 4 c 5 f 6 a 7 b
5	The sound /ð/ is written with the letters 'th' (the, this, that, these, those, they, there, their, they're, then, that, them).

UNIT 44 REVIEW

1	1 we 2 how 3 foe 4 thigh 5 this
2	1 coughed, laughed, lofty, soft, lift
	2 months, lengths, Judith's, naturopaths, tablecloths
	3 Swedish, sweeten, swum, swear, suite, swift
3	I ͜ʲasked you ͜ʷa question, Wesley.
	Oh ͜ʷI'm sorry ͜ʲI didn't hear you, Yasmin.
	You ͜ʷoften do that, and I ͜ʲalways get annoyed.
	Oh ͜ʷis that so? Why ͜ʲis that, Yasmin?
	It's just annoying! Why ͜ʲare you doing it, Wesley?
	Just to ͜ʷannoy you, Yasmin.
4	<u>va</u>lley <u>vi</u>llage beau<u>ti</u>ful <u>rail</u>way <u>Eu</u>rope per<u>haps</u> <u>hos</u>pital
	mathema<u>ti</u>cian <u>au</u>thor <u>lea</u>ther

Additional review task

Unit 37	funny, photographer, afternoon, Fred Phillips, photograph, myself, wife, Phillippa, fill, form, felt-tipped, prefer, full, front, profile, finished, sofa, comfortable, feels, fine, friendly, laugh, difficult, if, soft, beautiful, for, fifth, February, phone, office, after, five
Unit 38	view, Vander, lived, very, Victor, five, Vivienne, arrived, of, lovely, have, village, valley, love, living
Unit 39	walk, woods, William, Wednesday, Winona, well, what, we, went, wet, wasn't, Wednesday, were, wearing, warm, walked, railway, quiet, away, was, wild, squirrels, everywhere, twenty, with, afterwards, twelve, walnut, sweet, white, wine, wonderful
Unit 40	stupid, Yee, you, use, York, Young, yes, university, years, Hugh Yip, music, student, used to, yellow, beautiful, tunes, tuba, knew, news, millionaire, New York, produces, onion, stew, tubes, Europe, newspaper, yesterday
Unit 41	horrible, Hi, Holly, have, heard, happened, Helena's, husband, has, had, his, horse, how, he, he's, hospital, happen, hit, behind, house, having, unhappy, perhaps, he'll, hope
Unit 42	Catherine, Ruth, Samantha Roth, thirty, thought, thirty-three, Samantha's, birthday, Thursday, month, Roths', worth, thousand, three, author, moths, mathematician, thirsty, something, nothing, thank you
Unit 43	Miss Brothers, the, with, there, together, feathers, other, that, either, leather, another, than, smoother, rather, clothes
	Note: *with* can also be pronounced /wɪθ/.

UNIT 45 /m/ mouth

2c	The <u>mile</u> is very <u>old</u>.
	This is <u>mine</u>.
	He <u>loves</u> his <u>mummy</u>.
	I <u>want</u> a <u>comb</u>.
	He's <u>proud</u> of his <u>name</u>.
3c	2 met 3 remember 4 manners 5 come 6 make 7 maybe
	8 time 9 Mum 10 tomorrow
4c	1 ⌿ What did you say?
	2 → I'm thinking about what to say.
	3 ⌍ Yes.
	4 ⌿⌍ How nice!
	5 ⌿ What did you say?
	6 ⌍ Yes.
	7 ⌿⌍ How nice!
5	The sound /m/ is written with the letter 'm' (make).
	Other spelling: 'mm' (summer), 'mn' (autumn), 'me' (time).

UNIT 46 /n/ nose

2b	Pair 2:	1, 2, 2, 1, 2
	Pair 3:	2, 2, 1, 2, 1
	Pair 4:	1, 1, 2, 1, 2
	Pair 5:	1, 2, 1, 2, 1

2d   1 (2)   2 (2)   3 (1)   4 (2)   5 (2)

2e   Pair 1: c) oOoooO The <u>mile</u> is very <u>old</u>./The <u>Nile</u> is very <u>old</u>.

Pair 2: b) ooO This is <u>mine</u>./This is <u>nine</u>.

Pair 3: e) ooOo He loves <u>mummy</u>./He loves <u>money</u>.

Pair 4: a) oooO I want a <u>comb</u>./I want a <u>cone</u>.

Pair 5: d) oOooO He's <u>proud</u> of his <u>name</u>./He's <u>proud</u> of his <u>mane</u>.

2f   1 b – I want two cones, please.

2 b – I'll give you nine.

3 b – What a beautiful mane!

4 b – I only want sunflowers.

5 a – Please warm the children.

6 b – He loves his mummy.

3c   1 Nelson   2 Certainly   3 station   4 oven   5 garden   6 eleven
7 television   8 prison.

5   The sound /n/ is written with the letter 'n' (no).

Other spellings: 'kn' (know), 'nn' (funny), 'ne' (phone).

UNIT 47 /ŋ/ ring

Minimal pairs A

2b	Pair 2:	2, 2, 1, 1, 2
	Pair 3:	1, 2, 1, 1, 2
	Pair 4:	2, 2, 1, 1, 1
	Pair 5:	1, 1, 2, 2, 1
	Pair 6:	1, 2, 1, 2, 1

2d   1 (1)   2 (2)   3 (2)   4 (1)   5 (2)   6 (1)

2e   Pair 1: What a <u>win</u>!/What a <u>wing</u>!

Pair 2: <u>Why</u> this <u>thin</u>?/<u>Why</u> this <u>thing</u>?

Pair 3: <u>Ban</u> the <u>book</u>./<u>Bang</u> the <u>book</u>.

Pair 4: They <u>ran</u> for an <u>hour</u>./They <u>rang</u> for an <u>hour</u>.

Pair 5: She has never <u>run</u> be<u>fore</u>./She has never <u>rung</u> be<u>fore</u>.

Pair 6: Is it <u>Ron</u>?/Is it <u>wrong</u>?

Minimal pairs B

2b   Pair 2:   2, 2, 1, 1, 1

              Pair 3:   1, 1, 2, 1, 2

              Pair 4:   1, 1, 2, 1, 1

              Pair 5:   1, 1, 1, 2, 2

2d   1 (1)   2 (1)   3 (2)   4 (2)   5 (1)

2e   Pair 1: I'll <u>give</u> you a <u>wink</u>./I'll <u>give</u> you a <u>wing</u>.

              Pair 2: He's <u>sinking</u>./He's <u>singing</u>.

              Pair 3: The <u>rink</u> was a <u>perfect</u> circle./The <u>ring</u> was a <u>perfect</u> circle.

              Pair 4: What a <u>terrible</u> <u>stink</u>!/What a <u>terrible</u> <u>sting</u>!

              Pair 5: <u>Bank</u> it <u>quick</u>ly./<u>Bang</u> it <u>quick</u>ly.

2f   1 a – That's Ron.

              2 b – Somebody rang.

              3 a – Tom always sinks in the bath.

              4 b – What a beautiful wink!

              5 c – You should bang it.

              6 b – This is not the right place for sinkers.

3b   ~~evening~~ morning; ~~talking~~ singing; ~~putting~~ hanging; ~~saying~~ doing; ~~interesting~~ pink; ~~falling~~ going ; ~~whispering~~ shouting; ~~walking~~ running; ~~thinking about getting my revenge~~ sleeping

4a   1 What's Angus <u>Lang</u> doing? He's banging some nails into the <u>wall</u>.

              2 What's <u>Angus</u> doing? He's hanging some strong string on the <u>nail</u>.

              3 What's <u>Su</u>san Lang doing? She's bringing something for Angus to <u>drink</u>.

              4 What's <u>Mr</u> Lang doing? He's hanging from the <u>string</u>.

              5 What's <u>Mrs</u> Lang doing? She's ringing the <u>bell</u>.

              6 What's Duncan <u>King</u> doing? He's <u>sleeping</u>.

5   The sound /ŋ/ is written with the letters 'ng' (sing).

              Other spelling: 'n' (drink, English).

UNIT 48 /l/ letter

2b   Pair 2:   1, 2, 1, 1, 2

              Pair 3:   2, 2, 1, 2, 1

              Pair 4:   1, 2, 2, 2, 1

              Pair 5:   2, 2, 1, 2, 1

2d   1 (2)   2 (1)   3 (2)   4 (2)   5 (2)

2e   Pair 1: We need <u>no</u> tables./We need <u>low</u> tables.

              Pair 2: It's a <u>bright night</u>./It's a <u>bright light</u>.

              Pair 3: That <u>nine</u> is too <u>long</u>./That <u>line</u> is too <u>long</u>.

Pair 4: I <u>love</u> <u>J</u>enny./I <u>love</u> <u>j</u>elly.

Pair 5: That's a <u>sna</u>pping <u>noise</u>./That's a <u>sla</u>pping <u>noise</u>.

2f 1 a – Look! The moon's shining. What a lovely night!

2 a – There are no chairs here.

3 a – This shouldn't be on the bin.

4 b – It's a lot of string.

5 a – I'm wearing snow shoes.

6 b – I'm going to buy some slacks.

3c 1 early 2 o'clock 3 left 4 lamb 5 salad 6 olives 7 really
8 glass 9 slice 10 jelly

4d 1 beautiful 2 careful 3 special 4 sensible 5 gentleman
6 bicycle

5 The sound /l/ is written with the letter 'l' (like).

Other spellings: 'le' (apple), 'll' (all).

UNIT 49 /r/ rain

2b Pair 2: 2, 1, 2, 2, 1

Pair 3: 1, 2, 1, 2, 2

Pair 4: 2, 1, 1, 1, 2

Pair 5: 1, 2, 2, 1, 1

Pair 6: 2, 2, 1, 1, 1

2d 1 (1) 2 (2) 3 (1) 4 (2) 5 (1) 6 (1)

2e Pair 1: a) ooOO It's the <u>long</u> <u>road</u>./It's the <u>wrong</u> <u>road</u>.

Pair 2: c) ooO Is it <u>light</u>?/Is it <u>right</u>?

Pair 3: d) ooOO It's a <u>long</u> <u>load</u>./It's a <u>long</u> <u>road</u>.

Pair 4: f) oooOo Do you <u>like</u> <u>j</u>elly?/Do you <u>like</u> <u>J</u>erry?

Pair 5: e) oOoOo I'd <u>like</u> to <u>fly</u> it./I'd <u>like</u> to <u>fry</u> it.

Pair 6: b) OoO <u>There's</u> some <u>glass</u>./<u>There's</u> some <u>grass</u>.

2f 1 a – That sentence is long.

2 b – Susan likes Jerry.

3 a – There's some glass in the garden.

4 a – Please collect the homework.

5 b – We walked in the rain.

6 b – This is a free house.

4a 1 he's a <u>lorr</u>y driver.

2 she's a <u>wa</u>itress.

3 he's a <u>p</u>ilot.

4 she's a <u>sec</u>retary

5 she's a <u>lib</u>rarian.

5   The sound /r/ is written with the letter 'r' (red).

Other spellings: 'rr' (tomorrow), 'wr' (write).

UNIT 50 REVIEW

1   1 pang   2 mull   3 sun   4 Tim   5 rye

2   1 bridge, umbrella, brush, embrace, bride

2 wrongs, kings, springs, songs, thongs

3   eleven, forbidden, prison, certainly, kitchen, passenger, person, television, listen, suddenly, oven

4   Syllabic /l/ minimal, syllable, table, careful, central, example, little, special

Syllabic /m/ random, system, rhythm, madam, bottom, curriculum

Additional review task

Unit 45   Mum, muffins, Malcolm, Mrs MacCallum, may, Tim Mitcham, come, home, me, tomorrow, met, him, summer, small, remember, smart, charming, manners, family, from, Cambridge, make, some, home-made, tomorrow, mm, maybe, time, coming

Unit 46   accommodation agency, morning, name, Martin Nelson, manager, can, want, an, apartment, in, central, London, certainly, rent, no, than, £1,000 (one thousand pounds), month, don't, often, inexpensive, not, one, £2,179 (two thousand, one hundred and seventy-nine pounds), Notting Hill, down, near, station, Northend Avenue, furnished, unfurnished, kitchen, oven, forbidden, garden, friends, eleven, evening, noise, and, television, 11.15 (eleven, fifteen), prison

Unit 47   Duncan King, lying, trying, standing, watching, Angus Lang, bang, Langs, doing, morning, singing, banging, looking, hanging, strong, string, bringing, something, interesting, putting, happening, going, holding, fingers, shouting, helping, running, ringing, RING!, sleeping

Unit 48   early, lunch, Lesley, Lily Carpello, nearly, always, hello, only, eleven, o'clock, later, usually, left, like, leg, lamb, please, plate, salad, lettuce, black, olives, lovely, really, glass, lemonade, love, slice, melon, yellow, jelly

Unit 49   proud, parent, are all, children, grown, Ruth, Lara, Ruby, cleverest, librarian, library, very, interesting, Laura, secretary, central, railway, Rose, pretty, waitress, restaurant, Paris, married, electrician, Jerry, Roland, drives, lorry, everywhere in Europe, really, countries, drive, France, Austria, Greece, Russia, Australia, America

OVERVIEW

1   1 bit   2 could   3 A   4 T   5 show   6 V   7 pan

2   1

2

3   2 c   3 a   4 g   5 f   6 e   7 d

Track listings

CD A
Track A1 – A75
Duration: 70' 57"

CD B
Track B1 – B96
Duration: 76' 23"

CD C
Track C1 – C73
Duration: 71' 52"

CD D
Track D1 – D81
Duration: 70' 15"